AN AGE OF RENEWAL:
THE CATHOLIC REFORMATION

VOLUME 1

AN AGE OF RENEWAL: THE CATHOLIC REFORMATION

VOLUME I

Henri Daniel-Rops

Translated from the French
UNE ÈRE DE RENOUVENU: LA RÉFORME CATHOLIQUE
by JOHN WARRINGTON

CLUNY
Providence, Rhode Island

HENRI DANIEL-ROPS

THE HISTORY OF THE CHURCH OF CHRIST

VOLUME I
The Church of Apostles and Martyrs (2 VOLS.)

VOLUME II
The Church in the Dark Ages (2 VOLS.)

VOLUME III
The Church of Cathedral and Crusade (2 VOLS.)

VOLUME IV
A Religious Revolution: The Protestant Reformation (2 VOLS.)

VOLUME V
An Age of Renewal: The Catholic Reformation (2 VOLS.)

VOLUME VI
The Church of the Classical Age: The Great Century of Souls (2 VOLS.)

VOLUME VII
The Church of the Classical Age: The Era of Great Splintering (2 VOLS.)

VOLUME VIII
The Church of the Revolutionary Age: New Destinies (2 VOLS.)

VOLUME IX
The Church of the Revolutionary Age: A Fight for God (2 VOLS.)

VOLUME X
The Church of the Revolutionary Age: Christian Brotherhood (2 VOLS.)

CLUNY MEDIA EDITION, 2023

This Cluny edition is a republication of Chapters I and II and sections 1–6 of Chapter III of the 1962 edition of *The Catholic Reformation*, a translation of *Une Ère de Renouvenu: la Réforme Catholique*, published by E. P. Dutton & Co., Inc.

....

For this Cluny edition, citation and reference styles have been updated and developed, as needed, for the purposes of clarity and accessibility.

For more information regarding this title or any other Cluny Media publication, please write to info@clunymedia.com, or to Cluny Media, P.O. Box 1664, Providence, RI 02901

❦ VISIT US ONLINE AT WWW.CLUNYMEDIA.COM ❦

ISBN (paperback) | 978-1685952440
ISBN (hardcover) | 978-1685952464

NIHIL OBSTAT: Joannes M. T. Barton, S.T.D., *Censor deputatus*
IMPRIMATUR: E. Morrogh Bernard, *Vic. Gen.*
WESTMONASTERII, DIE 21 NOVEMBRIS, 1961

The *Nihil obstat* and *Imprimatur* are a declaration that a book or pamphlet is considered to be free from doctrinal or moral error. It is not implied that those who have granted the *Nihil obstat* and *Imprimatur* agree with the contents, opinions or statements expressed.

Cover design by Clarke & Clarke
Cover image: Peter Paul Rubens, *The Visitation*, detail from *The Descent from the Cross Triptych*, 1612–1614, oil on panel
Courtesy of Wikimedia Commons

CONTENTS

NOTE TO THE TEXT

M. Daniel-Rops dealt with the period 1350–1622 under the general title *L'Eglise de la Renaissance et de la Réforme*, in two volumes, from the second of which, *La Reforme Catholique*, this volume has been translated. (The Translator)

CHAPTER I

The Awakening of the Catholic Soul: St. Ignatius of Loyola

1. RENASCENCE, NOT COUNTER-REFORMATION

THE series of events which form the history of Catholicism in the mid-sixteenth century are most often depicted as follows. A violent shock causes the very foundations of Christendom to tremble, and whole sections of the Church's ancient edifice are swallowed up in heresy. Her rulers then drag themselves from their lethal indifference; they determine to oppose the Protestant menace; and at last take steps that should have been taken long ago.

Such is the pattern implied by the word "counter-reformation." The term, however, though common, is misleading: it cannot rightly be applied, logically or chronologically, to that sudden awakening as of a startled giant, that wonderful effort of rejuvenation and reorganization, which in a space of thirty years gave to the Church an altogether new appearance. What happened was a true renascence in the fullest etymological sense, more impressive from a Christian point of view than the Renaissance of art and letters upon which contemporary Europe was priding itself. The so-called "counter-reformation" did not begin with the Council of Trent, long after Luther; its origins and initial achievements were much anterior to the fame of Wittenberg. It was undertaken, not by way of answering the "reformers," but in obedience to demands and principles that are part of the unalterable tradition of the Church and proceed from her most fundamental loyalties.

2 I have remarked elsewhere[1] that in the second half of the fifteenth century every Catholic worthy of his salt, all who were alive to the situation, clamoured for reform, sometimes on a note of furious indignation, but more frequently as an act of faith in the eternal destiny of Mother Church. At the time of Luther's birth this longing for reform had begun to wear the look of agony. In the three departments of faith, morals and ecclesiastical discipline the Council of Trent did no more than supply answers to questions raised at least a century earlier, and even adopted some of those solutions which the more distinguished intellects had long since proposed. To say this is not to deny that Protestantism played a part, dialectically, in the Catholic renascence. *Oportet haereses esse*, as St. Paul says; and heresy obliged the Church to devise an exact statement of her doctrine upon certain points, to establish her position more securely than she would, in all probability, have been led to do, had she not been confronted with the challenge of error.[2] But the impetus which enabled her to join battle with her enemies was generated long before the Lutheran assault, and can in no way be considered a result of the upheaval caused by that event.

A general view of the history of the Church makes it clear that the sixteenth-century Catholic reform is not essentially different from other reforms, which have applied an irresistible law and thus serve as milestones on the road of time. The work of Cluny in the eleventh century, the achievements of St. Norbert, St. Bernard and others in the twelfth, the heroic undertakings of St. Francis and St. Dominic in the thirteenth—all these monumental and unending labours are of the same spirit and the same significance as those accomplished by the Popes and the Fathers of Trent, and by the religious founders of that period. Here indeed we have one of the most permanent features of Christianity, one of the most certain evidences

1. Henri Daniel-Rops, *A Religious Revolution: The Protestant Reformation* (Providence, RI: Cluny, 2023), Volume 1, Chapter IV, section: "Forces That Still Remained, and the Anguish of Reform."
2. In this respect the term "counter-reformation" is justifiable, especially after the Council of Trent, when Pius V and Sixtus V applied coercive and repressive means which can be hardly described as the noblest elements in the work of Catholic reform.

of its divine origin and of the reality of those promises which it claims to have received. For ever dragged downward by the weight of original sin, the baptised soul repeatedly falls back into darkness. Nevertheless, with equal regularity, there springs from her very depths, where primeval defilement cannot altogether mask, much less destroy, the supernatural resemblance, a force that impels her once more upward to light and life: a force whose name is Grace. Suspended for a time by such human events as the "Babylonian Captivity," the Great Schism and the Hundred Years War, this sublime game of seesaw was resumed in the sixteenth century, and the necessary reform was carried through exactly as in the past. If the means employed seem more drastic, the result more decisive, that is because the remedy had been long postponed and had therefore to act upon a sickness proportionately graver.

Whereas Protestantism marks a complete break in the history of Christendom, the most grievous and most tragic there has ever been, the Catholic reform stands in the direct line of ancient tradition. It is itself, in fact, the rediscovery of living Tradition. From whatever point of view it is considered, the same permanency is observed. The reforming decrees of Trent are in perfect harmony with the Gregorian Bulls, while those concerning faith look back constantly to the ancient conciliar decisions, to the decretals of the popes, to the Fathers and Doctors of the Church. Likewise in the moral sphere: Tauler, Suso and the great medieval mystics form an obvious link between St. Ignatius of Loyola and the *Imitation*, as do the Fraternities and Oratories of Divine Love between St. Philip Neri and St. Catherine of Genoa.

The Catholic reform, then, was in no respect a "counter-reformation" in the chronological order; nor was it any more so as regards the process of its development. Those who promoted it had no intention of combating Protestantism and halting its progress. St. Ignatius would have been very surprised, on that feast of the Assumption when he took the vow of Montmartre, had he been told that many historians were going to represent him as the man who recruited a body of shock troops entrusted with the elimination of heresy; and even the great bishops who, twenty or thirty years before the Council, took steps to reform their clergy were not primarily concerned to parry the furious Lutheran assault. The true reform was not directed *against* an enemy; it was undertaken *for* God, *for* Jesus Christ, as a protestation of unwavering loyalty. Before emerging as a body of doctrine, a disciplinary canon, an ecclesiastical code, it was an immense and prodigious movement of fervour, which uplifted the Christian soul almost everywhere (more especially perhaps in Italy and Spain), a kind of spiritual sublevation operated by the saints.

Here indeed is an altogether inexplicable phenomenon; it reminds us once again of the secret designs of Providence that guide the unrolling of history's scroll. For two hundred years there had been a sorry lack of effective witnesses to truth and justice, such as had arisen during the great centuries of the Middle Ages, in the hour when they were needed most. Why did they begin to reappear, in such numbers and so well suited to the times, early in the sixteenth century? What would have happened if men like St. Ignatius, St. Pius V and others had lived immediately before the tragic drama of the Schism? Things would certainly have been quite different. Again, why did God leave His Church to wallow for so long in slimy darkness before shedding His light upon her? Bossuet himself, aware of this enigma, could supply no answer.

At the critical moment when the Catholic, Apostolic, and Roman Church was about to recover possession of herself and regain her rightful aspect, it was as it had always been; her authentic history is written by the saints. The reform was brought about by means of a spiritual rebirth, that is to say, by a deepening of faith, a return to vital sources. The practice of prayer put an end to doubt and laxity, to the divorce between faith and life. It is characteristic that the really decisive personalities of the Catholic reform were all mystics, whose primary and indeed sole purpose was to know God, to love Him and to serve Him. Captain Iñigo, wounded at Pampeluna, wrote no treatise on anti-heretical strategy, but *Spiritual Exercises*; nor was it rage against the Lutheran thesis, but love of God, that lit up the face of St. Cajetan before the crib in Santa Maria Maggiore on Christmas night 1517. That the Catholic renascence originated in prayer is of profound significance. The whole difference between Catholic reform and Protestant "reformation" is summed up in these words uttered by a monk of shining faith, Giles of Viterbo, in 1512: "Men must be changed by religion, not religion by men." "Seek ye first the kingdom of God and His justice," said the Master, "and all these things shall be added unto you."

The most surprising feature of this interior movement, of this effort to obey the Gospel precepts of repentance and self-renewal, is the fact that it was not limited to the domain of conscience, where every man can, if he so wills, be sovereign. In the troubled years of the fifteenth century, mysticism retired within itself, isolating itself from the world of men[3]; the *Imitation,* for example, proposed the monastic enclosure or the more secret region of the heart as the proper field of spiritual endeavour. But the mystical leaders of the sixteenth century practised a form of spirituality directed to the science of God and to the demands of charity—a momentous change of outlook, the causes of which defy analysis. While fashioning a body of religious men dedicated to prayer and renunciation, they were almost unconsciously training an army of seasoned troops for the great battles in which the Church would find herself engaged. They became the most successful opponents of those heretics whom they had at first ignored; and the reform which they began by accomplishing within themselves overflowed and radiated its vigour in the larger realm of institutions.

It is this movement of renascent fervour, this tremor of awakening faith, that allows us to consider the sixteenth century, for all its blasphemy and bloodshed, as one of the fairest in Christian history. At a moment when the mind of man was everywhere scintillating with high intelligence and even genius, the human soul burgeoned also with sublime exaltation, in acts of faith, hope, and charity. It was indeed the pressure exerted by this distinctively religious phenomenon upon the Church's rulers that determined the reform of morals, institutions, and theological education, just as, by altering the climate of the period, it enabled the greatest of all councils to assemble and the Tridentine canons to become the lifeblood of a reborn Catholicism.

3. See *A Religious Revolution: The Protestant Reformation,* Volume 1, Chapter III, section: "Mystical Theology Comes into Its Own."

2. RELIGION A WAY OF LIFE

"THE evolution of Christian spirituality is often represented falsely in Protestant circles.... We may say that on the eve of the Reformation religion had become a way of life." These words, written by an eminent Calvinist,[4] are of deep significance, expressing an incontrovertible truth. Protestants had no monopoly of the desire to make direct contact with God through faith, to drink at the Gospel sources without being tied to external usages and formal devotions, to understand the word of God in all its fullness. Long before Luther translated the Bible into vernacular at the castle of Wartburg many editions of the sacred books had been published[5]; Cardinal Ximenes Cisneros had devoted immense labour to his Polyglot, and the French version by Lefèvre d'Étaples had proved a great success. As regards that craving for a purer religion, at once more exacting and more interior, which inspired the Augustinian of Wittenberg, it had been experienced well before his time by innumerable steadfast Catholics from Tauler to Ruysbroeck, from Suso to the unknown author of the *Imitation.*[6]

Would it were possible to describe in detail the tremor coursing through so many souls at the end of the fifteenth and beginning of the sixteenth century, a tremor that was to have so many different consequences! But the phenomenon will not yield to analysis; it is complex, contradictory, often ambiguous. The Christian conscience was examining itself, sometimes indiscreetly, and the prolonged silence of Rome allowed certain minds to go astray. The seeds from which the Protestant harvest later sprang did not at first seem very different from the fertile grain that would restore life to the Catholic Church. Before the hardening of attitudes and the erection of barriers that would soon be insurmountable, it was the whole body of the baptised, or at least the better members thereof, that

4. E. G. Léonard, *Calvin et la réforme en France* (1944).
5. See *A Religious Revolution: The Protestant Reformation*, Volume 2, Chapter V, p. 388.
6. TRANSLATOR'S NOTE: M. Daniel-Rops does not accept the attribution of this work to Thomas à Kempis.

sought to rid Christianity of all pollution and disfigurement. A general trend is clearly discernible; but there are notable contrasts of detail. One might just as well try to give an exhaustive account of the manifold processes of an orchard's blossoming in springtime to produce a whole variety of flowers and fruit.

This reawakening was apparent in all countries and in all classes of society; we can cite only a few names by way of example. In the ranks of the episcopate, and even of the Sacred College, we find Cisneros, Sadolet, Aleandro, Giberti, Carafa, Lippomano; in those of the secular clergy and the religious orders Cajetan, Zaccaria, Jerome Aemilian, Serafino da Fermo, Matteo di Bassi, Battista da Crema. Many intellectual laymen also were anxious to promote the interior reform, particularly such champions of Christian humanism as Marsilio Ficino and Vivès, Erasmus and Sir Thomas More. Of the women who played a large part in the spiritual ferment, some, including Marguerite of Navarre and Renée of Ferrara, were suspect; most, however, were true Catholics. Outstanding among these was Vittoria Colonna, the confidante of Michelangelo, of Reginald Pole and of Valdès. There was also her friend Catherine Cibo, who learned Hebrew and Greek with a view to the better understanding of Scripture, and the saintly Louise Torelli, Countess of Guastalla. But the same fervour is observed among the rank and file: the annalist Tassini gives us a picture of common folk discussing faith and dogma in the streets and squares of many an Italian town.

In many places there grew up small associations of the faithful, whose purpose was to study these grave problems, to read the Scriptures and to discuss theology and mysticism. Such groups were to be found at Alcala, Burgos, Palencia and even at the courts of Charles V, François I and Henry VIII. Another flourished at Naples under the aegis of Juan de Valdès, a Spanish mystic who sowed tares along with good grain, but died a Catholic. Giberti established others at Verona, in the Calabrian palace of Donatello Rubbo as well as beneath the arches of San Giorgio. The Oratory of Divine Love at Rome was founded by Gregorio Cortesi not long afterwards; and the circle formed by Briçonnet at Meaux was originally one of many such coteries, of which the Church had no reason to complain. Each of these small groups,[7] whose influence was considerable, may be compared with "La Chesnaie" in the great days of Lammenais.

Another mark of spiritual effervescence was the proliferation of religious books and methods of prayer. Fresh editions of the mystics, as well as new treatises, published between the end of the fifteenth century and about 1530, form an imposing catalogue. The *Imitation* was continually reprinted; so were Ludolph the Carthusian's *Life of Christ* and St. Augustine's *Soliloquy*. Harphius's *Mirror of Perfection* was translated into several languages; while the Charterhouse at Cologne specialized in the distribution of earlier works, an undertaking in which they were rivalled by the diocese of Granada and the abbey of Montserrat in Spain. It was at Montserrat also that Garcia de Cisneros published his *Exercises of the Spiritual Life*, which was afterwards studied by Ignatius of Loyola during his residence in the neighbouring city of Manresa. Meanwhile John of Avila's *Audi Filia* and Louis of Granada's *Guide of Sinners* found their way across the Franco-Spanish frontier. Other methods of prayer, drawn up by the Brethren of the Common Life and the canons of Windesheim, attracted the most fervent souls. In France Louis of Blois (1606–1666) was the author of many treatises, outstanding among which is the *Institution spirituelle*; and Catherine of Bologna's *Traité des armes spirituelles* enjoyed widespread popularity.

This passionate and uncontrolled ardour led in some cases to reprehensible extremes. Until the imposition of firm principles and the restoration of discipline by the Catholic reform, the Christian soul appeared to be feeling its way, groping hither and thither, in desperate longing for the light of certitude. Consider Spain. Under Philip II she emerged as the most impregnable fortress of the "counter-reformation," as the training-ground of St. Ignatius,

7. Many of them had offshoots in the shape of charitable confraternities similar to those which grew up during the second half of the fifteenth century. The most famous was the Charity of St. Jerome, named after the church in Rome which was the centre of its activity. To it Cardina Giulio dei Medici (afterwards Pope Clement VII) extended his patronage; and persons of all degrees, from members of the Sacred College to humble students, helped it to care for the sick and needy, visit prisoners and social outcasts, and bury the dead who had no relatives. A quarter of a century later the church of St. Jerome became the nucleus of St. Philip Neri's apostolate.

that great soldier of the Pope, as the school of St. Teresa and St. John of the Cross, those two most orthodox heralds of the mystical experience. But turn back the pages of history a mere thirty or forty years, and what a different scene, reminding us perhaps of molten metal! The idea of a return to genuine Christianity derived from Erasmus, according to whose "Philosophy of Christ" religion is to be "lived, not debated." And now the tide of his doctrine had swept over the peninsula: all "advanced" Christian intellectuals appealed to it, and the University of Palencia, quickly followed by that of Seville, became its centre. In Spanish Flanders, first at Louvain and then at Bruges, Erasmus found a rival rather than a pupil in the lofty mind of Luis Vivès (1492–1540), who later became one of the pioneers of educational theory. His *Enchiridion Militis Christi* ("Manual of the Soldier of Christ") circulated everywhere: its influence is apparent in the works of Luis de Leon and St. John of the Cross, who read it in the celebrated translation by Alonso Fernand. Many souls were overwhelmed with joy on reading this manifesto of the Christian life, so hostile to any kind of formalism; but the Franciscans and Dominicans were alarmed by its seeming unorthodoxy, and the Inquisition intervened. Diego de Zuñiga attacked the views of Erasmus in a pamphlet entitled *Blasphemy and Impiety*; but it cannot be denied, as Maldonado and the two brothers Vergara bear witness, that the Dutchman's philosophy was a true spiritual leaven.

There was yet another movement, affecting the rank and file no less than the intelligentsia of the universities. Illuminism, as it was called, included among its votaries simple laymen, parish priests and religious of both sexes. It was also favoured by such distinguished individuals as Juan de Valdès (before his flight to Naples) and Servetus, a future victim of Calvin's stake; and it won the approbation even of Cardinal Carranza. Illuminism, like Erasmianism, sought a more interior, a more spiritual type of Christianity, and rested its claim upon the vivid awareness of sanctifying grace. The guiding principle of its less exaggerated forms is explained in the *Third Primer* of Ossuna, a Franciscan. This was to create an absolute void in the soul, which God would then visit undisturbed and fill with His light. But contemplative teaching of this kind points the way to a doctrine of abandon, whereby men convince themselves that the conscience, illuminated by God, will no longer sin—a doctrine perilously close to Lutheranism. And indeed we find some peculiar fish among this haul of *Alumbrados*. There was Maria de Santo Domingo whose ecstasies lasted for hours at a time, with complete suspension of her faculties, and who, though ignorant and almost illiterate, held her own against the most eminent theologians. There was also Magdalena de la Cruz, a Poor Clare who made a pact with Satan! The brothers Vergara too, among other Erasmians, were attracted by these doctrines, while Blessed Maria Cazalla spoke of Luther with remarkable forbearance. In some respects the movement bordered upon spiritual aberration; in others it seems to have promoted an esoteric system for the use of certain high initiates. Still, its aim was the regeneration of souls, and it encouraged the desire that Christianity might conform more nearly to Christ. The Inquisition may often have had good cause to censure its adherents; but it is none the less true that without the uncertain strivings of Illuminism St. John of the Cross might never have developed and soared so far above it as he did.

Such phenomena reveal the pressure brought to bear by fervent souls upon the Church, whose leaders were thus at last compelled to shoulder the duty of reform. But they prove at the same time how urgent it had become to adopt clear-cut, uncompromising principles. It was no isolated danger that arose from the offensive conducted by Luther and other Protestant reformers and against the Roman Catholic Church. If the Holy See were to remain silent and inert, if authority would not decide to take in hand all those complex movements and to define the relationship between faith and life, there was no knowing into what wild thickets innumerable souls might not be led astray. Let Rome but speak, and all would be made clear; the voice of Rome, and no other voice, could bring order out of chaos. Notions which might originally have paved the way to misunderstanding would cease to be dangerous when circumscribed and defined by the Church; the partnership of truth and falsehood would be dissolved. This was the message proclaimed by Erasmus when, having broken with Luther, he declared: "I rely for certitude upon nothing but the sure judgment of the Church"; and the decisive steps towards reform were taken by those who "thought wholeheartedly with the Church." A period of intense spiritual unrest would terminate in an act of loyal obedience.[8]

It was indeed this ferment of ideas that produced men whose thought was in completest harmony with the Church, men of lofty spiritual aspirations but who never for one moment envisaged reform as a change of religion rather than a renewal of the human heart. They were firm in their allegiance to Mother Church, notwithstanding her unkempt appearance here and now. Most illustrious among them was St. Ignatius; Pope Adrian VI might have been another had he lived longer and possessed a little more ability. Others, however, there were—many others; and it was due to their very numbers that the whole Church was at length imbued with their longing, and accomplished her own reform.

Gaspar Contarini (1470–1542) is a particularly attractive example of this spirit. A Venetian senator, and consequently one of the governing body of the Most Serene Republic, he had represented his country in Rome and at the court of Charles V. He was also a distinguished humanist, a learned Greek scholar, and a friend of all who counted in European literature at that time. But he was no less a man of God, whose tender piety and exquisite charity remind us of St. Francis of Sales. His soul was haunted by yearning for the reform of Christendom, and he supported Valdès, Sadolet, Reginald Pole and Giberti in their efforts for the same cause. None had a closer view of Rome's corruption, of the decadence into which the See of Peter had lapsed; and yet he was a devoted son of the Church. He wished that the spiritual

8. It is precisely this spirit of loyalty which has led the Church to admit certain formulae while rejecting others scarcely distinguishable therefrom. We read, for example, in St. Ignatius's fourteenth "Rule for thinking with the Church": "it is quite true that no one can save his soul unless he be predestined, and have faith and grace." Now these words, taken at face value, are reminiscent of Calvin; but their sequel proves beyond a shadow of doubt that the founder of the Jesuits was in perfect harmony with the mind of the Church and had no part in the extravagances of the *Christian Institute.* So too with Seripando, General of the Augustinians from 1539 to 1551, and afterwards a member of the Sacred College and Papal Legate: his propositions on the role of faith seem to re-echo Luther. But as Canon Pasquier writes in the *Dictionary of Catholic Theology*: "We must not be perturbed by the different treatment accorded by the Church to the ideas of these two men [Seripando and Luther]... At every stage of her history the Church has reacted differently to theories expressed in very similar terms."

awakening which he endeavoured to inspire should take place within the framework of Tradition: it was for the Church herself to accomplish the necessary reform. After the death of his wife he was created cardinal, and became one of the most influential advocates of that reform.

Here is another example: and this time we meet a group of fervent Christians, or rather a whole collection of such groups, from whose ranks a number of great reformers would soon emerge. The Oratory of Divine Love used to meet, between the years 1510 and 1520, in the little church of Sts. Sylvester and Dorothea in the Trastevere district of Rome. It included persons of all sorts and conditions: clerics and laymen, devout burgesses and classical scholars. The original idea which brought them together can be traced to the "Fraternities of Divine Love," which, as we have seen, arose towards the end of the fifteenth century, thanks largely to the efforts of St. Catherine of Genoa. The oratory adopted St. Jerome as its patron, and among its principal members were St. Cajetan, Giovanni Pietro Carafa, Lippomano and Fr. Giuliano Dati, rector of the church where they assembled for prayers and meditation, as well as to study Scripture and the Fathers. Their first concern was to improve their own lives before thinking of ecclesiastical reform, to make of their own souls a fertile soil in which the grace of Christ might flourish. Their example was quickly followed, and similar Oratories of Divine Love were established at Venice, Brescia and Verona. These energetic associations produced founders of religious orders (e.g., St. Cajetan), a future pope in the person of Carafa, and Lippomano, who would one day preside in the Council of Trent. They were societies without statutes, a way of life without fixed rules; but their history affords a perfect illustration of the manner in which the reform itself took root in the Catholic soul. Their programme is well expressed in the sublime prayer taught to his little orphans by St. Jerome Aemilian, whose sole purpose was to bring about the reign of faith and charity: "Lord Jesus Christ, we implore Thee by Thine infinite goodness to re-establish the whole of Christendom in that state of sanctity which shall be most pleasing to Thy Divine Majesty."

3. EPISCOPAL REFORMERS[9]

"TO re-establish Christendom in the most perfect state of sanctity" was in fact the major preoccupation of many individuals long before the Council of Trent and subsequent papal decrees. Nor was that preoccupation confined to persons whose only weapon was prayer; it was found also among men whose duties enabled them to give effect to their purpose. The official Roman reformation was thus preceded by minor reforms in particular dioceses, abbeys and priories. These isolated movements prepared the way for the greater achievement, and in some cases supplied the means. True they were sporadic, often limited to the boundaries of a single diocese, more exceptionally to the frontiers of a kingdom. True also they depended on the life of one man, and were consequently of uncertain duration; but they are of considerable importance as signs of what was afoot.

It has been so often necessary to speak of unworthy bishops, greedy for prebends and leading far from exemplary lives, that we have not yet had the pleasure of showing that all heads of the Catholic hierarchy were not of this type. On the contrary, many of them derived from their faith a lofty conception of their duties, and tried to lead their clergy and people to a better understanding and more dutiful practice of true religion. They were very numerous and existed in all countries. Some were gentle, others violent in their methods; some were fortunate, others unsuccessful in the results which they obtained; but together they formed the vanguard of Trent.

One such precursor was the celebrated Cardinal Ximenes de Cisneros (1435–1517). He accompanied the Catholic sovereigns against Granada in 1492,[10] and used to say that he enjoyed the smell of gunpowder as much as that of incense. But it would be wrong to think of him merely as a prelate in armour. He died in 1517,[11] having devoted much of his tireless energy

9. In the fifteenth century there were printed a great number of treatises on the episcopal ideal; for example, those of Henry of Haguenau, Gerson, Denys the Carthusian, Laurence Justinian and Antoninus of Florence.

10. See *A Religious Revolution: The Protestant Reformation*, Volume 1, Chapter IV.

11. Luther was embarking on his career; the Council of Trent lay twenty-five years ahead.

 to the work of bringing back Christianity to its pristine holiness; and it is interesting to note that he shouldered this work not for theoretical reasons, but in consequence of a spiritual experience, an awakening within himself of religious fervour, as we find happening to many of his contemporaries. He was a secular priest and administrator of the bishopric of Siguenza when, at the age of forty-eight, he renounced the world and assumed the habit of the strictest Franciscan observance in the friary at Castanar. For more than ten years he lived a lonely and penitential life, dwelling in a wicker hut which he had built for himself in some desert place; and it seemed that he was destined to be no more than the ideal hermit whose virtues had quickly become famous far and wide. At length, however, he was summoned from his retreat by the queen, who made him her confessor and gave him the archbishopric of Toledo. He at once adapted himself to his new duties, and was soon able to devote an immense weight of authority to the service of God's cause. He personally visited each of the Castilian monasteries, urging them to reform, and strove to fashion the priests of his diocese into a model clergy. Realizing at the same time that the Church could play no effective part in the new world that was coming to birth unless she employed appropriate means, he endeavoured to make culture and humanism the allies of Christianity; while the University of Alcala, which he founded and which numbered as many as twelve thousand students, was entrusted with the formation of a Catholic élite in Spain. The six-volume Polyglot Bible was edited by a team of specialists, including Lopez de Zuñiga and Nuñez de Gusman, under the close supervision of the archbishop, who thus erected a monument of Catholic erudition anterior to the Protestant Bibles and the works of Erasmus. Nor did Ximenes relax his efforts until his death at the age of more than eighty years, though he had been exalted to the rank of Cardinal, Grand Inquisitor, Primate of Spain, Governor of Castile and Vicar of the Empire. It would of course be idle to pretend that he was everywhere successful. When, for example, he tried to force the common life upon his canons by obliging them to build houses near the cathedral, the new apartments remained empty, and the canons, in defiance of episcopal authority, went so far as to imprison the nuncio, Ortiz, who had come to excommunicate them. On the other hand it was due largely to his influence that Spain was able to resist Protestant encroachment, and the terrible Cardinal of Toledo set an example to the whole Church.

Such facts must not be overlooked. In Spain itself the current of reform initiated by Ximenes continued to flow after his death. In Andalusia, where John of Avila, a former student of Alcala, began his labours ten years after the cardinal's disappearance from the scene, the bishops showed themselves eager to continue the good work. For instance, when Pedro Guerrero, Archbishop of Granada, was summoned to the Council of Trent, he invited the apostle of the peasants to accompany him.[12] Again, St. Thomas of Villanova (1488–1555), Archbishop of Valentia, was the founder of charitable institutions to which he gave all the revenues of his benefices, and even his own bed. In addition, not only was he a great scholar and so eloquent in the pulpit, that Charles V appointed him court preacher, but his success as a reformer caused him to be surnamed in his lifetime "The New Apostle of Spain."

The Iberian Peninsula occupies a foremost place in this movement, but it was not the only part of Christendom to be stirred thereby. Italy was likewise affected. We tend to judge the entire Italian episcopate of that time by the worldly (and even more pernicious) character of some Medici, Farnese and Borgia cardinals. Yet it included many diocesan bishops whose lives were irreproachable, whose spiritual quality and achievement we cannot but admire. One man may suffice to represent all that was done, in many places, to rescue Mother Church from the bad example set by the Papal Court, and in view of his manifest sanctity it is surprising that he has never been canonized. I refer to Giberti (1495–1543), Bishop of Verona, "Master John Matthew, most revered and most rare," whom the Barnabite chronicler, Lorenzo Davidico, places in the front rank of the vanguard fighting for Catholic reform. Giberti is indeed a splendid figure: a mystic, a contemplative in high places. As a boy he had dreamed only of cloistered silence; and although circumstances obliged him to assume the responsibilities of ecclesiastical office, his constant purpose, wherever he might be, was to implant in men

12. On John of Avila, see Section 5 below.

that Gospel teaching which was the well-spring of his own life and activity. Placed by his father, the Grand Admiral of Genoa, in Cardinal Giulio de Medici's secretariat, he was entrusted with some delicate missions by Pope Leo X, and later became *Datarius* (i.e., virtual prime minister) of Clement VII, his former patron. But these onerous duties notwithstanding, he led the same fervent life of renunciation which he had once hoped to lead in the cloister; and the Oratory of Divine Love welcomed no more regular attendant at its meetings. His titles and honours weighed heavily upon him; and when at last, after the sack of Rome, he obtained the Pope's permission to resign them, he went to reside in his diocese of Verona, where in the space of about fifteen years he accomplished a remarkable transformation. Preaching by example, renouncing all his benefices and living like a monk in his palace, where a spiritual book was read aloud during meals, he managed to reimpose morality and discipline upon a clergy whose behaviour had been far from commendable. Journeying continually, visiting all the parishes of his diocese in turn, dismissing unworthy priests, encouraging the lukewarm and sluggish to do better, he revived faith and religious observance throughout his jurisdiction; and *vicars forane* were charged with the execution of his orders after he had gone. His regulations were printed and distributed to all parish priests; they were so perfect that many of their articles were afterwards embodied word for word in the canons of Trent. The religious orders were likewise an object of his constant solicitude, a fact which was not to the liking of all their members, particularly of certain refined ladies who appealed (unsuccessfully) to Rome. Mendicant friars were asked to moderate their zeal. There was scarcely a field left uncultivated by this amazing bishop. To develop piety among the faithful he established the Confraternity of the Blessed Sacrament, a forerunner of similar institutions. The liturgy was restored with all its dignity in the diocese of Verona, whose example was followed by others.[13] Preachers were invited not to abuse the

13. The Church owes to Giberti the custom of reserving the Blessed Sacrament in a tabernacle on the high altar, of ringing a little bell at the Elevation and the rule that priests must wear choir-dress and stole while hearing confessions. Many authorities also attribute to Giberti the invention of confessionals as used today.

claims of eloquence, to curtail the length of their sermons and not to revel in Latin quotations. The bishop was also a highly educated man, and gathered around him a study circle known as the "Gibertine Academy." Social and charitable, as well as a disciplinarian and moralist, he founded many orphanages, almshouses and hostels for poor girls and Magdalens, while his *Societas Pauperum* foreshadowed our Confraternity of St. Vincent de Paul three centuries before Ozanam. It is hardly necessary to add that these results were not achieved without fury, uproar and conflict; but it must be said to the honour of the popes that all of them strongly supported the Bishop of Verona, whom Clement VII had appointed legate. John Matthew Giberti died too early, too young, to witness the triumph of his ideas at the Council of Trent, but he had opened up the road; and the Carmelite Castiglione, who pronounced his funeral oration, had good reason to exclaim: "Our bishop lived and died as a saint."

Giberti was by no means the only one of his kind. What he accomplished at Verona—where Lippomano continued his work with unrivalled energy—others were doing elsewhere, or would do later: Cornaro at Brescia, Ridolfi at Vicenza, Ercole Gonzaga at Mantua, Contarini at Belluno, Vida at Alba in Lombardy, Pisani at Padua, Aleandro at Brindisi, Doria at Genoa, Cles at Trent. Results varied and in no case attained the same level as at Verona; but it was significant that so many dioceses were handled in this way. The same trend was noticeable everywhere, more or less impetuous, more or less effective. In Germany, where all the bishops did not attain the stature of Hermann von Wied or Rupprecht von Simmern, the movement was nevertheless headed by holy prelates such as Johann von Eich, Friedrich of Hohenzollern and Berthold Pirstinger. Excellent bishops followed one another in the See of Basel, among them Cristof of Utenheim, ably assisted by some energetic auxiliaries. England had John Fisher, than which no more need be said. In Poland, too, Stanislaus Hosius, Bishop of Cholm and a future cardinal, fought Protestantism not only with his pen but also by his example. Nor indeed must we omit from this concise and incomplete list the team of French bishops whom we have already seen at work, deriving from the deep wells of fervour strength to contend for the reform of their dioceses. Two in particular come to memory: the radiant Sadolet of Carpentras and Briçonnet of Meaux. The latter's doctrine was momentarily suspect, but no one ever criticized his moral eminence or the courage with which he strove to regenerate the Church.[14]

4. REFORM OF THE OLD ORDERS: THE CAPUCHINS

PARALLEL with this episcopal reaction against the forces of decay rose another, which had long been part and parcel of ecclesiastical history: reform of the religious. In every crisis experienced by the Church in course of centuries, it had been the monastic Orders that had embodied the forces of resistance; and it remained to be seen whether these ancient organizations were capable of doing once again what had formerly been accomplished first by the Benedictines and Cistercians, then by the Franciscans and Dominicans. Outwardly at least they seemed to retain plenty of vigour. There were still numerous abbeys of both black and white monks; the Friars Minor continued to exercise a strong influence upon the people; and it was to the Dominicans that Paul III entrusted the restored Roman Inquisition. Generally speaking, however, as is only too well known, these old Orders had declined sadly from their primitive fervour. True they still included in their ranks a number of pious religious. But these existed side by side with a host of dubious companions, who had been admitted to vows by an inadequate system of recruitment. Obliged to live among brethren whose conduct was often unedifying, the better elements came to feel themselves altogether ineffective, and the resulting situation gave rise to frequent discord and even violent conflict. The question was whether the good could prevail over the bad, whether those who observed the rule and the traditions of sanctity would manage to convert the others; a question all the more grave because these old Orders were to become the object of the most furious assault by Protestant critics, while new Orders rose up alongside, full of energy and ready to supplant them.

14. See *A Religious Revolution: The Protestant Reformation*, Volume 2, Chapter VI.

There was a strongly marked tendency, which later became an integral part of the Catholic reform, to subject the religious Orders more strictly to ecclesiastical authority: to the Holy See as represented by the Congregation of Religious, and to the bishops by reducing various monastic privileges. In 1516 Pope Leo X placed all religious, even the Mendicants, under episcopal jurisdiction when ministering outside their own houses; and on the many occasions when conflict arose between reforming bishops and the monks (e.g., at Verona in the time of Giberti) the Holy See invariably upheld the bishops; this policy foreshadowed not only such Tridentine decrees which terminated abuses, made the black Benedictines a congregation, and regulated the official poverty of the Minors, but also the stern measures taken by Paul IV against gyrovague monks, who were sent to the galleys or to prison.

These conciliar and papal measures would have been useless if a sincere and spontaneous will to reform had not existed at the heart of the Orders themselves. Exist, however, it most certainly did; in fact, it had never disappeared. In the worst days of the fourteenth and fifteenth centuries, the deepest loyalties had produced reforms of which some had been efficacious.[15] St. Colette, St. Catherine of Siena, St. Andrew Corsini, St. John Capistran, St. Antoninus and many more had striven courageously; but the task had once again to be resumed, for human nature is such that even when sustained by the triple vow, it repeatedly falls back.

There was hardly one of the old Orders that did not give striking signs of revival during the forty years preceding the Council of Trent. In all, or nearly all, as in the case of diocesan bishops, men and women found in themselves the strength to war against everything that imperilled not only their respective Orders but also the very bases of their spiritual life. This revival among the regular clergy is one of the most impressive aspects of the "pre-reform" which heralded the official reform and prepared for it both strategy and troops. Almost everywhere the process is identical. A man of God establishes within the bosom of an old Order, which has become more

15. See *A Religious Revolution: The Protestant Reformation*, Volume 1, Chapter III, section: "Will the Church Reform Herself?" and Chapter IV.

or less degenerate, a new congregation or community resolved to live in complete fidelity to the rule. After various difficulties the small nucleus survives, prospers and is joined by many fresh units; sometimes indeed the whole or a substantial majority of the older body transforms itself accordingly.

We should pay homage to those brave men who rekindled the fire; they are less renowned than their contemporaries—St. Ignatius and St. John Capistran, for example—who founded new institutes. Their memory was not preserved by the zeal of young formations anxious to obtain a protector in Heaven, with the result that few of them have been canonized, though they richly deserved the honour.

Among the Benedictines there was the magnificent effort of the Congregation of Bursfeld in Germany, heir to the impulse given by St. Nicholas of Cusa. At the head of the famous Spanish abbey of Montserrat, near Barcelona, stood a great mystic who was to influence St. Ignatius of Loyola: Garcia de Cisneros (1455–1510), nephew of Cardinal Ximenes, who restored the splendour of the divine office as well as monastic discipline. The noble humanist Gregorio Cortese (1488–1548), first at Mantua, then at the ancient monastery of Lérins, and finally at San Giorgio in Venice, revived, together with religious fervour and good order, a taste for intellectual studies, which exercised a profound influence on his brethren of Monte Cassino. He was appointed Bishop of Urbino and created cardinal by Paul III.

Among the Camaldolese, the venerable order of St. Romuald, the movement was headed by Blessed Giustiniani (1476–1528).[16] First in the Apennines and later in the plain of Ancona, his spiritual sons lived their austere lives in small separate huts, like true hermits; their example was such that the entire Order quickly followed suit, and under his relative, Pietro Giustiniani of Bergamo, Monte Corona on the upper Tiber afterwards became the centre of reformed Camaldolese.

We find the same stirring, the same will to be reborn, among the various orders of Mendicants. If the Dominicans lacked outstanding reformers

---

16. He belonged to the same Venetian family that gave the Church the holy patriarch St. Laurence Justinian and the Benedictine *venerabilis* Nicholas.

at this period, it was because their Order had already been reformed since 1493, by the celebrated congregation of San Marco at Florence, which was fostered by the archbishop St. Antoninus, and also perhaps because the work of Savonarola, despite his ultimate defeat, had continued to make itself felt long after his ashes were thrown into the Arno. The Black Friars, however, possessed a man of wonderful energy in the person of Battista da Crema, whose voice was scarcely less powerful than that of Friar Jerome; while at Pavia and Alba, Prior Ghislieri (afterwards Pope St. Pius V) was distinguished by his immense authority. It was rather on the intellectual plane, in conformity with their vocation, that the sons of St. Dominic laboured for reform. In Spain, for example, Francisco de Vittoria (1480 or 1492–1546), master of Salamanca,[17] put new life into Thomism by discarding its scholastic subtleties, and was followed on this road of positive dogmatics by his pupils Melchior Cano and Domenico de Soto.

The Augustinians, upon whom Luther was to confer such unpleasant notoriety, included in their ranks some remarkable men, no less preoccupied with spiritual life and reform than was the monk of Wittenberg himself, but never thinking for a moment of leaving the Church. Giles of Viterbo (died 1532), an outstanding humanist and fascinating preacher, delivered a sensational address in the Lateran Council, scourging the vices of the Church and proposing a real programme of reform. His disciple Jerome Seripando (1494–1563), a member of La Carbonaria, the most austere branch of the Augustinians, was of such exemplary life that he was appointed its secretary at the age of twenty-one. He later became General of the whole Order, and visited all its houses as far afield as Spain and Portugal, bringing them back to a higher standard of morality, ridding them of Lutheran influence and breaking all resistance. Among those who profited by his unwavering support was Thomas of Villanova. Another was Gaspard Casai, future Bishop of Coimbra, who was ultimately appointed Archbishop of Salerno; created cardinal, he served as Papal Legate at Trent, and was one of the most vigorous personalities of his age.

17. He is the father of international law, and is still much quoted in the universities.

There is scarcely an Order, congregation or institute of religious in which we do not find the symptoms of this ferment; the "reformers" were acquainted one with another and influenced one another without regard to differences of rule or degrees of enclosure. Thus, for example, Fr. Serafino da Fermo introduced the Canons of the Lateran to the ideas of Battista da Crema. At Bologna another canon regular, Pietro de Lucca, did similar work; while the Premonstratensians of Spain and Lorraine became imbued with notions of reform that were realized immediately after the Council of Trent.

But in no Order did these notions give rise to such dramatic incidents or to such determined opposition as among the Franciscans, the most numerous and decidedly the most influential Order at that time. Masters in almost every university, preachers in every pulpit, the sons of St. Francis displayed their familiar habit throughout Christian Europe. It is useless, however, to pretend that they were not the target of criticism that was often no less justified than severe. The skill with which they wormed money from the faithful was proverbial, their moral conduct not always beyond reproach. Cardinal Nicholas of Cusa and St. John Capistran had frequently complained of them, and in Spain they were severely treated by Ximenes. It is well known that since the morrow of the founder's death two tendencies had been apparent in the Order of St. Francis: one favoured a strict interpretation of the Poverello's Rule and Testament; the other demanded some relaxation, without which, they argued, no great Order could function. This cleavage had resulted in the famous crisis of the "Spirituals."[18] Having been soothed and reorganized the party of Strict Observance was represented mainly by the Celestines (1294), or Clarenines, in Italy; by the Colettines (1406) in France; by the Amadeans (1457) in Savoy; in Spain by the Bretheren of the Cowl (1487). During the mid-fifteenth century Bernardine of Siena, John Capistran, James of La Marche and Bernardine of Feltre all belonged to the Strict Observance, which therefore seemed to be the party of the saints. Under its influence there began to flow within the Order a current directed to the recall of lax convents to the Rule and thus to the reunification of the

18. See *The Church of Cathedral and Crusade*, Volume 2, p. 697f.

great Franciscan family. In 1516 Leo X allowed himself to be persuaded that circumstances favoured a decree which would suppress the old denominations and bring all the sons of St. Francis under the single name of "Friars Minor." The attempt, however, failed; a certain number of houses declined to renounce collective ownership. Leo X yielded, and gave official recognition to the Friars Minor Conventual, who thenceforward wore black. The Order as a whole was sadly disappointed, but disappointment here had one good result: it whipped up the energy of individuals, and there began to appear in many sectors of the Franciscan world a host of men determined to apply the principles of St. Francis in all their rigour and to live in heroic poverty. Among the most famous of these was St. Peter of Alcantara (1499–1562), an austere Spanish ascetic, whose lofty mysticism caused King John III of Portugal to summon him to court, and St. Teresa to take him as her adviser when she contemplated the reform of Carmel. Under his direction, too, the "Alcantarines" enjoyed great spiritual advancement and numerical increase. Their custom of establishing "houses of recollection" or retreat for the periodical or permanent residence of those who felt the urge to asceticism became widespread; and in France these members of the Strict Observance became known as Recollects.

At about the same period an analogous design for returning to the original observance begat yet another type of Franciscans, whose unfamiliar habit caused them to be known by a new name. "Capucini! Capucini!" the street urchins of Camerino used to shout when they caught sight of these odd, bearded monks, strolling along in their rough habits with fantastic square hoods. The nickname "Capuchins" passed into usage and still denotes one of the three branches of the Franciscan Order. But the humble Matteo di Bassi (1495–1552) certainly had not the least idea of founding a new congregation when, in 1525, he came down from his friary at Montefalcone to beg Pope Clement VII, with gentle obstinacy and simple heart, for leave to wear a habit which he maintained was the authentic dress of St. Francis. He begged also to be allowed to go and preach throughout the world, exhorting all, by example rather than by word, to turn their steps into the paths of God. Son of humble parents though he was, Matteo was already known as a model religious. He had distinguished himself by his devoted service to the plague-stricken during an epidemic in 1523, and was admired by the virtuous Catherine Cibo, Duchess of Camerino. It was rumoured that St. Francis had several times appeared to him: "I want my Rule observed literally; yes, to the very letter!"; and since on these occasions the founder wore the quadrangular hood as used by the peasants of Ancona, Matteo had adopted it notwithstanding criticism and even an express prohibition on the part of his superiors. He won Clement's approval; but it was given by word of mouth only, and the good friar, who had now been joined by two companions, met at first with strong resistance from his Order, even to the point of excommunication. However, Louis of Fossombrone, one of his disciples, had heard tell that Giovanni Pietro Carafa, a future pope and at that time influential in the Curia, was a resolute supporter of anyone working for reform. He therefore went to Rome, and prevailed upon Carafa to obtain a papal Bull which withdrew Matteo from Franciscan jurisdiction and made him subject to his firm friend the Bishop of Camerino. Such was the origin (1528) of the Franciscan hermits, called thenceforward Capuchins. The new formation quickly proved its worth. The strange houses of these new Minors began to arise on all sides, with doors so low that one had to stoop to enter, and narrow windows devoid of glass. The friars themselves ate nothing but bread, fruit and herbs, drank nothing more tasty than water, while their habit was made of coarsest fustian. But they also emerged from their convents, especially into heavily populated districts, and, as we learn from the *Mémoires* of Castelnau, were "frequently met travelling through towns and villages, visiting private houses to reprimand the occupants...reminding the people of the excellence of the Catholic faith," renewing in brief the far-flung and fruitful apostolate of the earliest Franciscans. Their charity was inexhaustible, in flagrant contrast to the rapacity of some other Mendicants, and earned them much goodwill. After the sack of Rome, when Italy was ravaged by the soldiery, then by famine and epidemic, they rose to magnificent heights; and the Hospital for Incurables, in the Piazza del Popolo, preserves the memory of their generosity. Having been organized as a congregation under the kindly and little more than nominal jurisdiction of the Conventuals, and with their Constitutions approved by Rome in 1529, the Capuchins seemed destined for nothing but success. Severe trials, however, awaited them. First to launch a violent attack were the Friars Minor Observant, maddened by the zeal (somewhat excessive at times) of the new-born institution. The attack failed, and some of the most celebrated Observant preachers actually joined the Capuchins. A second offensive from the same quarter was thus provoked, and the fact that it did not succeed was due entirely to the influence of Catherine Cibo and Vittoria Colonna. Paradoxically assisted by the Conventuals, the Capuchins were able henceforward to live almost independently under their own vicar-general.

Alas, however, a worse misfortune lay in wait for the hermits. The most illustrious of their recruits, whose arrival had been hailed with such delight and who had been quickly promoted to the rank of vicar-general, was none other than Bernardino Ochino. This wonderful man, this born leader, this splendid orator—"he would move stones," Vittoria Colonna used to say—went over to Protestantism. The scandal of his departure may be imagined. The head of the Capuchins become a Lutheran, and married! It was enough to lay the whole edifice in ruins beneath the blows of its adversaries; and Paul III, hearing the news, went so far as to exclaim: "Soon there shall be no Capuchins at all." But the devoted protectress of the congregation intervened once more, helped by Giberti and Cardinal San Severino. A careful inquiry revealed that Ochino's was an isolated case. Could one condemn so many on the strength of one man's error? And so the Capuchins, saved from the pontifical thunderbolts, were enabled to go ahead and prosper. A hundred years later they numbered thirty thousand, in one thousand four hundred houses; and to these were subsequently added the Sisters of the Passion, founded by Maria Laurentia Longa and known commonly as Capuchines.

Such was the magnificent process whereby the old religious Orders were regenerated and made ready to enter fully into the effort for which the Church would soon call upon her sons. That process, however, was as yet far from complete: it would assume larger proportions on the morrow of

Trent,[19] receive fresh impetus and produce many another saint. Even while Rome recovered herself and prepared to undertake reform on a world-wide scale, Teresa of Avila, afire with mystic love, was already contemplating the reform of Carmel and laying the foundations of her great achievement.

5. BIRTH OF NEW ORDERS: THE CLERKS REGULAR

It appeared that revival and reorganization of the old Orders was insufficient for the end proposed. A new formula was required to meet new demands, and was found in the institution of clerks regular. This, however, was an institution that evolved quite naturally from earlier beginnings. Long ago, in the thirteenth century, the Franciscans and Dominicans, laying much less emphasis than their predecessors on cloistered contemplation, had made close contact with the faithful, particularly through the medium of preaching. The new leaven introduced into the Christian lump by the Mendicants had undoubtedly caused it to rise; but the results of their labour had not been as decisive as could have been wished. Their many examples of priestly virtue had been far from consistently followed by the parochial clergy, and it appeared, generally speaking, that in order to be a good priest one needed to join a religious Order. Surely it was possible to go a stage further by establishing a body of priests with the same spiritual quality as the regulars, and equally subject to vows, but living as part of the ordinary clergy, wearing their dress and leading their life. These "clerks regular" would help the parish priests in their task and devote themselves to the same ministry, but they would also provide the faithful with a living example of priestly virtue in the world. Trained to methods of prayer and thus deepening their spiritual life, but exempt from the choral office to which even the Mendicants were still bound, these new priests would labour to make their faith an integral part of life. It was a momentous innovation, one that would play an

19. At which time the Observant Franciscans had no fewer than one hundred sixty-five thousand members.

important part in the work of ecclesiastical reform; and it continues fruitful to this day.

The first of such bodies was that of the Theatines, an offshoot of the Oratory of Divine Love. It resulted from the meeting of two men whose characters were entirely different. One of them, St. Cajetan of Tiene (1480–1547), was a refined and devout soul, of retiring disposition, full of meekness and moderation. The other was Giovanni Pietro Carafa (1476–1559), "a Calabrian firebrand," who afterwards displayed the same temperament on the papal throne, but also those gifts of leadership which had revealed themselves in the years of his early manhood. The idea was Cajetan's. Having attended many meetings of the Oratory of Divine Love, he decided that the pious exercises of that closed circle were having no influence upon the Church, whereas its methods of spiritual perfection might well prove more effective if adopted by an army of zealous priests. He dreamed therefore of creating a sacerdotal community whose members would forgo honours and lucrative positions, bind themselves by vows similar to those taken by religious, and work in collaboration with the rank and file of the secular clergy. The gentle mystic must inevitably have failed without the backing of Carafa's more practical qualities. But agreement between them was not easy. Cajetan did not altogether trust the other's impulsive nature; and having embraced a state of poverty he suspected that the episcopal benefices held by his destined ally might prove a serious obstacle to the realization of his plans. There is a story that Carafa fell on his knees before the future saint, begging him to accept his services, whereupon the astonished Cajetan knelt in turn and embraced him, weeping. Be that as it may, the two men were thenceforward close associates. In 1524, thanks to Giberti, who was at that time head of Clement VII's chancellery, they obtained permission to found a society of clerks regular, and secured the privilege of its dependence upon the Holy See alone. Carafa magnanimously resigned his two bishoprics, but as he had been titular of Chieti (Latin *Theatinum*) in the Abbruzzi, the members of the new Institute soon came to be known popularly as Theatines. Except for their white stockings and larger tonsure, they were in no way distinguishable from other priests; but they strove to be present wherever there was need of preaching, charitable work or other form of service. Their undertaking very quickly prospered. Obliged to flee after the sack of Rome, they forgathered at Venice, whence they were summoned to Naples by the patriarch Caracciolo. Back once again in the Eternal City, at the church of St. Nicholas of Tolentino, they gave public proof of their holiness and zeal during months of famine and misery. Within a period of about twenty years the Theatines spread over the whole of Italy, and from there to Spain, Poland, Austria and Germany. The election of Carafa as Pope Paul IV contributed greatly to their success, and they became a regular nursery of bishops, more than two hundred of whom issued from their ranks. They also produced some distinguished preachers, among whom was St. Andrew Avellino, and mystics such as Lorenzo Scupoli. The Theatines were once on the point of incorporation with the Jesuits, to whose rule their own, though less exacting, bore some kinship. The proposal never materialized, and their influence steadily declined; but we ought not to forget the work that they accomplished.[20] The canonization of St. Cajetan in 1671 was the Church's official homage to an initiative which had opened up for her a new road on the eve of the Council of Trent.

Along that road, or along parallel roads, others quickly set out. A young doctor at Cremona, St. Antony Zaccaria (1502–1537), was disturbed by the sight of his people's misery and increasing immorality; he was already active before his ordination to the priesthood, insisting upon the need for penance, like St. Paul, with whose doctrine he was deeply imbued. He was soon joined by a number of disciples; and the citizens of Milan and other towns beheld these new preachers marching through the streets, with ropes around their necks, carrying enormous crosses, and halting at crossroads to proclaim the love of God. The movement gradually became organized.

---

20. St. Cajetan and the Theatines are credited with various customs and devotions, which were introduced first at Naples and became universal. These were the Forty Hours, the Christmas Novena, popularization of the crib (invented by St. Francis of Assisi), wearing of the surplice by preachers, segregation of men and women at Mass. This last custom is extinct in France, except at funeral Masses, but is still quite common in Germany.

Ludovica Torelli, Countess of Guastalla, told Zaccaria about Cajetan and the Oratory of Divine Love, and a small community was formed, to which a papal Brief (1533) granted the same privileges as those enjoyed by the Theatines. So began the "Clerks Regular of St. Paul," known popularly as Barnabites because their first house in Rome stood on the site of an ancient church dedicated to St. Paul's fellow apostle. The Barnabites differed somewhat from the Theatines in their taste for liturgical splendour (which appealed so strongly to St. Aloysius Gonzaga), in their use of such devotions as Perpetual Adoration, and in their work as teachers. They too spread, despite the premature death of their young leader at the age of thirty-five; and it was to them that St. Francis of Sales had recourse when he planned to reorganize the education of his diocese.

The radiance of the Oratory becomes once more apparent in yet another of its disciples: Jerome Aemilian[21] (1481–1537), founder of the Congregation of Somascha. He likewise adopted the system of clerks regular when he decided to gather round him a body of men equally obsessed with the general misery and resolved to fight it with the charity of Christ. Orphanages, hospitals, refuges for prostitutes—all that could render the sufferings of mankind less cruel was their domain. Approved in 1540, the "Clerks Regular of St. Mayeul" were thus named after their house at Pavia; but they subsequently established themselves in the little town of Somascha, between Milan and Bergamo, and were thenceforward known more commonly as Somaschi. A fresh field soon opened to their apostolate, and they devoted themselves to the education of youth a hundred years before John Baptist de la Salle.

Theatines, Barnabites and Somaschi: those names are far from representing the whole creative activity of which the Church gave evidence at that time. The idea of "clerks regular" was so plainly in the minds of all that it took concrete shape almost everywhere, without any apparent influence of one such institution upon the next. In various parts of Christendom, and distinct from the larger formations, a number of priests would meet

21. This was his name in religion. His father was Girolamo Miami, a Venetian senator.

together for prayer and for mutual instruction with a view to the impending struggle on behalf of Christ; and some such groups even bound themselves by religious vows. The history of these small nuclei is obscure and will probably never be written; but we know, for instance, that Cardinal Sadolet was at the head of one at Carpentras, and Cardinal Fisher of another in England. One of the most energetic was formed in Spain by John of Avila (1500–1569), author of the mystical treatise *Audi Filia* and a tireless apostle of the spoken word. In the cities and even the poorest villages of Andalusia he and his companions, forerunners of our rural and factory missions, spent themselves without counting the cost. The whole country was familiar with their threadbare cassocks, the burning eyes in their shrunken faces, which put to shame the harshness of the rich and the weakness of proud prelates. Huntsmen of Christ, they ran down such game as Louis of Granada, John of God and Francis Borgia. In the Sierra Morena they built churches which can be seen today, and anticipated by fifteen years the first endeavours of St. Ignatius and his companions.

John Ciudad, a young Portuguese, is one example of the profound influence exercised almost everywhere by initiative of this kind. Returning to his home at Evora, after distinguishing himself in a long series of campaigns, he heard John of Avila preaching in nearby Andalusia, and was converted. Known thenceforward as John of God (1495–1550), he determined to form a group of laymen, like himself, who would take vows and lead the same sort of life as the clerks regular. Thus there was born at Granada, in 1540, the little Congregation of John of God, dedicated to the hardest tasks in the hospitals and asylums. In France its members came to be known as Fathers of Charity,[22] in Germany as Brothers of Mercy. Their selfless generosity continued to spread, and is still in evidence today.

Women were somewhat less prominent in this movement, but far from inactive. Female congregations were established whose principles were in many respects identical with those that had given rise to the clerks regular.

22. At Paris they founded the Hôpital de la Charité, in the Rue des Saints-Pères; when this was laicized they moved to the Rue Oudinot.

Instead of their traditional confinement to the cloister, where they were limited to the necessary but exclusive work of contemplation, female religious were now more practically engaged in the daily combat of the Church, assisting the clergy in works of charity, education and even of apostleship. The appearance of these "secular nuns" provoked surprise and resistance. "Women need a husband or a cloister," was a common saying; but the innovation was destined to bear good fruit.

The "Angelicals of St. Paul," for instance, owed their existence to Ludovica Torelli, and were fostered by St. Antony Zaccaria and his Barnabites. They devoted themselves to the care of orphans and penitent girls; and it was largely upon them that St. Francis of Sales afterwards modelled his Order of the Visitation. Reorganized by Pope Benedict XV in 1919, the Angelicals are known today as Sisters of St. Paul, and flourish particularly in South America. Somewhat later, again thanks to Ludovica Torelli, appeared the Daughters of Mary; they were concerned mostly with education, and were commonly called "Guastallines."[23] Thirdly, there was the female branch of the Theatines, established at Naples by Ursula Benincasa. But none of these institutions was destined to so glorious a future as was that founded at Brescia in 1535 by St. Angela Merici. As a young woman still living in the world, but favoured by God with ecstatic visions, she beheld in the sky a Jacob's Ladder upon which virgins holding lilies ascended and descended. She therefore resolved to form an association of girls, who, though bound by monastic vows, would continue to live in the world, striving to bring God into the lives of men. The new institute took St. Ursula as its patron, and was so successful that it was obliged before long to assume a more official character, to accept constitutions[24] and to become step by step a fully fledged religious order. This was the origin of the Ursulines, who received papal approval in 1544, and afterwards did for the Christian education of girls what the Jesuits did for that of boys on the morrow of Trent. The order

23. Ludovica Torelli was Countess of Guastalla.
24. Even today the "Angelines" of Brescia observe usages that date from the time of Angela Merici; they have not accepted the Ursuline constitutions.

spread far and wide, until it included no fewer than ten thousand religious. We shall find them later, in the person of Mary of the Incarnation, riding with the king's officers through the dread forests of Canada, to plant the Cross beside the fleur-de-lis.

Such then was the prodigious quickening that became apparent in many sectors of the Church, long before the Holy See undertook to direct the work of reform and determined to summon a council which would embody the results of that work in social and ecclesiastical institutions. An intense spiritual fervour revealed itself in the manifold achievements of evangelization and charitable endeavour no less than in the sphere of discipline. Countless men and women of goodwill were offering their services, and effective means were already available. This reawakening of the Catholic soul, this return to "a religion become life," as Léonard calls it, was undeniably rich with promise. To effect the synthesis of all those efforts and aspirations, to confer upon the resurrected Church her dowry, was the heroic destiny of a genius, of a mystic who was also an administrator—St. Ignatius of Loyola.

6. IÑIGO THE BASQUE IS CALLED BY GOD

DURING the spring of 1521 war was resumed between France and Spain, that is to say, between François I and Charles V. The French troops, under Comte André de Foix, crossed the Pyrenees without mishap, for their adversaries had been called away by a revolt of the grandees of Castile. Their purpose was to recover Navarre,[25] and restore it to King Jean d'Albret. The fortress of Pampeluna was ill defended: the garrison amounted to no more than a single company of pikemen and arquebusiers, under the command of a thirty-year-old captain. Finding themselves encircled by such powerful forces, the city fathers at once began to talk of opening their gates; but

25. Ferdinand the Catholic had seized it nine years earlier, while Louis XII was preoccupied with his Milanese adventure.

the young military commandant would not agree. The Duke of Najera, as viceroy, had entrusted him with the defence of this place, and he would not surrender without a fight, however unequal the contest might prove to be. Shut up in the citadel with a handful of loyal troops, he had held out for six days, as a matter of honour, when a bullet suddenly ricocheted off a wall and struck him in the legs, one of which was gashed and the other broken. With him resistance collapsed. His name was Iñigo Lopez de Recalde; he was born at the castle of Loyola, in the heart of Guipuzcoa, one of the Basque provinces.

War in those days had its peculiar refinements. The French officers behaved with great gallantry towards their brave prisoner: they got an army surgeon to dress his wounds and make some sort of an attempt to reset the broken bone; then they had him carried in a litter along the rugged roads of Navarre to his birthplace, where the grateful victim presented his escort with some fine specimens of inlaid armour. But the body set down by its bearers in the ancient hall was indeed a sorry thing. The wounds showed no signs of healing, and the broken tibia, so badly set, had been displaced by the jolting of the litter. It was unthinkable that a Spanish officer should be thus permanently disfigured, and the wounded man gave orders for a second operation, which he endured with clenched fists but without a groan—"sheer butchery" as he afterwards described it. Moreover it was unavailing; for the bone, broken a second time and reset, continued to protrude below the knee. So they had to saw off the point, then stretch the shortened leg with boards, ropes and weights, while Iñigo de Loyola suffered in stoic silence.

What had been his motive? Pride and concern for his appearance no doubt. What good is an invalid soldier, a well-bred captain become bandy-legged and lame? Providence, however, apparently intended to oppose a barrier to his vain desires, and he was soon obliged to bow before the inevitable. He would never again be the handsome cavalier with his embroidered doublet and gleaming breastplate, the cynosure of female eyes. He had dreamed of life in the style of *Amadis des Gaules*, full of doughty deeds, but must now reconcile himself to being no more than a cripple. But physical suffering, and this kind of humiliating experience which deprives a proud man of bodily strength, are often the means employed by God to bring him back to a sense of moderation and requisite humility. Iñigo's long convalescence within the frowning walls of the ancient *castillo* was quickly transformed into a spiritual retreat. At first he felt a stirring of rebellion against his absurd fate, against a future devoid of hope. Haunted by idle dreams of a worldly life, of love and battles, his thoughts turned to the lady of his heart, for, like every *hidalgo*, he was devoted to a lady, and his was of most illustrious birth. He asked himself "what he would have to do in her service, what words he would speak to her, what feats of arms he would accomplish on her behalf." But stern reality dragged him from such fantasies. All that was finished: never would he enter the distant castle and rescue the Infanta Catalina from her dismal fate, unhappy Catalina, daughter of Joanna the Mad, whose secluded life she was condemned to share. What then? What destiny awaited him? It was at this point of his journey that Christ lay in wait for him, to conquer and enlighten.

In his father's library, to which he hobbled along the corridors, he had exhausted all the romances of chivalry. A few books still remained on the niggardly shelves, pious treatises covered with dust. He took them down: *The Flower of the Saints*, a Spanish adaptation of Jacobus de Voragine's *Golden Legend*; Ludolph the Carthusian's *Life of Christ*, which Cardinal Ximenes had had translated into Castilian. Opening these volumes simply because he had nothing better to do, the invalid was surprised to find himself absorbed. He was, as it were, locked in conflict with himself: two currents of thought opposed one another, two contrary dreams fought for mastery of his soul. The history of St. Dominic and St. Francis, above all, roused in him a strange sense of exaltation. Why should he not do what the saints had done? Might not divine assistance enable him to satisfy that thirst for greatness which he could not quench by human means? It was the first summons of the ineffable Voice, as yet ill-defined and unobtrusive. "God was beginning to overcome the devil in my soul," he afterwards said of this period. It was not spiritual anguish, such as had ridden Luther, that was driving him to seek a new road, but a sort of inverted pride, of native arrogance. The ways of the Lord are incomprehensible. In the fine summer nights of 1521 Iñigo de Loyola, having climbed to the summit of the castle, would spend long hours watching the sky with its myriads of stars; and there he came to understand that a force more powerful than his will had taken charge of his life. He knew he had been called.

It would be false to say that he had not been hitherto a Christian. In his country at that time there was no one who did not stand fast by the Christian faith, even when faith did not exclude the gravest moral shortcomings. A man is no true Spaniard unless he is a Catholic, and in that land, where the Reconquista had been completed only thirty years earlier with the capture of Granada, the faith was such an integral member of the national conscience that a young knight, swashbuckler and libertine though he might be, would simply not have understood the question if asked whether he believed. The cripple of Loyola was a typical product of his race as well as of his country. Though a son of the Basques, who while attaching themselves to Spain had kept their pride and the certitude of accomplishing a great individual destiny within the Iberian kingdom, he was yet a brother of those crusaders who, in the course of centuries, had rewon their country from the Moors, brother likewise of those conquistadors who were even then winning new worlds for their king, as well as of those mystics who, at the same time, were undertaking the perilous ascent of the high peaks of the soul. His Christian name, Iñigo,[26] was that of a venerable Benedictine abbot who had governed a monastery in the neighbourhood of Loyola. His family, long rooted in the vale of Urola—in its stony hillsides rather than among the maize and apple trees of the plain—had been from time immemorial a nursery of soldiers. The seven red bendlets of their arms recalled the exploits of their ancestor, Juan Perez, who, with his seven sons, had spent a lifetime in the battlefield. Iñigo had eight sisters and four brothers. Of the latter, one had fallen before Naples, another before Mexico City, while a third was later killed fighting against the Turks on Hungarian soil. His childhood was

26. He afterwards abandoned it to call himself after the great martyr St. Ignatius of Antioch—a name better known throughout the world and more significant perhaps of his own designs.

similar to that of many boys of his rank: his early education was backed with liberal use of the rod; his parents vaguely intended him for the Church, but he was soon driven to embrace a career of arms and placed in the service of a high personage. None of those factors, however, had prepared him for his ultimate destiny. The pious influence of his mother had been withdrawn too early, and he used to say that he had found little among the whole warrior class but traditions of sin; only one of his brothers took holy orders, and his conduct was far from edifying. Yet it was precisely from these elementary fidelities, in this brand of faith confused with the sense of honour, in this ancestral violence on behalf of just causes, that he would derive the strength which urged him forward along a new road. The crusading spirit which he had inherited was leading him, more determinedly than he himself was aware, towards the crucial decision he was about to take. All his life he would remain a soldier, but henceforward a soldier of God.

The interior debate was resolved. "The discernment of spirits" took place little by little, not in the gloomy resignation of an invalid disgusted with life, but in the choice of a new vocation more exacting than that which Iñigo renounced. All the attractions of life in the world appeared to him insipid compared with those he was beginning to discover in another life. Copying "lovingly" whole pages of the spiritual treatises he was reading—the words of Our Lady in blue, those of Christ in red—praying ceaselessly, with ever-growing fervour, he came to feel within himself the operation of a silent decision, a tranquil obedience to the summons he had heard. Heaven itself assisted him. "Lying awake one night," he later told a friend, "I saw clearly an image of Our Lady with the Child Jesus. From this vision, for a considerable space of time, I received such consolation as to be completely overwhelmed. And immediately I experienced such disgust with my past life, especially with my wickedness, that I seemed to feel my soul scraped clean of all that had been so deeply imprinted there." All that he had found strongest within himself—the warlike spirit, sexual temptations, the pride of a nobleman and a soldier—was henceforth transformed and directed to other goals. As yet he knew not how he would employ these new forces, whether on crusade or in the extreme asceticism of the Charterhouse;

but he was determined to "perform those great feats which the saints have accomplished for the glory of God."

Caballeria a lo divino, divine chivalry: Christ's cavalier was now inwardly prepared. So he left the castle that had been his home, "dressed according to his rank, armed and accompanied by two servants." After spending a whole night in prayer in the church of Our Lady of Aranzazu, dear to the folk of Guipuzcoa, he set out for the celebrated Benedictine abbey of Montserrat, in Catalunya, one of the main centres of Spanish loyalties. An unfortunate incident on the road made him realize how far he still was from the love of God. A Muslim gentleman, with whom he travelled part of the way, called in question the virginity of the Mother of Christ. Iñigo's first reaction was to challenge him to a duel and kill him; second thoughts, however, stayed his hand, and he knew not what to do. From this embarrassment he escaped by the pleasant expedient of leaving it to his horse, like another Balaam's ass, to show him the will of God. At the next crossroads he allowed it to choose whether it would take the same route as the Moor or follow another path, and the animal chose the way of meekness. God's cavalier had still to learn, among many things, the charity of Christ.

The old Adam still clung to him, but was sloughed off at the end of a short retreat, which, though it lasted for only three days, was conducted with exemplary thoroughness and determination. On that fantastic mountain whose Wagnerian rocks might have concealed the Holy Grail, at the feet of that statue of Our Lady which was said to have been miraculously preserved during the Muslim invasion, young men kept vigil before their admission to the ranks of knighthood. So too did Ignatius of Loyola—not to gird on arms at break of day, but to put them by once and for evermore. He laid his sword and dagger before Our Lady of Battles, divested himself of doublet, breastplate, all the trappings of this world, and donned the humbler garb of a pilgrim—sandals, staff and all. He handed a written confession, detailed and exhaustive, to one of the monks (a Frenchman named Jean Chanones), and at last obtained peace of mind. His new guide gave him in return Garcia de Cisneros's *Exercises of the Spiritual Life*, a book that would lead him faithfully on the road he wished to follow.

What was that road, and through what country would it pass? As yet he did not know, and he sought it in a strange direction. Having, like some anchorite of the Thebaïd, assumed the dress of a penitent, with long beard, hair and nails, he went and took up his abode at Manresa, a large market-town of Catalunya. Here he spent a year of terrible asceticism—he who was afterwards so moderate, so prudent in this respect—endeavouring to carry renunciation and mortification to a degree seldom attained. He would not accept the hospitality of the Dominicans, who had welcomed him with open arms; he would not even shelter beneath the roof of the hospital where he devoted himself to caring for the worst cases. For weeks on end he lived all alone in a cave near the River Cardoner, eating scarcely anything, kneeling seven hours at a time absorbed in mental prayer. This régime caused his health to deteriorate and he fell sick. At the same time, however, new certainties dawned upon his mind, and it was God Himself who roused him from his reverie. Here now is his own account, taken from the impassioned *Pilgrim's Narrative*, wherein, long afterwards, he described the graph of his spiritual experience. "One day I was going to pray in a church about a mile from Manresa, on a road which follows the bank of the Cardoner. I sat down, with the river flowing deep before me, and there the eyes of my conscience began to open. It was no vision that was granted me, but an understanding of many things—of the mind, of faith, of human knowledge—and in so clear a light that all seemed renewed from top to bottom." What had he understood in that moment of inspired insight? He had learned that God had not called him to the eremitical life, that he was destined for other tasks which Providence would lay upon him in its own good time. He therefore decided to eat meat again, to comb his hair and bring to man the fruits of his experience. A new man came forth from the cave of Manresa.

This time of superhuman trial was by no means wasted. In long hours of silent meditation Ignatius had discovered the secret of the most difficult of conquests, the victory which every man must gain over himself. First for his own use, and later with the idea of helping others too, he recorded its elements in minute detail. "The pilgrim," he says, "saw such and such a thing in his soul, then such and such another, deciding that it was useful; and so, in the belief that he would be helping others, he wrote a book." This book, with whose precious leaves Ignatius would never part during the remainder of his life, this little book which sprang from the depths of one soul's personal experience, and which would become one of the master-works of the age, the most effective manual of warfare and conquest ever possessed by the Church, is known as the *Spiritual Exercises.*

7. A METHOD OF PRAYER BECOMES A CODE OF ACTION

IN order fully to penetrate the significance of the *Spiritual Exercises*, to understand them above all in relation to the author, we must place ourselves as far as possible in the climate in which Ignatius lived during those months of unimaginable tension, where in solitude and penance he saw himself at once the battleground and the stake in a terrible conflict between good and evil, between Christ and the Devil, and where by a clear effort of will he made his choice. We have, in one of his favourite phrases, to "make the composition." Each paragraph, every one of those formulae whose elliptical simplicity is sometimes baffling, sums up an experience, denotes a vital means to victory discovered by the writer himself. No Christian book—not even the *Imitation*, infinitely more moving though it is—gives so poignant an impression of direct experience as does this slender volume with its atmosphere of a military manual written at the height of battle.

When Ignatius of Loyola quitted Manresa, he certainly carried with him the matter of the *Spiritual Exercises.* The form may have left much to be desired; its shape, as we have it now, is not that of the original. During the twenty-seven years between the saint's conversion and the publication of his book[27] the text was constantly retouched and enriched. Meticulous scholiasts claim to have detected traces of St. Bernard, St. Bonaventure and

27. He would not allow its publication until 1548, but by that time it had been recopied and translated by a host of retreatants.

such moderns as Fray Alonzo of Madrid, with whom the author cannot have been acquainted until later. All that, however, is mere detail: it suffices to read the book itself, better still to follow its teaching, in order to feel that it was written in a climate of fire—in the Santa Cueva, the cave on the banks of the Cardoner.

Innumerable specialists have analysed the "sources," trying to discover from what books the hermit of Manresa derived the living sap of his own. Certainly and above all from the Gospel, whose most striking passages he had copied out and kept always by him; from such works as *The Flower of the Saints* and the Carthusian Ludolph's *Life of Christ*, which had first given him food for thought during his convalescence; from the *Imitation of Christ*, with which he is known to have nourished his mind during the year of his retreat; doubtless also from Cisneros's *Exercises of the Spiritual Life*, to which he had been introduced by Dom Chanones at Montserrat; and an echo has even been detected of Battista da Crema's *Self Conquest.* Each of these books may have done something to set in train the mysterious process accomplished in the soul of Ignatius, but none has left a direct imprint of any importance. Literary exegesis gives no account of the unique originality of the *Spiritual Exercises.*

It was not in books but in the depths of his own soul that Ignatius found the essence of what he had to say, and that fact alone is quite remarkable. Considering how difficult it is for any man seeking self-knowledge to express himself in writing, one may well ask how a young officer, who could do little more than read and write, and who had only just abandoned the world and a career of arms, was able to advance so far in the most intimate knowledge of the soul and to formulate his discoveries in terms so clear, so powerful and so profound. The keyword is contained in this short precept: "Study yourself, analyse what goes on within you, for there you have the lists where the spirit of good confronts the spirit of evil." It was by thus analysing himself, noting his particular difficulties and the means whereby he had managed to overcome them, writing down his examination of conscience, that Ignatius eventually produced his book. Even so he must have had an extraordinary sense of inward sovereignty, of the spiritual drama, of the call uttered by God in the secret place of every man's soul, and of the mysterious means set in operation by grace. Genius he certainly possessed, but he also enjoyed divine inspiration, the direct working of the Holy Spirit on a human intellect. Ignatius himself admitted that he had on several occasions benefited by supernatural enlightenment, and a tradition confirmed by papal authority states that it was *dictante Deipara*, at the dictation of the Mother of God, that he wrote that "perfect code of every good soldier of Jesus Christ."[28]

Materially the *Exercises* form a very small volume, a mere booklet running to no more than a hundred pages, one-third the length of the *Imitation*, four times less than the *Christian Institute* in its original form and a mere nothing in comparison with the final edition of Calvin's monumental work. But a soldier is used to expressing himself briefly. The *Exercises* were written first in Castilian, the rugged and uncouth Castilian of the Basques, heavy with obsolete or inaccurate words, but alive at the same time with forcible phrases, concise and unforgettably to the point. Subsequently, in 1534, Ignatius translated his book into Latin, after which he adjudged his own version unsatisfactory, and entrusted the work of preparing another to Père André de Freux. This final recasting of the *Exercises*, however, has no literary appeal: it seems calculated rather to discourage simple curiosity.

As we have it today the book is divided into four parts. But the fourth, consisting of a set of rules on the discernment of spirits, on the giving of alms, on scruples and on the manner of "thinking with the Church," is evidently much later than the Manresa period; it reveals the cares of a spiritual director, of a religious ruler, while the concluding section on orthodoxy appears to reflect the decrees of the Council of Sens (1528). The three fundamental elements of the work are the "Annotations," the "Exercises" properly so called and the "Meditations." Without any wish to please his reader, Ignatius begins by explaining in great detail how he must "acquire some understanding" of the Exercises and put them into practice. This advice runs to no fewer than twenty pages; nothing is left to chance. After a brief,

28. Pius XI, *Letter Apostolic to the General of the Jesuits*, December 3, 1922.

closely packed and all-important passage entitled "Principle and Foundation," which summarizes the meaning of Christian life and experience, the Exercises begin. They are intended to cover a period of four weeks. During the first week the reader's attention is directed to the ultimate ends, and having learned the rules of self-examination and meditation, he will concentrate his mind on Sin and Hell. In the second week he will place himself in the presence of Christ and His kingdom, so that, by fully understanding the achievement of the Incarnate Word, he may "make choice" of a life faithful to His principles, to which he will be led on the final day. The purpose of the third and fourth weeks is to constrain the soul to set out without further delay upon the chosen road, by meditating the sorrowful mysteries of the Passion, then the glorious mysteries of the Risen Christ, all of them pledges of the Creator's infinite love for His creatures. The third part of the book, called "Meditations," is in fact a series of rather dry formulae, devoid of comment, each element of which contributes material for a comprehensive meditation on the life of Christ, step by step from His birth to His glorious Resurrection, and thus provides as it were the skeleton of mystical experience, or the evangelical index of a spiritual treatise.

So much for the externals, the schema of the book; but it would be a mistake to call a halt at this point in the belief that it has been adequately summarized. The *Spiritual Exercises* were not written to be read, however carefully, but to be translated into reality and lived; they came from the pen of one who had himself been first to practise and live them with his whole soul. They require a man who would follow their method to give much of his own being—or rather his whole self. All the powers of the soul, heart, intelligence and sensibility must come into play. Each of the meagre formulae of which the several chapters are composed seems austere, dry and often abstract; but if one manages to charge it with sufficient spiritual passion it becomes the gateway to a whole world of imagination, to a whole field of meditation. And so to make the *Exercises* properly it is not enough to read the paragraphs one after another in order to understand their meaning; one must release within oneself such powerful stirrings—love or hate—that every word produces thereafter in the conscience a driving force which urges the will irresistibly along the chosen road. The soul which has accustomed herself to seeing Christ, hearing His words, tasting the sweetness of His presence and sharing the atrocious sufferings endured by Him in expiation of the iniquities of men will be restrained from yielding to evil by the very love she has cultivated within herself; and if she is not entirely preserved from sin she will be the less willing to incur its guilt when she considers the horrors which await a sinful soul—hell-fire, everlasting corruption, the malediction of the damned. Thus accustomed to bathe in love or freeze in terror, according as she looks upon light or darkness, the soul will be trained to confront life with its dire risks and daily temptations, and she will be able to emerge victorious from the combat.

For here indeed there is question of combat; the word "exercises" must be taken in the strictest of military senses—that of training for battle. This little book, presented as a treatise on prayer, is more properly a series of "regulations," a code of strategy for the waging of a terrible war whose issue is nothing less than eternity. Captain Iñigo, now become the hermit Ignatius, still thinks and writes as a soldier. For him Christ is the king who calls upon men to enlist in His army, in order to fight nobly at His side. The climax of the four weeks' retreat is reached on the fourth day of the second week, with the meditation on the "Two Standards." Here Ignatius shows us the two hostile armies confronting one another: that of Christ "in the great land of Jerusalem" with all those who serve under His banner, and that commanded "in the great land of Babylon" by Lucifer "seated on a kind of lofty throne of fire and smoke." The true Christian is he who has given Christ the King his total loyalty and fights on His behalf. His offensive weapon is the particular examination of conscience repeated twice daily, by means of which the vices will be vanquished one by one. Strict discipline is enforced; there must be no faint-heartedness.

This notion of combat is fundamental in Ignatian spirituality; it presupposes and underlies a whole system of theology diametrically opposed to that of the Protestant reformers. What would be the use of expending so much effort in order to teach Christians the laws of combat if, in fact, the result depended solely upon God, without any co-operation on the part of man? Ignatius certainly declares that God, in his omniscience, knows what the result will be, and that without grace human strength is incapable of victory. But to the quietistic fatalism of Luther and the predestinationism of Calvin he opposes a spirituality of effort which is the main characteristic of his doctrine. Molina afterwards fashioned it into a theological systemization when dealing with the relationship of grace and free will,[29] but the principles are apparent in Ignatius's own book. One of his confidants tells us that he often used to say: "We must work as if success depended on ourselves and not on God." Though no less stern with men than Calvin—"without Christ," he said, "all would go down into hell"—Loyola believed in the possibility of curing the sick soul of renewing it by means of interior labour co-operating with grace. There you have the essence of his message, a lucid and constructive optimism which has proved to be one of the most effective weapons ever wielded by the Church.

Thus it is completely wrong to consider the *Spiritual Exercises* as an instrument employed by Catholicism in the war against Protestantism. Although substantially anti-Protestant, the thought of St. Ignatius owes nothing to dialectical reaction against that of the "reformers" of Wittenberg, or later of Geneva. "By the favourite word 'reform' he means nothing else than the necessity for everyone to change himself before wishing to change the world.... Loyola passes no judgment on the profane and complicated questions that were troubling the whole world; rather he seems, with his advice to 'think with the Church,' not to be concerned with the external aspects of religion—doctrine, hierarchy, liturgy, sacraments, ecclesiastical customs.... While Calvin begins his reform in the opposite direction, by a general revolution of the whole structure of the Church, Loyola is content to effect a reformation in the depths of her soul.... Far from hypnotizing him, the confessional struggles seem for a long time to have occupied no more than the background of his thought. The effort of conquest, implied by submission of the whole world to the 'eternal and universal King,' pursues as its unique object the individual salvation and liberation of souls, of *all*

29. See Volume 2, Chapter VI, p. 442.

souls, by the sole arms of sacrifice, humility and charity in Catholic truth."[30] No career shows us better than does that of St. Ignatius what the Catholic Reformation really was—a fundamental movement of spiritual rebirth, not a counter-attack upon the Protestant positions; none demonstrates more convincingly that it was not at first a "counter-reformation," but a revival proceeding from the deepest loyalties.

What was the ultimate goal of this combat in which, according to St. Ignatius, the Christian is engaged? Only one answer is possible: the glory of God; all the rest is vain and laughable. On the threshold of the *Exercises*, in the first line of the "Principle and Foundation," we read this tranquil and categorical assertion: "Man is created to praise, adore and serve God Our Saviour, and thereby to save his soul." The two purposes are inextricably linked: interior reform, the means of salvation, is at the same time a testimony rendered to God in His perfection. Like Calvin on this point, Ignatius was literally haunted by the rights of God, by the adoration of His power, by the recognition of His sovereignity, by His glory which must for ever increase. *Ad majorem Dei gloriam*: the celebrated phrase flows constantly from his pen; in his writings and correspondence it occurs at least a thousand times. But the difference between Calvin and Loyola is that the former conceives God in fear and trembling, and causes man to cringe beneath the rod of a terrible master, while Ignatius, on the contrary, wishes gently to subject human freedom to "infinite Goodness, the divine Mercy, eternal Wisdom and Love, the Charity of Christ Our Lord." This man, who has so often been represented as hard, unyielding, pitiless, sums up his doctrine in three lines of a letter to the scholastics of Coimbra. He speaks neither of discipline nor of the holy fear of God, but simply says: "Above all, I want to arouse in you the pure love of Jesus Christ, the desire for His honour and for the salvation of souls redeemed by Him."

It remains to say to whom he addressed this little book, and to what classes of souls he thought it would be "useful." Theoretically, I think, to all Christians. "Exercises," runs the subtitle, "to lead man to conquer himself, to

30. A. Favre-Dorsaz, *Calvin et Loyola* (1951).

 detach himself from all inordinate affection, to lead a Christian life." Such a programme is exactly that which every baptized person must set before himself; and it is indeed true that *everyone*, provided he holds the Christian faith, finds in the *Exercises* something wherewith to nourish his religious life, to help him to a better understanding of himself and to control over his own soul. Upon whatever rung of the spiritual ladder one may stand, one can derive much profit from this teaching compounded of interior joy, self-discipline and obedience to high principles. For four centuries, too, the method has been used in countless ways and for the most varied purposes, giving rise to "closed retreats," "Manresas" and "Treatises on Meditation." If innumerable saints from Francis Xavier to Alphonsus Liguori, from Charles Borromeo to Vincent de Paul, have expressed their gratitude to this little book, there is no Catholic who, though perhaps unconsciously, is not indebted to it for having taught the world the importance of recollection and silence, the necessity for spiritual concentration, and for having given him that warmth of communication with the supernatural world without which there is no true religious life.

In practice also then—and herein lies their richness—the *Exercises* are addressed to all souls without exception. They do good to the most ordinary, to those who possess neither great spiritual ambition nor a wealth of means. They also help those who have already "made choice" to conform their lives to their vocation, and it is thus that St. Francis of Sales, in his treatise *On the Love of God*, advises bishops, priests and religious to use them. More important still, as Henri Bromond had rightly observed, far from being a mere method of asceticism, they can guide the most earnest souls to the highest summits of mystical experience; they lead by way of prayer to contemplation and even to the unitive life; and it is no accident that so many contemplatives, from St. Francis Borgia to Père Surin, from Balthazar Alvarez to Père Lallemant, became what they were by the simple practice of the Ignatian method. But this glory itself, this universal extension, is liable to obscure the true goal of their author. It was unintentionally, and because he carried within him the fire of exceptional genius, that St. Ignatius was able to make himself understood in so many ways. His initial purpose was not so ambitious. "As he wrote them," says Père de Grandmaison, "the *Exercises* had a definite end in view; their purpose was to enable a man, still free to dispose of his life and excellently endowed for the apostolate, to hear clearly and follow generously the call of God." All good prayer should be translated into action, and the contemplative must be at the same time an apostle. Such is the logical conclusion of the spirituality of effort.

Thus, it seems, by working simply to reform the interior man, St. Ignatius created a type of man of action whose effectiveness proceeds directly from the effort accomplished first at the level of conscience. Corneille's principle, "I am master of myself as of the universe," might well sum up the purpose of that cripple who was going to produce new men to the service of God and of the Church. Or perhaps he would have said rather: "I shall master the world to the extent that I first master myself." Even so, while the ancient world collapsed around him St. Benedict intended his Rule as a method for training monks to be perfect servants of God, whereas in fact he also proposed a body of heroes who would reconstruct Western society during the "Dark Ages."

When he left Manresa Ignatius carried with him, probably without knowing as much, the instrument which would enable him to endow Catholicism with the most efficient of her troops. He would now put it to the test, and gather around him the first of those innumerable men who would answer the summons issued by God through his voice.[31]

31. Like everything connected with St. Ignatius and the Society of Jesus, those permanent signs of contradiction, the *Spiritual Exercises*, have been heavily attacked; and not only by such unbelievers as Michelet and Quinet, the last of whom said that they professed "to create ecstatic automata in thirty days." Catholics too have found fault with them, possibly because their rigorous method of reform interfered with too much comfortable routine, but perhaps also because the precision of that method exceeded anything else of the kind and thereby roused jealously. When their influence began to be felt they incurred such hostility that in 1545 St. Francis Borgia asked Pope Paul III to examine them. That Pope's explicit approval was the first of many which have since emanated from Rome. One of the most famous is that of Pius XI, who in 1929 wrote to Cardinal Dubois that he himself had experienced "the holy benefits of the *Exercises*."

8. PILGRIM AND STUDENT

It often happens that an idea is slow to find its objective, that the genius who forged it gropes among a variety of means and must await the hour and the event appointed by Providence. So it was with Ignatius of Loyola. Leaving Manresa at the end of February 1523 he thought of pilgrimage to the Holy Places, after the manner of St. Francis of Assisi, as prelude perhaps to some kind of crusade. It was long before he finally abandoned this medieval dream.

Accordingly he took ship at Barcelona. Travelling by way of Gaeta and Rome, where he was received in audience and encouraged by the austere Pope Adrian VI, he reached Venice, which was the usual point of departure for Palestine. His health was none too good, but Ribadaneira informs us that it was improved by seasickness which "got rid of the humours." Six months of this stern therapy set him on his feet once more. Landing at Jaffa he performed the customary round of a pilgrim: a night of prayer at the Holy Sepulchre, visits to Bethany, Bethlehem and the Jordan ford where John baptized. Was this where God wanted him? Ought he to remain and carry the faith to Jew and Muslim? When he broached the subject with the Franciscans who looked after the Holy Places, they quickly discouraged him, unwilling that this strange Spaniard should hunt in their preserves. The Islamic authorities, they assured him, would never agree to his proposals. So Ignatius once again took ship; Christ had not called him to convert the Infidel.

What next then? He tells us in the *Pilgrim's Narrative* that "he frequently asked himself what he ought to do; and in the end he came to the conclusion that in order to be useful to souls he would first have to study." And so, as an elderly scholar at the age of more than thirty-three, he bravely applied himself to grammar at the University of Barcelona, leading of course at the same time a life of prayer and penance, and trying his hand at the apostolate—with more courage than moderation. It was at this time that there occurred one of the most charming episodes in his career. The fervent Basque, having found some lax nuns, won these ladies back to better ways and the observance of strict enclosure—but got beaten up by their admirers for his pains. Then, at Alcala, he devoured with frenzied but over-hasty joy all that he could of philosophy, literature, science and theology, meanwhile visiting hospitals and religious houses, and talking to his fellow students so ardently of life in God that four of them became his inseparable companions. Here again his zeal was too impetuous, and questions were soon being asked about these strange young men who always wore brown homespun, like hermits, and who went about preaching although they were not priests. When a rumour began to circulate that they were "Illuminati," the ecclesiastical authorities bestirred themselves. Ignatius was arrested and held in custody for forty days, and though examination of his doctrine discovered nothing reprehensible, he was forbidden to dress like a religious or to give public instruction. Things were hardly better at Salamanca, the intellectual centre of Spain, which was controlled by the Dominicans. These latter were even more seriously alarmed by the Basque preacher: twelve days after his arrival Ignatius was apprehended and wrought before the Inquisition, doubtless on suspicion of being a secret *alumbrado*, if not a Lutheran or an Erasmian. After three long weeks, during which the *Exercises* were subjected to careful scrutiny, the judges announced that they could find no trace of error in the thought or life of the student and his companions, who were therefore authorized to continue preaching and teaching the catechism within prescribed limits. These trials, however, had determined Ignatius to look beyond the Spanish border for a field in which liberty of thought and action would be less precarious. Notwithstanding the remonstrations of his friends, who pointed out the dangers that lay in wait for him in a distant country, of whose language he was ignorant and which was even then at war with Spain, he set out for France and eventually reached Paris.

His sojourn in the French capital was decisive. The great city was in the throes of intellectual and emotional ferment: the humanism of Guillaume Budé was opposed to the old scholasticism; Luther's books were passed from hand to hand and eagerly read, despite their condemnation by the Parlement and the Sorbonne. It was said that François I and his sister Marguerite were sympathetic towards the new ideas. The Collège des Lecteurs

50 Royaux was about to open its doors alongside the Sorbonne, the Collège de Navarre, and the Franciscan and Dominican schools. It was not, however, to this intellectual excitement that Ignatius responded, but to the more solid element of sober wisdom in the life of Paris. The climate of the Île-de-France exerted a moderating influence upon the fiery Spaniard, and rid the medieval hidalgo of his wilder dreams. He came to realize that the spiritual knowledge he had acquired in solitude at Manresa must be associated with other forms of learning, such as are obtained by study and hard work. At Alcala and Salamanca he had been in too much of a hurry. Embarking therefore upon a regular course of studies, and attending the Dominican classes at Saint-Jacques as well as those of the Lecteurs Royaux, he set himself to follow the same way of life as that led by students half his age. He registered as a day pupil, first at Montaigu, the famous college of which Béda was president, and then at Sainte-Barbe, which provided a more thorough course in philosophy. Despite his maturity he had the wisdom and strength of mind to spend no fewer than seven years rebuilding his foundations. At a later period this long and meticulous preparation seemed to him so necessary that he made it obligatory when drawing up the Constitutions of the Society.

9. IGNATIUS AT THE AGE OF FORTY

LET us now take a look at this aging scholar as he limps through the narrow streets of La Montagne Sainte-Geneviève. Some of his young classmates were already beginning to see him as a leader, but it was certainly not to the prestige of money or of birth that he owed this increasing ascendancy. A younger son from Guipuzcoa had no standing in Paris; and during these seven years Ignatius remained as poor as he had been when, with his few belongings loaded on a mule, he climbed from the banks of the Seine in search of board and lodging. In order to earn his daily bread and defray the cost of his studies, he had to make do as best he could, and was obliged on days of utter penury to go begging like the Franciscans. In the summer, for at least two years running, he betook himself to Flanders and even to England, where some Spanish merchants took pity on him and loosened their purse-strings. He was actually so destitute of means that after obtaining his B.A. in 1533 he had to wait a year before receiving the doctorate, because he could not pay the necessary fees, let alone provide the customary banquet. No one would have guessed that this needy student, who had to share his room with another, was already destined to a most glorious future.

His outward appearance was equally unimpressive. Apart from that poor leg whose shortened bone gave him a permanent limp, he was far from what is commonly called "handsome." He was not tall, and seemed at any rate to be devoid of strength; one could only describe him as a little fellow from the mountains, gnarled and lean, his face sunburnt and deeply furrowed. Yet his countenance was remarkable, perhaps on account of a lofty brow whose effect was heightened by his lameness; perhaps because of those strange ears, or the blood vessel that throbbed at his temples. Most surprising of all were his eyes, half veiled by heavy lids, and which, in the astonishing portrait by Sanchez Coello,[32] gave so powerful an impression of looking into the beholder, of considering only tHe inner man.

He was not a "good speaker," as the words are used of an orator or a skillful dialectician. Even in Spanish he retained the accent of his native province, its manner of speech and even many of its peculiar phrases. His Latin was clumsy; when speaking French or Italian he lapsed quickly into patois. And yet in private conversation, or when addressing a small gathering or a crowd, he held the attention of his hearers from the very start. A countryman, used to slow and solitary reflection, he was able to condense the fruits of his thought into the most striking sentences. As Cardinal Carpi observed, "he could hit the nail on the head." It is in these brilliant flashes that his intelligence is revealed, an intelligence, however, more solid than sparkling, more original in substance than in appearance.

There was nothing of Calvin in Ignatius of Loyola. He was not one of those towering geniuses who move with sovereign grace among ideas and

---

32. In the cathedral at Madrid.

forms, and upon whom the gifts of intellect seem to have been conferred by destiny. In order to learn and to understand he needed patient research, conducted with modest means and suspicious of intuitive perception. One thing, however, he possessed in common with Calvin, with Luther, and indeed with all the most influential figures of history. This was an enormous, an unlimited, capacity for work. He could spend the whole day attending lectures, helping his neighbours, discussing the most abstract themes—and then pass most of the night reading and writing in the circle of his lamp. We possess no fewer than 6,742 letters from his hand; they fill twelve large volumes, and doubtless represent less than one-half of his entire correspondence. As General of the Society he was never more devoted to his task than as a student at Sainte-Barbe or Montaigu.

It must be admitted that when we of today approach these letters with our twentieth-century outlook, they seem rather cold and slightly dull. Yet, though they lack the impetuous flash of Luther, the hidden flame of Calvin, we must admire their sovereign calm, their logic and their *moderation*. Here perhaps we have the epithet most characteristic of Ignatius. He is serene, firm, wonderfully self-controlled. Luther was prone to ungovernable rage; and it has been said of Calvin by Doumergue, his most enthusiastic panegyrist, that "he gave way too frequently to hysterics." The *Spiritual Exercises* would not be what they are if their author had not possessed a conscience absolutely self-assured, trained to army discipline and capable of applying military principles in the spiritual domain. "Ignatius," says one witness, "was never heard to abuse anyone or use a scornful word. In adversity he showed only joy." Later on, when he found that the Archbishop of Toledo was endeavouring to destroy his work in Spain, Ignatius merely said: "This trial proves that the Lord expects great things of us." There is no trace of umbrage, rancour or envy, any more than of fear, doubt or excitability. "He seemed," Ribadaneira tells us, "to be free of all interior trouble, of all that can disturb the soul." When Pope Paul IV attacked him with merciless criticism, Ignatius only smiled and said: "Let us remember Pope Marcellus, who was a saint and loved us." The same moderation is evident in his personal relationships. One of the Society's first historians wrote of him with perfect truth:

"He loves his sons, but with good sense and reserve; he is roused, but with prudence and discrimination; he punishes, but with calm and moderation."

He has been accused of "hardness," and hard indeed he was if that word is taken to mean that he never gave way on fundamental issues. He was hard as a soldier must be, for it was no easy war that he was called upon to wage. As head of a great institution he would have to eliminate without fear or favour every doubtful element, all who were weak, hesitant or rebellious; and it was these measures, together with penances which seem to us unfair, that drove Zapata to exclaim: "I would rather obey fifty superiors than one Ignatius." But this kind of hardness involved no hardness of heart, from which he was as far removed as it is possible to be. One of his companions took advantage of his confidence and robbed him; yet when Ignatius heard that the thief had fallen sick, he hurried to his bedside, embraced him and forgave him. When, as head of the Jesuits, he learned of the apostasy of Ochino, General of the Capuchins, far from making fun of the affair and giving vent to bitter mirth, as did so many others, he wrote to assure the miscreant that if he desired to return to the Church, he (Ignatius) and all his brethren would be there to welcome and assist him. The charity of Christ is no empty phrase for one who conceives "the greater glory of God" as an extension of love and justice. "It is not in words but in deeds that love must first express itself," he says in the *Exercises.* This notion of charity undoubtedly goes far to explain the radiance of his personality and his ascendancy over others. Later one of his spiritual sons, Gonzales de Camara, paid him this tribute which certainly represents the common opinion: "Our Father Ignatius is so universally loved that there is no member of the whole Society who does not love him and who is not sure of being equally loved by him."

But the mysterious prestige of this little gnome-like man rested upon something more than beauty of character; it arose chiefly from the manifest quality of his soul, as is testified by all who knew him well. Once in his student days, while begging in Spanish Flanders, he was received and assisted by the great humanist Luis Vivès, who murmured on parting from him: "That man's a saint; one day we shall see him at the head of a new Order." His young fellow student Pierre le Fèvre exclaimed: "Through this man Our

Lord has enabled me to see deep down into my own conscience." No truer word was ever spoken. In his company a man felt raised above himself, placed quite naturally in a climate of heroic greatness—the selfsame perhaps (on a spiritual level) as that of Spain under the Catholic sovereigns and Don Quixote, the climate of St. Teresa and St. John of the Cross. Because he himself was filled with God, Ignatius radiated God and the Spirit which animated him; and if he loved any man, any one of his brethren, it was only "in order to make him serve and glorify God."

Such was the secret of Ignatius, a poor student at the age of forty, in whose unfurnished room there gradually assembled two, three, and soon six or seven, enthusiasts. He talked to them all; but he did more than talk. In order to teach them how to live he allowed them to copy his first written work, with which he never parted. Surely indeed it was there that the secret of his influence lay, there in those hundred or so pages of military regulations. As soon as a man had understood the lesson and absorbed its substance, he was launched upon a new way of life. The Inquisitor at Paris, having had occasion to examine the little book, was so filled with admiration that he begged the favour of a copy. The *Spiritual Exercises* form a single entity with the personality and very soul of Ignatius: they are inseparable. And it was thus that there gathered round the crippled Basque of Montaigu and Sainte-Barbe a nucleus from which would spring the Society of Jesus.

10. THE VOW OF MONTMARTRE AND THE BULL OF PAUL III

ON the morning of August 15, 1534, the feast of Our Lady's Assumption, along an arduous and stony road that lay through vines and rabbit warrens, seven men, nearly all of them young, were climbing the slope of that isolated hillock situated about one and a quarter miles beyond the city wall and known to Parisians as Mont des Martyrs. Having left Mont Sainte-Geneviève at first light, they had walked for nearly two hours reciting prayers, while about them hung an air of mystery and urgency. On the summit of

"Montmartre," as if to show them their goal, the windmills turned white sails in the rising sun. These seven students were bound for the crypt-like chapel in the ancient Benedictine Abbey, which commemorated the Holy Bishop Denys who was supposed to have been beheaded on this spot. Lameness notwithstanding the eldest among them was in the lead.

The little band represented a fair cross-section of society: it included rich and poor, sons of peasants and noblemen of high rank. Pierre le Fèvre, a Savoyard, had been sent by the Bishop of Geneva to study for the priesthood at Paris, and he had just celebrated his first Mass. His room-mate at Sainte-Barbe, Francisco de Yasu, a native of Xavier in Navarre, was noticeable because of his aristocratic bearing. There were also three Spaniards: Diego Laynez, son of a tradesman at Almazan and a former student of Alcala; Nicolas, surnamed Bobadilla from his native village, more wealthy in brains than in hard cash; and little Alonzo Salmeron, whose precocious learning could not obscure the gaiety of his nineteen years. Lastly there was the Portuguese Simon Rodriguez, a man of noble descent, obsessed with the dream of vast lands to be won for the Gospel along the routes opened up to his countrymen by Henry the Navigator. All of them acknowledged as their head the lean, limping man who was now showing them the way, and who was senior to the eldest of them by fifteen years. They were indebted to him for the grand design which directed their steps to the chapel on Montmartre.

He had won them over one by one, in the course of passionate arguments such as have been beloved by students in every age. It is a strange sight, and one that says much for the reputation of Ignatius, to see these brilliant youths, many of them rich and all talented, bow before an elderly student and receive from him words of command that would decide their vocation. One after another he had taken them in hand, picking out with unerring sagacity those who would be able to appreciate his design, and displaying the ability to talk to each one in the language that would appeal most to him. Having first shaken them out of complacency, he had gone on to explain his famous method to them, requiring them in turn to perform the *Exercises*; and in each case the effect had been conclusive. Pierre le Fèvre, hitherto unsure of his vocation, had determined to receive Holy Orders. Francis Xavier, obsessed with temporal ambition, had come to understand the Gospel saying that it profits a man nothing to gain the whole world if he loses his soul. Thus was formed this little band, linked together by love of the interior life, a fraternal group without rule or formal obligations, wherein each would strive to help the other in the difficult warfare against self, pooling their slender resources, their knowledge and their prayers.

This small circle, formed for the purpose of mutual aid in the spiritual field, had no idea whatever of constituting themselves a body of shock troops, that fanatical army for the crushing of heresy, which too many historians have pretended to discover in the Society of Jesus. It was much more like one of those small associations which the Oratory of Divine Love was even then establishing in many villages up and down Italy, though perhaps with the additional clear-cut aim of evangelization. The seven companions seemed to pay little attention to the dramatic events precipitated by religious issues in the French capital. There is no mention in their writings and correspondence of the first executions of Lutherans and that of the humanist Louis de Berquin in 1529, of the vitriolic sermon preached on the feast of All Saints 1533 by the rector of the university, or of Calvin's flight; nor do they refer to the tragic affair of the Placards which broke out two months after the vow of Montmartre.[33] No, these young men had nothing to do with the various groups of Evangelicals, Bible punchers and Lutherans who were beginning to swarm throughout the kingdom. On that point they had satisfied the Inquisition, which, though momentarily suspicious, had approved their life and teaching. If they had any share in the strange religious fervour which troubled so many souls at that time, it was not with a view to altering the foundations of the Church, but to labouring "for the greater glory of God."

33. The only point at which it is possible to detect an influence *a contrario* exerted by current ideas on the little Ignatian group was their unanimous undertaking that they would never, as priests, accept stipends for their Masses or other sacerdotal functions; "Not," says Simon Rodriguez, "that they considered the practice illicit, but in order to shut the mouths of heretics."

As to the precise manner in which they would employ their vocation, they had as yet reached no final decision. The plan which Ignatius had formed is described in the *Memoirs* of his Portuguese companion, Simon Rodriguez, the fellow countryman of Bartholomew Diaz and Vasco da Gama: "Having all decided, in a wonderful outburst of spiritual joy, to devote themselves even unto death to whatever might increase the glory of God, they agreed unanimously that they would all start for Jerusalem, leaving the decision to Him." Several years, however, and a wealth of experience were necessary before they came to understand that old Europe offered the heralds of the Gospel as vast a field as pagan territory. Before climbing Montmartre they had resolved to take a vow binding themselves as champions of Christ in distant lands.

In that tiny chapel, remote from the crowds, they heard Mass. Pierre le Fèvre, the only one of them as yet ordained, was the celebrant. Just before receiving Communion, Ignatius, in the name of them all, pronounced the triple vow to observe evangelical poverty and perfect chastity, and to go to Jerusalem in order to labour for the conversion of the Infidel. But in obedience to what must have been a supernatural intuition he added that if their efforts to reach the Holy Land had proved unsuccessful at the end of a year, they would go to Rome and place themselves unreservedly at the Pope's disposition. It was this last vow which, though they knew it not, would direct them to their true path. "They spent an entire day in boundless fraternal joy, assuring one another of their common desire to serve God; and at sunset they returned home, blessing and praising Him." On that memorable day, August 15, 1534, the Society of Jesus may be said to have been born, although it had to wait some time before receiving its name and official Constitutions.

It remained to be seen how the seven companions would employ themselves, whether they would obey their missionary vow or invite the Pope to make use of them. Ignatius was unable to set out at once for Italy on the first stage of the journey to Jerusalem and the goal of their desire. He had been taken ill, and had been ordered by his doctors to seek a change of air at Loyola, his home. Here humility forbade him to revisit the ancestral castle; he lodged in the Magdalen hospital, resuming his former life of almsgiving, penance, visits to the sick and preaching. Once again too there were snarls, suspicions, and even importunate entreaties on the part of his family, who disapproved of their shabby relative. As soon as he was able therefore he resumed his travels, turned his back on ungrateful Spain, which he never revisited, and made for Venice where he would be able to rejoin his friends.

The latter, despite his absence, had deviated no whit from the line he had appointed. So deep was the impression made upon them by their leader and by the *Exercises* that it would never have entered their heads, in the words of Laynez, "to abandon the rule left by our Father and Master Ignatius," which was administered in his name by "the excellent Master Pierre le Fèvre." They held frequent meetings at which they encouraged one another in their spiritual effort, and helped one another to the necessities of life. The little company actually increased: on August 15, 1535, when they solemnly renewed their vows for the first time, Le Fèvre introduced his compatriot Claude le Jay. Next year two new recruits were admitted: Paschase Broet, from Picardy, and the Dauphinois Jean Codure. Life was a gay and joyous experience. In the autumn of 1536, notwithstanding cold, hunger and the insecurity of travel in time of war, they set out through eastern France, southern Germany and Switzerland—regions full of Lutheranism—preaching wherever they could. So grave and modest was their bearing that a peasant of Lorraine, who saw them pass, called out in his expressive lingo: "They're off to put some foreign place to rights."

At Venice they rejoined their leader, who had been waiting there for eighteen months and had made some useful conquests: Pietro Contarini, nephew of the cardinal; Gaspar de Doctis, an auditor at the nunciature; John Helyar, an Englishman, secretary to Cardinal Pole; and, above all, three Spaniards, Diego de Hoces and the brothers Eguia. The reunion took place in January 1537. Some months later Ignatius and those of company who were not yet priests were ordained at Venice; and the officiating bishop afterwards declared that of all the ordinations which he had ever conducted none had made so deep an impression upon him as had this.

The critical hour was at hand. War was raging. The Mediterranean, a prey to Barbary pirates, was also the scene of conflict between the imperial navies and those of Genoa in the service of France. Ignatius had withdrawn to a tumbledown house at Vicenza, seeking in prayer and contemplation an answer to his problem. Thither he summoned his companions, who suggested that, while waiting to start for Palestine, it might be useful for them to enter the universities so as better to prepare themselves for the great tasks of the apostolate. Though separated from one another they would be none the less united by their vows, by fraternal love and by the very organization imposed upon them by their leader. 59

This was all very fine; but the grand project of missionary work in Palestine was proving unrealizable, and Ignatius was beginning to see that they would have to fall back upon the final clause of their vow. At this juncture too he experienced another flash of enlightenment such as he had had years ago at Manresa, on the banks of the Cardoner; it came to him one day as he was praying in the church of S. Pietro in Vivarolo at Vicenza. Accordingly he set out for Rome, and as he neared the journey's end he distinctly heard two phrases ringing in his ears: "I want you to be My servant." "Go, I will be favourable to you at Rome." These messages could surely proceed from none but Him in whose name the Apostle had established the Church upon the Seven Hills. Moreover, as we learn from Bobadilla, Pope Paul III had said to some of his companions who had arrived in the Eternal City ahead of him: "Why are you so anxious to go to Jerusalem? Italy is just as good as Jerusalem if you seek to benefit the Church of God."

The problem was now solved. These soldiers of Christ, so faithful to their vow and determined to place themselves at the service of the Pope, could not but listen to the call of a pontiff who had been roused by the reiterated appeal of the entire Church, who was anxious to begin the work of reform regardless of all the obstacles in his way, and who would at long last summon the oft-promised Council.[34] Besides, the Holy Father was using the companions of Ignatius in confidential missions even before their

34. See below, Chapter II, section 2.

status had been canonically established by papal Bull. In 1539 he sent Fr. Broet to reform a monastery at Siena, Fr. Bobadilla to pacify the island of Ischia, Frs. Laynez and Le Fèvre to inspect the city of Parma and then to teach in the recently founded College of the Sapienza. Next year Fr. Le Jay was entrusted with a mission to Brescia. Soon afterwards Fr. Le Fèvre accompanied the diplomat Pedro Ortiz as official theologian at the Diet of Worms; and while Frs. Francis Xavier and Simon Rodriguez started on their missionary undertaking in the Indies, at the invitation of King John III of Portugal, there was a question of appointing Frs. Salmeron and Broet apostolic nuncios in Ireland and Scotland. It was a curious situation: a religious institute which as yet had no canonical existence and included a mere handful of men was nevertheless already playing an important role in the Church.

Success of this kind inevitably failed to please everyone. Ecclesiastical jealousy is well known to be inventive, and care for God's glory often adopts the most extraordinary forms. The fame of their sermons—particularly those delivered in Spanish by Ignatius at the church of S. Maria de Montserrat—did not win the unqualified approval of the Dominicans and Franciscans. The infant order of Theatines, after briefly considering amalgamation with these vigorous newcomers, proved no more friendly; one of its leaders was the powerful Carafa, with whom Ignatius had dealt somewhat brusquely in an open letter. Even the commission of cardinals[35] entrusted by the Pope with preparations for reform and the summoning of a council looked with a jaundiced eye upon the emergence of a new religious order, especially one that rejected choral office and wore no distinctive habit.

Eventually, however, the various obstacles were removed. By skillful use of all the powerful friends he could muster,[36] and by procuring the celebration of three thousand Masses for the success of his cause, Ignatius held his ground and finally won the day. Constitutions were drawn up, creating an

35. It included Contarini, Sadolet and Reginald Pole.

36. Pietro Contarini interceded with his uncle, and Ortiz, hitherto mistrustful, showed himself a firm supporter.

apostolic order to be governed by an elected superior in a spirit of military discipline, which would undertake to serve no end other than the will of the Pope. "Thus," wrote Bobadilla, "Divine Providence had changed the vows of Montmartre into others more fruitful." Paul III saw clearly what a marvellous instrument had been offered him for the tasks he meant to undertake. On September 27, 1540, the Bull *Regimini militantis Ecclesiae* canonically established the Society of Jesus. In the written oath taken by this new organism it was said that the members engaged themselves to go wherever the Pope might send them, either among the Turks or other infidels, or among heretics and schismatics, as well as among the faithful. The Church could henceforward rely upon this *corps d'élite* in the struggle that lay ahead.

11. THE CONSTITUTIONS

THE elements of organization submitted to the Pope were merely an outline: more detailed Constitutions were indispensable. Ignatius was unanimously elected head of the Society by his friends in 1541, despite the reluctance inspired by his humility, and he now bent himself to a task which was to take him ten years. First he carefully studied the rules of other Orders, meditated the lessons of experience, having in view the work which already occupied his spiritual sons in various fields, and listened to the objections and suggestions which many of them put forward. Then, with the help of Fr. de Polanco, his secretary, he drew up a body of regulations at once so firm and so moderate, so simple and so clear, that a Protestant historian[37] has seen fit to pay him this tribute: "As an organizer, its author is undoubtedly one of the greatest geniuses that have ever lived."

Created by a soldier for the purpose of spiritual warfare, the Society had several elements of a military nature. We must not of course overestimate them, as has been done by certain of his enemies, who have compared his spirit with that of Prussian militarism; but they are nonetheless apparent.

37. H. Böhmer, *Les Jesuites* (1909).

 Ignatius himself used to say: "I do not consider myself as having retired from military service, but only as having come under the orders of God." As in the army then, his essential principle was obedience. The Constitutions declare that anyone desiring to enter the Society "must strip himself of all earthly affection towards his family, in order to love them only with that well-ordered love required by charity; for being dead to the world, he lives only for Our Lord, who has taken the place of his parents, brethren and all else besides." He must incline his whole will, submit entirely to his Superior, "out of respect and love for Jesus Christ, whom he represents. He must be utterly docile in the Superior's hands, must abandon any and every occupation at his command, leaving unfinished even a single letter of the alphabet. He must obey his orders promptly, earnestly and with interior joy; he must be convinced, in brief, that in living under obedience one ought to allow oneself to be led by the will of Divine Providence, through the agency of the Superior, like a corpse—*perinde ac cadaver*—which can be carried anywhere and handled in any way, or, rather, like a staff which an old man holds to use at his discretion."[38]

Perinde ac cadaver. These celebrated words have given rise to much debatable comment. To attribute them exclusively to St. Ignatius, either as praiseworthy or as reprehensible, is equally absurd. The necessity for obedience is in full accord with the most ancient tradition as represented by St. Basil, St. Augustine and St. Benedict; and it was probably from Franciscan tradition, perhaps from Thomas Celano's charming life of the Poverello, that the founder of the Society of Jesus derived the idea that subjects "humiliated, moved from one place to another, ill-treated or honoured, must remain, like corpses, imperturbable in their humility." It may also be asked whether the terms of the Constitutions quoted above are any more severe than those of Christ Himself, which bid a man "leave his father and mother," to consider himself "dead to self" and "to lose his life in order to save it." Absolute dependence, in the view of St. Ignatius, was a free obedience based upon the man's will to conquer himself, to reform himself, and to give himself

38. Thomas of Celano attributed these words to St. Francis.

entirely to an ideal which transcends him. Though a reaction against the individualism preached by the spokesmen of the Renaissance, the Jesuit discipline tended to the highest of all human attainments—the clear-sighted and resolute sacrifice of self. Far from being a slave in the hands of more or less unknown masters, as many still profess to believe,[39] the Jesuit was a man raised above himself in order to serve of his own free will.

Ignatius devoted a large part of the Constitutions to this matter of selection and training. "As regards recruitment," says Böhmer, "perhaps no other congregation has shown itself so cautious as the Society of Jesus in the reception of new members. Ignatius considered no one fully qualified unless he were healthy, in the prime of life, of good personal appearance, intelligent and of a disposition at once energetic and serene." Just so, an army will accept none but vigorous and healthy men. The Constitutions are devised to exclude those who are fainthearted, hesitant, excitable or mediocre. Above all, the Jesuit must be well balanced, moderate, prudent, mistrustful of exaggeration in any form. Likewise Ignatius refrained from imposing rigorous asceticism and long fasts of the Cistercian type, or privation of sleep; he feared that excessive austerity would enfeeble the body and occupy much valuable time, so that the Fathers would be unfit for work "and spiritual fervour grow cold." For the same reason, with a view to making full use of all their faculties in whatever work they might undertake, he would not have his spiritual sons bind themselves to choral office, sung or recited. Their training would have to be such that they might profit by the teaching of the breviary without communal psalmody, and unite themselves

39. This and other still more ridiculous fables derive from a pamphlet entitled *Monita Secreta Societatis Jesu*, written about 1612 by one Jerome Zanorowski, a Pole who had been expelled from the Society and sought a contemptible revenge through the medium of the printing press. According to the *Monita*, the Society is governed by a small clique whose members hold certain secrets and are bound to one another by terrible oaths. Zanorowski also declares that the Jesuits have orders to win the favour of the powerful and the confidence of the rich, in order to impose their influence and to amass useful wealth. "It is unfortunate," says the Protestant Harnack, "that falsehoods such as the *Monita Secreta* are still used to denigrate the Society." But the practice continues. Many an honest man still believes in the "Secrets of the Jesuits" as well as in the "black Pope" who controls the white Pope and even gets rid of him if he resists.

 month by month with the Life and Passion of Christ without communal participation in the ceremonies of the liturgical cycle.

This training assumed capital importance, and it must be admitted that no Order or Institute has ever envisaged anything so solid or detailed. The fundamental idea was such as can be discovered in the *Spiritual Exercises*, that the most efficient man is he who is most completely master of himself. It was for this absolute mastery that the future soldiers of Christ must be prepared; nor did the wise founder think seventeen years an unnecessarily long period for the formation of a perfect Jesuit. The postulant would therefore spend some weeks or months under observation, after which he would be admitted to the novitiate; and this novitiate would last for two years, as against the twelve months required by most other Orders. During it he would be trained in spiritual exercises, in examination of conscience and in meditation, as well as being subjected to trials or "tests"—in the kitchen, for example, or the infirmary—in order to see whether he were capable of adapting himself to all circumstances. At the end of this period of probation the novice would pronounce simple vows of poverty, chastity and obedience, like all other religious, and then begin his scholasticate, during which he would receive his training properly so called. This would involve two years of classical studies, three of philosophy, four of theology and lastly several years (five at the most) of practical testing, generally in one of the Society's educational establishments. Meanwhile, having completed his theological studies, the future Jesuit would be ordained priest, at the age of about thirty to thirty-five; but he would still have to undergo a final period of probation, the "third year," in a special novitiate. He would not be a fully fledged Jesuit until the solemn and public renewal of his vows. Even then he would be only what the Constitutions called a "spiritual coadjutor"; higher still there would be a select few, numbering perhaps one Father in every thirty or forty, who would take a fourth vow of total obedience to the Pope and be known as the "Professed of Four Vows." Naturally such training could be given only to subjects of the highest quality, with outstanding intellectual gifts. The Society, however, did not close its doors to men who, though less richly endowed, might wish to serve as soldiers of Christ. Ignatius admitted them as "temporal coadjutors," bound by the three vows. They would act as door-keepers, gardeners or cooks, and would look after the material needs of the community; but the Constitutions laid down that they were "forbidden to learn more than they knew on joining the Society." This admirable logic and methodical genius appear yet again in the organization of the Society. Once more like an army, it was to have a clearly defined system of command, but the whole hierarchy of officers was established with a view to action, to warfare in God's cause. At its head would be the General, or rather, since Ignatius thought of the word as an adjective rather than a noun, the *praepositus generalis*: "superior-general." He was to be elected for life by an absolute majority of the General Congregation, itself consisting of the Provincials and two Professed from each province. Helped by five or six assistants, he would be the truly monarchical head of the Society, but a monarch whose authority was clearly defined as intended to be exercised in a paternal spirit and in full agreement with the whole body of members. Personal power and oligarchic power must control and balance one another. On the administrative plane the Society was divided into provinces, to be governed by Provincials appointed for three years and assisted by Counsellors. Jesuits were forbidden to accept positions of authority outside the Society; they must be "at the service of the Holy See, and not usurp its place." Hierarchical relationships were to be both confident and strict. The inferior must at regular intervals make "manifestation of conscience" to his superior, "that is to say, he must reveal the whole of his interior life, his temptations, difficulties and progress"; and the Constitutions even provide for an *admonitor* on the staffs of the General and the Provincials, specially entrusted with the sanctification of others and having for this purpose access even to the "manifestations" made to superiors.[40] It is hard to imagine a stricter organization, a closer centralization, a securer discipline. Most recent of the great religious Orders, the Society of Jesus appeared to discard as far as possible

40. These two regulations have done more than anything else to provoke criticism of the Society by those who refuse to understand the spirit of charity and faith with which they were to be applied.

the ancient characteristics of monachism. Broadly democratic, it showed none the less, in its will to perfection, as well as in its firm determination to serve God above all, those essential tendencies to which in the course of centuries monachism had owed its development.

The hierarchical system and discipline of the Jesuits were destined to speedy and violent criticism, which has persisted into our own day. Michelet has said that the Jesuit is a mere cog; in the enormous machine of the Society; but that is to misunderstand the spirit in which St. Ignatius conceived the whole gigantic system. Far from being a prisoner of the hierarchical and administrative framework the Jesuit feels himself all the more free because that very framework protects him against danger and temptation. Within the principles laid down by the Constitutions, and freely accepted, he enjoys a considerable degree of autonomy that may sometimes appear surprising. Sent into the world, he preaches, teaches and campaigns in the way that seems to him most appropriate to his purpose and best adapted to his temperament, without the presence of an immediate superior to direct and control him; government is exercised at a higher level, in the sphere of more ultimate responsibility.

Perfectly trained, the soldiers of Christ as recruited by Ignatius obeyed no other criteria than zeal for souls, with the essential motive for which their leader could feel confident of having equipped them. United by a grand overall design, they would adhere to the strict discipline imposed by their Society, sure that they were serving a cause which transcended them all, and which had been expressed once for all by their founder in the phrase *Ad majorem Dei gloriam.*[41]

---

41. It must be observed that St. Ignatius never made provision for a female congregation. "Women," wrote St. Francis Xavier, "would be more trouble than profit to confessors; I advise you always to concern yourselves rather with their husbands." Between 1543 and 1547 a few communities of female Jesuits tried to establish themselves in Italy, Spain and Portugal, but without success. One at Barcelona, under a certain Isabel Roser, turned out so badly that Ignatius brought an action against the foundress. It was not until much more recent times that religious Orders of women adopted the Ignatian spirituality and the substance of the Constitutions (e.g., the Helpers of the Holy Souls, the Ladies of the Cenacle, the Ladies of the Sacred Heart and the Society of the Holy Child Jesus).

12. THE MEANS OF PEACEFUL RECONQUEST

THE Society of Jesus, thus established, was intended for action in the service of God. Its members, outwardly indistinguishable from secular priests,[42] were destined to mix with the people and rub shoulders with those to whom they had to deliver their message, obeying, in short, the celebrated commandment of St. Paul which is the motto of every missionary undertaking: "A Jew among the Jews, a Gentile among the Gentiles." They were an immediate success—too much so perhaps for the liking of some. It is well known that the outstanding qualifications of the Jesuits are no less proverbial (and decried) than their ability to adapt themselves to circumstances and the readiness with which they can find common ground with every sort of mentality. So also in the matter of their iron discipline: it has provided material for countless tales which have been going the round of ecclesiastical circles for the past two or three hundred years. It was by agreeing to share in everyday life (which incidentally raised for them a number of very real problems) that the sons of St. Ignatius exercised their widespread influence. They were daunted by no task or difficulty. Their apostolate was no less pliant than universal. We shall find them later on serving as astronomers and geographers in China, adopting the manners of men of caste in India,[43] but mixing just as easily with the slaves of America in the person of St. Peter Claver. Writers, preachers, lecturers, professors, missionaries—they were all these things, and much else besides, according to the precept of St. Ignatius: "You must above all offer yourselves generously for the tasks in which charity also plays its humble part."

The efficiency of the Jesuits quickly manifested itself on the strictly religious plane, where they had at their disposal a remarkable weapon forged by St. Ignatius. I refer, of course, to the *Exercises.* The Fathers gave the *Exercises* wherever they were sent, and on many occasions made truly miraculous draughts. Novices of excellent quality soon flowed in: Italians, Spaniards,

---

42. Less even than the Theatines, who retained certain small details of dress peculiar to themselves.

43. On Fr. de Nobili, see Volume 2, Chapter V, pp. 375–79.

 Portuguese; then Frenchmen, Belgians and Germans. Wherever Le Fèvre, Jay, Bobadilla or Francis Xavier spoke, souls on fire with this ideal offered themselves without reserve. Such was the Dutchman, St. Peter Canisius, afterwards the apostle of Germany. Such too was the Spanish grandee and viceroy of Catalunya, St. Francis Borgia, who became third General of the Society and whose holiness washed away the disgrace incurred by others of his name.

But in addition to those who actually became Jesuits, many others experienced the influence of that enchanting little book. It was at this period that there emerged and gradually developed the custom of "retreats" (analogous to the sojourn at Manresa), during which the soul withdraws into solitude and silence, to consider its last end and its hope of salvation. Individual retreats at first, then collective, were preached ever more frequently, summoning their hearers to conversion. The practice of an annual eight-day retreat soon established itself in religious houses and seminaries, and eventually was made obligatory for all priests. When the decrees of the Council of Trent became part of the Church's life, this use of the *Exercises* became one of the principal means employed by numerous monasteries in the work of reforming themselves and developing a life of prayer among their members.

The Jesuit influence exerted itself far beyond the cloister, reaching out to persons living in the world. Spreading everywhere the practice of frequent confession, and installing in all their churches a newly invented piece of furniture known as the "confessional," which guaranteed absolute secrecy, the Fathers began to refine the very technique of confession. This they did by examination of conscience, and also by the use of "casuistry," an art much decried by their opponents, but which enabled them to apply with more flexibility, more moderation, and consequently with more justice, the great principles of Christian morality to particular cases that were often extremely complicated. Thanks to their intellectual eminence, it was not long before the Jesuits supplanted the seculars and Mendicants as confessors to princes.

Their activity in the purely spiritual domain made use of devotions and practices which cannot be described as original, but to which they gave new emphasis. The meditation on our Lord's life in the *Exercises* helped to exalt the love of God made Man and the sacrifice of Calvary, a love which soon found expression in devotion to the Sacred Heart. Linked with the worship rendered to her Son, the Blessed Virgin was also held in high honour by the Jesuits; so much so that in the following century St. John Eudes paid them this tribute: "Among all the religious Orders none shows more zeal or more ardour than does the Society of Jesus for the honour and service of the Queen of Heaven." These two forms of devotion, to which St. Bernard had owed much of his success in the twelfth century, contributed also to that of the Jesuits. Among their principal labours was the encouragement of frequent communion, which had fallen into disuse and which St. Ignatius strove energetically to restore. In several of his spiritual letters he lays great stress upon the importance of the Eucharist and the advantage of receiving the Holy Sacrament very often.[44] The profound change thus inaugurated by the Jesuits added to their prestige. When Teresa entered the convent at Avila, in 1534, the hundred fifty Carmelites were not allowed to communicate more than six times a year, or at the very most once a month. Eight years later, thanks to her Dominican confessor, she obtained permission to do so every fortnight, and in 1554 the first Jesuit whom she met advised her to communicate each morning.

Of all the activities pursued by the Jesuits, from the earliest days of the Society and in the lifetime of St. Ignatius, that which they favoured most was the work of education. It was not peculiar to them, for it had already been undertaken by such institutes as the Barnabites and Ursulines; but they made such advances in the science of teaching and youth training that within a hundred years of their foundation they held, if not a monopoly, at least a marked predominance in this field. The educational work of the Jesuits was carried on at two wisely chosen levels. First, they left elementary instruction to others, and concentrated upon the religious formation of children in every class of society as well as of illiterate adults, a task all

44. He experienced such emotion when celebrating Mass that he used to prolong the ceremony far beyond the half-hour prescribed for his subjects. Sometimes he was so overwhelmed that he would not ascend to the altar.

the more indispensable because it had been badly neglected. The first Jesuits, and St. Ignatius above all, were zealous catechists. St. Peter Canisius's *Summary of Christian Doctrine*, compiled in three stages adapted to the pupil's age and proficiency, was an enormous success: published in 1555, it was reissued four hundred times in a century, and translated into twelve languages, including Japanese and Ethiopian. It was surpassed, however, by the catechism of Bellarmine, with its fifty translations (six or seven in India alone) and world-wide circulation. After the Council of Trent there was talk of making one of the Jesuit catechisms the official catechism of the Church.

The second and very different level of Jesuit education was the formation of a social élite, that is to say, the development of a new type of teaching. Here again their interest was not original. The Brethren of the Common Life had been making serious efforts in this direction for more than a hundred years, and their success was apparent in the flourishing Collège de Montaigu at Paris. Their teaching methods, however, remained archaic, scholastic and often brutal, if we may believe Erasmus, Calvin and Rabelais. The new Jesuit educational system, taking account of contemporary trends, gave the ancient languages pride of place in the curriculum; at the same time, while maintaining strict discipline and morality, it made use of a technique of encouragement and rewards to stimulate rivalry among pupils, paid attention to cleanliness and physical exercise, and undoubtedly enjoyed greater success than the forbidding schools that were normal at that time. This idea formed no part of St. Ignatius's main plan; but when he saw its good results he adopted it. The earlier Jesuit colleges were simply the lodgings of the Society's scholastics who were attending university courses. Soon they began to take in young men who were not destined for membership of the Society; then these college seminaries became regular homes of learning. St. Ignatius understood so clearly the importance of this matter that he inserted in the Constitutions a body of rules governing education.

Thus, long before Calvin founded his notorious academy at Geneva,[45] the Jesuits erected so many colleges that by the end of the sixteenth century

45. See *A Religious Revolution: The Protestant Reformation*, Volume 2, Chapter VI, p. 545.

three-quarters of their houses were schools, and four-fifths of their own number were teachers. This new type of educational establishment spread to every country of Europe and even to India: Coimbra in 1542, Alcala in 1543, Valencia in 1544, Barcelona in 1545; but others were founded simultaneously at Gubbio, Messina, Perugia, Bologna, Ferrara, and also at Goa. The first Jesuit college in France was opened at Billom in Auvergne (1550); others followed at Pamiers, Toumon, Mauriac, Dole and Dijon. The Collège de Clermont, founded at Paris in 1565 through the generosity of Guillaume Duprat, Bishop of Clermont, afterwards became the famous Lycée Louis le Grand. Elsewhere in Europe the Society reorganized the high schools at Vienna, Ingolstadt and Dillingen; they settled at Louvain, where, despite fierce resistance, they subsequently did much to revive the celebrated university; at Douai and Rheims they founded special colleges for English Catholics who were determined to bring back their country to the Roman faith. In the Eternal City itself the German College aimed at producing zealous and well-educated priests for Germany; while the Roman College, founded in 1551 and now the illustrious Gregorian University, became the model seminary. The goal of Jesuit pedagogy, then, was twofold: to train priests for their tasks, and to produce Christian gentlemen who would exert a beneficial influence in their various walks of life. The Jesuits borrowed their technique from contemporary humanism, but not its anti-religious and unduly individualistic spirit. It is impossible to overestimate the part which they thus played in the revival of Catholicism. Attracted by the quality of their teaching and by the novelty of their methods, as well as by the free instruction offered in many cases by the Society, children thronged these "good houses"[46] to the great scandal of the synods. Jesuit Colleges were in process of turning out a new Christian élite, such as we shall find throughout most of the Catholic world in the seventeenth century.

The foregoing achievements of the Society by no means exhausted its activities, and we must say something here about its missionary undertakings

46. "In vast herds" said a disgruntled Calvinist, for the sons of many non-Catholics also frequented them.

 properly so called. In Europe, notably in those parts overrun by the Protestant heresy, the work of the Jesuits was at many points crowned with success[47]; but we must not overlook the tremendous impetus given by them to the missions in pagan territory, the epic of St. Francis Xavier,[48] and the exploits of so many Fathers from the Zambesi to Monomotapa, from Macao to Mexico, at the court of the Negus and among the slaves in Morocco.[49] We must likewise remember their creative role in the very different field of art. From 1568, when Vignola began the "Gesù" their famous church in Rome, their influence was so strong that the Society alone of the great Orders has given its name to a form of art, "the Jesuit style,"[50] which continues to flourish. It may in fact be said that there is no department of human affairs (even politics, economics and finance) in which the Jesuits have failed to discover means for the advancement of God's glory.

Of all these means one characteristic is particularly striking: all are constructive, none is negative or polemical. They reflect the essence of St. Ignatius's thought: that it was necessary, before and above every other task, to refashion the Christian man. This did not mean that the Jesuits would not later become involved, like the Dominicans, Capuchins and other Orders, in the rough and tumble of the counter-reformation, where they had many battles to fight. Their primary purpose however lay elsewhere: what they sought to do was to rebuild the very structure of Catholicism, its substance and its outlook; the rest would be a mere corollary. Nothing is more absurd than the oft-repeated assertion that "the Society of Jesus was founded to extirpate heresy"—excepting perhaps the old cliché which links "the Jesuits and the Inquisition" in a single formula of reprobation. On the contrary, the Society of Jesus kept strictly aloof from the Inquisition, even when the latter had been reorganized by Rome and made an important part of the ecclesiastical organism.[51] No one has ever ventured publicly to declare that

47. On the work of St. Peter Canisius in Germany and Poland, see Volume 2, pp. 429–30.
48. See Volume 2, Chapter V, section 8.
49. See Volume 2, p. 354.
50. See Volume 2, p. 500.
51. See above, Chapter II, p. 110.

St. Ignatius was responsible for the death of any man, and he himself never prosecuted an adversary with a view to his execution by the secular arm. All the first Fathers were remarkable for their spirit of gentleness and charity, the spirit of true apostles, and not for that fanatical zeal which is attributed so unjustly to their Society. It was a Jesuit, St. Peter Canisius, who coined the beautiful phrase "our separated brethren," to denote those who are not of the faith. In any case, until the death of Loyola, the Jesuits were very little concerned with polemics and the struggle against Protestantism; they intended to use other weapons in order to oppose and checkmate heresy.

13. EXPANSION OF THE SOCIETY AND DEATH OF ST. IGNATIUS

WHEN the saintly Cardinal Cervini was elected as Pope Marcellus II, in 1555,[52] one of the first things he did was to summon Ignatius of Loyola and ask him to appoint two Fathers who would live in the papal palace and act as his immediate advisers. "Do you," he said, "muster troops and train them for the struggle; We will employ them."

Those words are a perfect description of the part played by the Society from the day of its foundation, and which would soon become of capital importance in the history of the Church. With its strong organization, the spirit of discipline and enthusiasm which inspired its members, together with their moral, intellectual and spiritual excellence, it was a providential instrument which the Church could use to halt the advance of Protestantism and try to recover lost ground. The popes understood as much, and did their best to foster the growth of the young institute. The Bull *Regimini Militantis Ecclesiae*, while giving the Society canonical status, had confined the number of its members to sixty. Three years later (1543), Paul III's Bull *Injunctum nobis* suppressed this restrictive clause and allowed unlimited recruitment. Better still, in 1545, the same pontiff signed a brief exempting

52. Unfortunately for the Church he died after a pontificate of only twenty-two days.

 the Jesuits from episcopal jurisdiction, and empowering them to preach and confer all the sacraments wherever they might exercise their ministry, without having to ask the permission of parish priest or bishop. Julius III, one of those who had presided at Trent, had made friends with the Jesuit theologians[53] attending the Council. Immediately after his election he promulgated the Bull *Exposcit debitum*, confirming and "renewing with added force" the privileges of the Society, pronouncing upon it a solemn panegyric, and formally declaring that it was placed "under his immediate protection and that of the Apostolic See." The election of Marcellus II, as we have just seen, ratified these measures.

Thus encouraged by the popes, and officially recognized as the spiritual army of Rome, the Society of Jesus was on the threshold of prodigious increase. Its expansion was exactly similar to that of the Mendicants at an earlier date, and perhaps even more impressive when we consider the difficulty of admission to its ranks and the meticulous training of its members. In 1540 there were ten Jesuits; in 1556, at the death of their Founder, they numbered one thousand in one hundred houses spread over twelve provinces. Forty years after their canonical establishment, twenty-one provinces included five thousand members; a census taken in 1616 yielded thirteen thousand, one hundred twelve members, four hundred thirty-six houses and thirty-seven provinces; while the second centenary of their foundation brought the membership to twenty-two thousand.[54]

There was immediately unleashed a veritable "Jesuit offensive," which had begun, it will be remembered, even before the Society existed as a canonical entity, and whose multiform and planetary character is something of a marvel. It seemed that the Jesuits wished to be everywhere and to have a hand in everything. Some of them were present at the Council of Trent, where their learning made a deep impression. Others served as legates at the court of Charles V, or as nuncios in Ireland and Scotland. When it

53. Laynez, Le Jay, Salmeron and Canisius.

54. On January 1, 1954, they numbered thirty-two thousand, making them the second largest religious Order after the Franciscans (forty-one thousand), though the latter are divided into three branches. The Jesuits far outnumber the Dominicans (eight thousand).

became necessary to make a visitation of Corsica, where faith and morals were at a very low ebb, the duty was entrusted to a Jesuit. Meanwhile the Society's schools were multiplying, and Jesuit missionaries were at work in every quarter of the globe. One asks where they found sufficient men qualified to shoulder simultaneously so many different tasks; for others again were commissioned to revise the Bible, and to draw up the canons of Trent. Ignatius controlled the threads of all this huge tapestry from his office in Rome. In 1551, having finished work on the Constitutions, and believing his task fulfilled, he offered his resignation. But the Professed were unanimous in refusing to accept it; the chief was indispensable to the army. So he continued his labour to the end, writing innumerable letters to his subjects who were scattered over the face of the earth, as well as to correspondents in religious houses, to laymen, and even to the Emperor of Ethiopia.

Success of this kind was bound to have repercussions, and watchful jealousy reared its head. When the Theatine Giovanni Pietro Carafa succeeded Pope Marcellus II, Ignatius could not hope for the same benevolent interest as had been shown by his predecessor; the two men were at once too much alike in the inflexibility of their characters and too different in their manners. Thus Paul IV tried to impose traditional religious usages upon the Society, particularly the choral office. He also disliked the idea of such paramount authority at the head of an Order, and therefore suppressed the clause in the Constitutions which provided that the General should be elected for life. Ignatius, simple and modest as ever, submitted without a murmur to the papal decision: he was entitled to remind himself that popes are mortal, and that what was done by one could be undone by another. This in fact is what actually happened on the accession of Pius IV. Moreover, in the closing months of his pontificate, the harsh Carafa showed signs of relenting, and even helped in the foundation of various Jesuit colleges, notably at Ingolstadt and Prague.

The Society met with resistance in many lands, especially in France. What, men asked, were these Spaniards, subjects of their enemy Charles V, doing in the kingdom of the fleur-de-lis? Would not the ultramontanism of the Professed, as evidenced by their fourth vow, tend to circumscribe the rights of the Gallican Church? Many bishops, particularly Eustache du Bellay of Paris, thought their privileges extravagant. Parlement and Sorbonne made themselves the spearhead of this opposition, and the first of these great corporations even refused to register the edict of Henri II authorizing the foundation of a Jesuit College in Paris. In spite of all the Society installed itself under the patronage of the Cardinal of Lorraine and Guillaume Duprat, Bishop of Clermont. The first Fathers arrived almost clandestinely, on the pretext of having come to study, and lodged in the house of their episcopal protector. Opposition gradually died down, so that they were able to make their projected foundations; but it was never fully appeased.[55]

More surprising was the resistance offered to the Society in Spain, the land of their origin. Whereas their success had been rapid and triumphant in Portugal, which Francis Xavier had reached in 1540, trial and tribulation awaited them in the most Catholic of all territories. These difficulties sprang from various causes, partly perhaps from the jealousy of the all-powerful Dominicans, who did not much care for the presence of such competent rivals on their home ground. Again, it may be that Charles V and Philip II, staunch Christians though they were in faith and utterance, mistrusted a body of religious who professed to serve none but the Pope. The fact that the Society was primarily Roman rather than Spanish may likewise have told against them. The result was something more than unfriendly maneuvering: there were acts of open hostility, such as the decree procured by the Dominicans from Philip II forbidding any Spaniard to study abroad—a direct blow at the Society. At Salamanca, the most eminent Dominican theologians, Vittoria and later Melchior Cano, his disciple, did not hesitate to attack the Ignatian spirituality on the grounds that it was tainted with mystical excess and even with illuminism. Nevertheless the Jesuits obtained a foothold in the land of St. Ignatius: by 1554 there were three Spanish provinces (Aragon, Castile and Andalusia) with more than three hundred

55. Henri IV drove them from the kingdom after the attempt on his life by Jean Chatel, because they had been more or less associated with the League. But he soon recalled them.

Fathers. The most striking feature of this achievement was the entry into the Society of Francis Borgia (1510–1572), Duke of Gandia, whom the *Exercises* had won for Christ and His new militia. He sought admission after the death of his beloved wife, and even before he had secured the future of his eight children.[56] In 1554 he was appointed "commissary" of the three Spanish provinces, a position which he held for eleven years until his election as General.

As Ignatius looked into the measureless distances that now revealed themselves, what did he care for resistance and ill will? To attacks that were often furious he replied only with meekness and prayer, counselling his Fathers, if they met with opposition, "to commit their adversaries to God, and do everything with a view to touching their hearts, not with fear of the contradictions or of the difficulties they might cause, but with charity." His serenity was indeed admirable; but he knew that the work God had given him to do was now established on unshakable foundations. He could die, and those who succeeded him at the head of the Order would be able to follow his lessons and example, and to continue the forward march. He was in fact succeeded by a distinguished line of Generals, whose work was a splendid continuation of his own: Laynez, his companion; St. Francis Borgia; the Belgian Mercurian; the Neapolitan Aquaviva, whose genius for organization gave the Jesuits an even stronger impetus.[57] If Ignatius had not been so profoundly humble he could have finished his life with this tribute to himself, which has been paid to him in our own day by a Protestant author: "The Church is indebted to him for most of her victories and for the recovery of her vitality."[58]

His end was marked by the quiet simplicity befitting one who, in the second week of the *Exercises*, recommends Christians "always to think of

56. The Pope granted a special dispensation enabling him to exercise his functions as viceroy during three years of his Jesuit scholasticate, so that he might make arrangements for the future of his family.

57. It was he who published the educational principles of the Society in a work entitled *Ratio Studiorum*, which remained in use until the nineteenth century.

58. G. Monod, Introduction to the French translation of Böhmer's work.

 themselves as if they were on the point of death." He had long since made the "necessary dispositions" and taken the "necessary steps"; almost forty years ago he had made a "sound and wholesome choice." On July 1, 1556, he fell sick; the physicians declared that his indisposition was not serious. Warned, it may be, by the Spirit of Light who had so often guided him, he replied gently that he was under no illusion and that he was going to die. At his bidding, his secretary Polanco left for Rome, to offer Paul IV a last greeting from his faithful son and to ask the papal blessing. That was on July 30. A few hours later, on the morning of the thirty-first, Ignatius of Loyola died peacefully, attended by only one of his Fathers. He had so loved solitude, and had spoken much of its spiritual benefits. At about the same time news reached the Eternal City that far away, on the other side of the world and looking towards China which he had longed to evangelize, Francis Xavier also was dying. He too was alone. From the vow of Montmartre to these solitary deaths, what a journey had been accomplished in the space of twenty years![59]

13. THE PAPACY INTERVENES

St. Ignatius and his companions represent the high-water mark of that tidal movement towards reform, which lifted up the Catholic soul and drove it to confront the perils of the age. The experience of the Jesuits, even more than that of other orders and congregations which came into being or were reformed at about the same time, proved the existence of a widespread and determined craving for personal perfection. It showed likewise that this interior urge, so far from leading Christians to shut themselves away behind the bastions of prayer, was preparing them to take action in accordance with their faith, that is, to become effective in the sphere of human contingency and human conflict. These profoundly mystical souls, like all the men of the

59. Beatified in 1609, Ignatius of Loyola was canonized by Gregory XV in 1622, together with St. Francis Xavier. See the final paragraph of Chapter V.

Renaissance, considered it their main business to live more intensely and for themselves. In their view, however, living meant living in Christ; and because they understood the demands made upon them by the charity of Christ, instead of retiring to a monastic cell, after the example of Ignatius at Manresa, they were resolved to carry their testimony into the world, where the cause they held more dear than life was at stake. The necessary reform of institutions and morals could have had no better instruments than these men who had reformed themselves.

Moreover the very conditions in which this reawakening had come about was a guarantee that any such reform would not deviate from the straight and narrow path, that it would not end in one or other of those anarchical movements which were becoming so numerous and which pretended to rebuild the Church outside herself, in opposition to herself. None of these Catholic reformers had dreamed of innovation, but only of a return to the sources, of rediscovering a tradition more alive in respect of its two main principles of progress and fidelity. None of them, however clearly they might perceive the glaring defects of Mother Church, had sought to remedy those defects by means of a system proceeding from their own minds, but merely to lay firm hold of eternal principles and apply them more effectively. Nor indeed had any of them advocated a rupture with the ecclesiastical hierarchy, even when that hierarchy was at its worst. Rejecting the dangerous pride that exalted men such as Luther and Calvin, they all submitted humbly to authority, especially to that of the Pope, who, being responsible to God for the Church, could alone take the initiative and render it effective.

All the prerequisites of a Catholic reformation were thus present. The men who would be its instruments were ready. The spiritual and moral climate demanded it. What more was required for its accomplishment? Something which had always been indispensable in matters of this kind: the intervention of supreme authority, that is, of the Papacy. Whenever the Church has had to pull herself together and lead the world back to the Gospel, the popes have always been, in short, the effective agents of reform. That was true in the sixth century under Gregory I, in the ninth under Nicholas I and later still in the eleventh and thirteenth under Gregory VII and

Innocent III respectively. Great as were the saintly founders of religious Orders—Bernard, Norbert, Bruno, Francis of Assisi, Dominic and their like—they would never have managed to repair the Church but for the presence over them and at their side, throned in Peter's curule chair, of men invested by the Holy Spirit with infallible authority to recall Christians to their duty.

At the beginning of the sixteenth century, in a world seething with passion and aspiration, when Europe seemed tottering to its fall, the papal role appeared more important than it had ever been. Only the popes could undertake the work of reformation in all its fullness. Christendom had ceased to be; nationalism, growing everywhere, was turning its back more and more resolutely upon the ancient idea of Christian unity. Unless therefore personal initiative was taken in hand by Rome, it was powerless and might actually result in cleavages. There was no longer a lay sovereign capable (as Charlemagne, for example, had been) of controlling even the spiritual interests of the Church. The emperor was no more than a shadow. The popes alone survived.

So long as the Vicar of Christ hesitated to embrace the cause of reform, with the firm determination to crown it with success, nothing could be done; the broad stream of fervour and generosity then flowing through the Church would remain untapped. It is remarkable that all those who had occupied the Apostolic throne during the past hundred years or so had been fully aware of their primordial duty; even those whose mere presence in Rome seemed to demonstrate the necessity of reforming the Church, "both in her head and in her members"; even those pontiffs whom we have seen caught up in the allurements of art, of politics, or of the flesh—all had spoken of performing that duty. One after another, to quote but a few examples, men had heard Nicholas V, supported by Nicholas of Cusa and John Capistran, declare himself about to correct the vices of the clergy; Pius II, terrified by the scourges threatening Christianity, drawing up a huge scheme of reform which began with Rome and the Curia; Paul II fulminating against simony and the laxity of religious houses; Sixtus IV proclaiming that monks should labour to sow the good grain of wisdom and uprightness in the souls of men; even Alexander VI himself, for a few fleeting months, summoning a commission of reform and directing it with noble ardour to prepare the cleansing Bull, *Flatus vocis.* None of these splendid projects got beyond the stage of design, of fine words or at the very most of tentative beginnings. True the Ecumenical Council of the Lateran (1512–1517),[60] under the presidency of Julius II and then of Leo X, had promulgated some discerning observations on the evil of reserves and the accumulation of benefices, reminded cardinals of the duties of their state, and decreed wise measures on the subject of clerical morality; but its work had remained altogether incomplete, and its decisions were applied half-heartedly. The danger was clear for all to see. Leo X had rightly said "that Christian truth was in peril, and that the hour had come to defend it"; only the courage and determination was lacking—above all, courage and determination on the part of Christ's Vicar to put in motion the machinery of reform where it was most indispensable, that is, in his own domain.

Nevertheless a wind of change was blowing. For what mysterious reason? Was the pressure exerted by the reawakened Christian soul upon the whole Church and even upon her leaders so powerful that it forced the new decision? Once again we can but remind ourselves of those secret intentions of Providence, whose ways are impenetrable by human reasoning. At long last the tiara was to be set upon the brow of popes not all of whom were saints, but who proved themselves more faithful to their vocation and lent a ready ear to the repeated summons of the universal Church. The reform which had appeared so hard to undertake would be carried through in the space of about twenty years, not without effort and serious difficulties, but without violent shocks or startling innovations, simply by means of Catholicism's return to her true principles. "An empire is easily conserved by the same means which created it." These profound words of Sallust must have been familiar to many in an age so enamoured of ancient literature. Let them only be applied to the Church, and her true countenance would reappear.

60. See *A Religious Revolution: The Protestant Reformation*, Volume 1, Chapter IV, p. 312.

CHAPTER II

The Council of Trent and the Work of the Saints

1. A CORPSE IN SHREDS

TOWARDS evening on Sunday, May 5, 1527, sentinels keeping watch on the walls of Rome suddenly beheld along the slopes of Monte Mario the gleaming weapons and breastplates of a large armed force, and heard menacing shouts borne on the gentle spring breeze. They were not surprised; the blow had been expected for at least a month. It was known that the imperial troops were marching against the city at the almost incredible speed of eighteen or twenty miles a day; but it remained to be seen whether they would dare attack and violate the capital of Christendom, where lay the bones of St. Peter. Whatever happened the papal units, inefficiently commanded by Lorenzo de Ceri, would certainly not be a match for them. One of the most appalling tragedies in Christian history was about to be enacted.

The enemy were a mixed lot, including Spaniards, Italians, and Germans—many Germans. The fifteen thousand lansquenets, Lutherans for the most part and with Frundsberg at their head, believed themselves engaged in a holy war, and were convinced that by overthrowing the Pope of Rome they would triumph over Antichrist. The rest, the great majority, were driven to fanaticism by less exalted motives: desire of pillage and an appetite for violence. Months had passed since these men last received any pay from their commander-in-chief, who, when they yelled "Money! Money!" showed them the opulence of Italy by way of answer: "If you have ever dreamed of pillaging a town and laying hold of its treasures, here now is one, the richest of them all, queen of the world." The speaker was the Constable de Bourbon, a traitor to his king, a Frenchman in rebellion against France, who lent himself to the crime of sacrilege, in hope no doubt of winning for himself a principality.

The affair was not long delayed. Bourbon was killed during the assault by a bullet which Benvenuto Cellini used to boast of having fired; but that did not prevent the mercenaries infiltrating through the gardens, scaling the walls and smashing down the gates. The doom of Rome was settled in a few hours, and it was a dreadful doom. Unchecked, mutinous and obeying no one, the troops of the Catholic emperor Charles V gave themselves up to an orgy of bloodshed. None can tell whether the taciturn Hapsburg had willed this thing—or tolerated or suggested it. For seven days the city was delivered to sack, to rape, to pillage. "Hell," said one diplomat, "is nothing to what happened then." Convents were the theatres of revolting obscenities in which the nuns were involuntary actresses. Fathers were seen to stab their daughters rather than allow them to be taken by the soldiery.

Palaces and churches were rifled, their contents broken or mutilated. Then it was the turn of the merchant classes, from whom parties of troops exacted enormous ransoms at dagger-point. Ridicule was added to cruelty. The aged Cardinal Araceli was paraded through the streets in a coffin; bishops and other prelates were dragged like slaves for sale in the common market; drunken lansquenets, arrayed in liturgical vestments, brawled in the taverns. The sack went on until there was nothing left to steal or to destroy, and until the insufferable stench of corpses called for police measures.

From the narrow windows of the castle of Sant' Angelo, where he had taken refuge, Pope Clement VII watched this nightmare spectacle. He had managed by sheer good luck to save himself; but he was a prisoner, and before long his jailer would arrive: Alarcon, the same who had kept watch upon François I at Madrid. It was not so much his own situation, however, that grieved the pontiff as the horror of the spectacle. Violence had been unleashed and seemed likely to continue indefinitely; it reached all the Papal States and the Kingdom of Naples. And so, turning to the man who, whether or not responsible for the tragedy, derived the benefit therefrom, Clement VII wrote to Charles V accepting the harsh conditions imposed upon him. He would surrender the States of the Church, he would pay a huge ransom, he would agree to everything provided the frenzy ceased: "Dearly beloved son," he cried, "we have nothing before our eyes but a corpse in shreds...."

If it be asked whether he himself did not bear some responsibility for this catastrophe, the answer must be yes undoubtedly—at the political level; his own policy had been simultaneously too deeply committed and too hesitant, too temporal and too lacking in energy. After Pavia, alarmed by the progress of Charles V, he had determined to rely upon François I, encouraging him to denounce the clauses of Madrid and assuring him in writing that "treaties concluded through fear are not binding." He had also allied himself with the League of Cognac, formed to drive the Spaniards from Italy. He had in short done everything to attract the thunderbolt, but without taking the steps necessary to avoid the danger. Supported half-heartedly by the King of France (who was more generous of kind words than of material reinforcements), and attacked in Rome itself by the Colonna clique, he—and the city with him—suffered the consequences of that Italian policy in which the popes had entangled the Holy See too deeply during the past hundred years.

But it is not only political responsibility that can be ascribed to Clement. The outrage committed upon Rome by Bourbon's *reiter* was symbolic: it reflected for all the world to see those numerous other affronts to which the Church and all Christendom had been subjected in recent times. The sky was dark in so many directions. In Germany the Lutheran heresy was prospering and had just brought about the bloody upheaval of the Peasants' War. In Switzerland a new reformer had appeared, Zwingli, who was even more radical than Luther. In England a royal passion, which was common gossip, would soon raise the problem of divorce, a very difficult question. In France suspect trends were discernible, as also in Bohemia, in Poland and everywhere. Finally, on the eastern frontiers the Turkish peril was more grave than ever: Hungary had lately been overwhelmed by the blows of Solyman at Mohacs, and it looked as though the Muslim corsairs would soon dominate the Mediterranean. Providence seemed filled with wrath against the Church. And why all this, why this crowning tragedy which had now drenched the Eternal City in blood? Many could find but one answer: chastisement from heaven.

The weakness, frivolity and even unworthiness of too many recent popes were openly declared to be the supernatural but decisive causes of those innumerable woes. What else but this weight of anger could be expected of God in return for the Papal Court, the Curia, and even the Sacred College packed by one pope after another with their unworthy nephews and contemptible parasites? Surely the sword of Divine Justice had been brought upon the Church by Alexander VI, prey to the temptations of the flesh; by Julius II, devoured by ambition and the will to power; by Leo X, who allowed himself to become intoxicated by the delights of art to the detriment of higher interests; in fact by all those pontiffs who had proved unequal to their duties. Many courageous voices had denounced the manifold stain that disfigured the Mystic Spouse, yet what had the popes done to wash it out? Charles V, with gloomy countenance and feigned distress, exclaimed: "It all happened by the judgment of God rather than by my order"; and many minds were ready to accept this excuse. A lampoon went the rounds, written by some scribbler in the imperial pay, in which each one of the sufferings endured by Rome was represented as the punishment for a particular piece of wickedness. St. Peter's turned into a stable—what a striking symbol of so many Roman souls in whom dwelt none but the vices! Sacred hosts profaned by the soldiery—what an image of the outrages perpetuated on the Sacrament by so many unworthy priests! There were some of the opinion that this pamphlet told the truth.

Poised thus on the slope, the Church seemed destined to slide into the abyss. Could no one check her fall, seize hold of her and compel her to climb back? After the death of Leo X there was reason to think that one man might be capable of fulfilling this herculean task: Adrian VI (1522–1523), formerly tutor to Charles V, Adrian of Utrecht,[1] an austere priest,

1. Contrary to custom he retained his baptismal name on the apostolic throne. He was incidentally the last non-Italian pope.

rigid and of unassailable morals, whom the Conclave had elected almost unwillingly as a result of one of those polite maneuvers which sometimes determine the outcome of a scrutiny. On the morrow of his coronation the brave Dutchman had undertaken the work of reform. He was known to lead the most edifying life in his palace, dismissing suspect persons from his court, together with every element of pomp. In a number of sternly worded allocutions he denounced scandals and criticized the venality of justice, the corruption of officials and the misconduct which was rife among the clergy. A few examples had provided an effective lesson. His excellent intentions, however, had not been supported by those qualities of prudence and sagacity which the situation had required. To grapple with all scandals at once was to invite unanimous opposition. Powerless to arrest the progress of Lutheranism[2] any more than that of the Turks, who had just taken Rhodes from the knights of Villiers de l'Isle-Adam, and equally powerless to halt the intrigues of Francis of Sicily, Adrian VI soon showed himself unable to discipline the pawnbrokers and profiteers. The cardinals whom he had ordered to modify their ostentatious way of life, the holders of benefices to whom he had forbidden the practice of accumulation, the *datarii* and other secretaries whom he had tried to prevent from lining their pockets—everyone in fact, or nearly everyone, had quickly agreed to treat him as a "churl" and a "Teutonic barbarian." Some unfortunate remarks of his, too, had caused scandal. Gazing, for example, at the wonderful examples of ancient sculpture collected by his predecessors, he had exclaimed: "*Proh! Idola Barbara.*" And then inevitably, as we learn from a Venetian ambassador, because of his origins he had come to be regarded "not as the common father of the Christian republic, but as an agent of the German Caesar." Vast unpopularity had ended by enveloping this good man who, immediately before his death, had murmured this avowal of disappointment: "It is sad that there are some periods in which the most upright of men is forced to succumb."

Such then was the situation which confronted the Dutchman's successor, Clement VII (1523–1534), a very different man. Neither evil intentions

---

2. The German princes were beginning to secularize bishoprics and abbeys.

nor degrading passions had any place in the distinguished mind of this humanist cardinal who had been trained to public life. The very opposite is true. The first acts of his pontificate had made an excellent impression. He had sought advice from Sadolet and Giberti, the two leaders of the reforming movement; he had appointed a commission of cardinals to study the necessary measures; he had kept himself well informed on the affairs of Germany, and had sent his legate to try and settle matters. But this refined intellectual was devoid of character; it has even been said that he suffered "from a sort of anemia of the will." Vacillating, irresolute, incapable of making up his mind and sticking to it, he was bound to appear as lacking in sincerity. Besides, he was a Medici—son of Julian who had been assassinated in the Pazzi conspiracy—and could not refrain from mingling the interests of his family with those of the Church, or in taking a hand in those Italian intrigues where Florentine birth was no guarantee of success.

And so his entire reign is one long story of hopeless confusion, and produced nothing but a succession of defeats. Reconciled with Charles V, who needed him in order to defend his aunt Catherine of Aragon against the machinations of Henry VIII, he set about persuading the emperor to re-establish a Medici at Florence. Next, seeing the increase of Spanish influence in Italy, he prepared a new series of alliances; having performed the solemn coronation of Charles V at Bologna, he approached François I and arranged to marry his niece Catherine to the future king Henri II. Wholly preoccupied with Italian politics and family concerns, he could not handle the real problems of the Church amid the hurly-burly of the great conflicts that were shaking Europe. In the affair of Henry VIII's divorce he has the credit of having stood firmly by his principles, but his maneuvering and hesitation contributed something to the Schism. In Germany, apart from addressing some strong language to Charles V, he allowed the imperial policy to tolerate the Lutheran advance for too long. As regards the Turks, the situation was absolutely catastrophic: Solyman occupied all Hungary, and laid siege to Vienna with three hundred thousand men. Gregorovius has called Clement VII "the most unfortunate of popes"; but he himself bears a measure of responsibility for those misfortunes.

And what of reform? How had it been progressing in such circumstances? The commission of cardinals, after numerous sessions and many valuable reports, dispersed without having accomplished any of those things which had been expected of it. Faced henceforward with the Lutheran doctrines, Catholics were everywhere clamouring for measures that would put an end to scandals and rob the heretics of their arguments. Rome was silent. The most serious point was that an idea sprang up in various quarters according to which some power was needed in place of the Holy See, since the latter was incapable of taking the indispensable decisions. But *what* power? Pens in the service of Charles V declared unequivocally: "If the emperor reforms the Church—and everyone knows how important such reformation is—he will not only render service to God, but will also earn for himself the greatest glory that any prince has ever enjoyed." The danger was not illusory. Charles V was haunted at this time by the desire to reconcile the adversaries and thereby restore peace to the Empire. Now if he were to decide to summon a council, what would the Pope do? When an imperial proposition to this effect was made in more explicit terms (1534) Clement VII had the strength to refuse. But what a nonsensical situation! The Vicar of Christ refusing to take steps demanded by the best minds in the Church, forbidding another to answer the appeal and yet doing nothing about it himself!

Was all lost then? Must men despair of the future of the Catholic Church? No reply was forthcoming from the hesitant Medici pope, from his lily-livered Curia, or even from the Germanic emperor whose good Christian intentions hardly concealed his very definite ambition. It was given by all those fervent souls who were even then making ready for the decisive awakening by their return to their true loyalties. It was during the pontificate of Clement VII, remember, and with his encouragement, that there began many of those individual enterprises which we have seen at work refashioning the army of the Church. Theatines, Capuchins, Barnabites, Somaschi; it was Clement's reign that witnessed the birth of these and numerous other orders, institutes and congregations whose activity would prove decisive. This was not the fruit of mere chance. A few weeks before Clement VII's death, on September 25, 1534, Ignatius of Loyola and his six companions had vowed (August 15) in the little semi-subterranean chapel on the hill of Montmartre to devote themselves body and soul to the Church. That Church appeared to have reached the nadir of her existence, but her recovery was at hand. The "corpse in shreds" would soon come to life again.

2. POPE PAUL III (1534–1549)

ON October 13, 1534, Cardinal Alessandro Farnese was unanimously elected Pope, and took the name Paul III. He was certainly no saint. Farnese belonged to one of those powerful Italian clans which used to dispute among themselves for the tiara; and that is why thirteen years earlier, on the death of Leo X, his candidature, opposed by the Colonnas and Medicis together, had not succeeded.[3] Must we attribute his easy election to his age, to his sickly and infirm appearance? One can hardly believe, in any case, that it was due to his prestige. No doubt his way of life had been regular since his ordination to the priesthood in 1519. But the Romans did not forget that he had been created cardinal by Alexander VI at a time when his sister, the beautiful Giulia Farnese, was believed to have refused the Borgia nothing, and on this account Alessandro had been nicknamed Cardinal Petticoat. They remembered also that in the course of a rather stormy career he had begotten three bastards, Pierluigi, Ranuccio and Constanza, whose legitimation by Julius II did not perhaps suffice to excuse their existence. Alessandro Farnese was from top to toe a man of the Renaissance—cultured, a patron of the arts and a lover of pomp—and would remain so in the chair of Peter. One day he would be heard to let fall some words that sound strange indeed on the lips of a pope. Referring to Benvenuto Cellini, who was guilty of many crimes: "An artistic genius," said Paul III, "is above the laws of morality." He would still be seen attending brilliant hunts, entertaining the women of his family at table, and giving noisy parties in his palace

3. He obtained twenty-two votes in a scrutiny instead of the necessary twenty-four. It was thanks to those squabbles around the urn that Adrian VI was elected.

with female singers, dancing girls and buffoons. His enlightened taste moreover would lead him to have painted on the walls of the Vatican, and above all in the castle of Sant' Angelo, frescoes of a strongly pagan flavour. The inclinations of the new pope were only too well known. Besides, when he began his pontificate by raising two of his grandsons (modestly described as "nephews") to the Sacred College—Alessandro Farnese, aged fourteen, and Ascanio Sforza, aged sixteen—those true Christians who longed with all their souls for the reform of the Church were stricken with grief and believed that everything would continue as before. But they were wrong.

Paul III would prove himself neither a Clement VII nor a Leo X nor a Borgia. The man whom we still see in his portrait by Titian[4] at the age of sixty-seven, bent, almost hump-backed, with long aristocratic nose and white beard, possessed a character of enormous strength together with the shrewdest intelligence. Violent, but able to control the irascible instincts which sometimes blazed in his piercing eyes, he had succeeded in remaining at court throughout six pontificates, and in holding the balance so evenly in his relations with France and the Empire that François I and Charles V both declared themselves pleased with his election. Where Adrian VI had exhibited so much clumsy haste, and where Clement VII had shown himself so unskillful a diplomat, a man as firm, subtle and worldly-wise as Pope Farnese would be able to work wonders, no matter how little he understood the significance of the immense drama in which Christianity was then engaged. Now in point of fact Paul III did understand it, and thanks to him the Church would take the decisive step that had been so long awaited.

In the Bull which he later sent to the Council of Trent he gave a perfect summary of the situation as he found it on ascending the papal throne. "In those days all was full of hatred and dissension. Princes were everywhere at loggerheads one with another, princes to whom God had entrusted government. The unity of the Christian name had been shattered by schism and heresy. The Turks were advancing on land and sea; Rhodes was lost,

4. At present in the Museum at Naples. It shows Paul III between two of his grandsons, Cardinal Alessandro Farnese and Ottavio, Duke of Parma and Piacenza.

Hungary devastated, Italy, Austria and Slavonia threatened. The divine wrath lay heavy upon all us sinners." This clear-headed man understood that it was time to take a stand against the threefold danger of the Turks, political dismemberment and religious dissolution. But he also detected something even more serious: that sickness which was ravaging the Christian soul, that universal treason which was calling down God's ire upon the Catholics. Cries of fury or of desolation were rising from all parts of Christendom, imploring him or commanding him to put an end to the tale of scandal. While crossing the bridge of Sant' Angelo he had heard the voice of a strange man named Franz Titelmans, a former teacher at the universities of Angers and Louvain who had abandoned all, students and professorial chairs, to come to Rome and make his solemn protestation: "To hell with sinners! To hell with adulterers!" This great humanist of Louvain, a keen opponent of Erasmus, had surrendered his chair in 1535 in order to take the Capuchin habit at Rome, where he died in the odour of sanctity on September 12, 1537. The Flemish Capuchin's cry was no solitary voice in the desert. There were countless men and women begging the Pope, as the jurist Caccia de Novara puts it, to restore to the Church "her evangelical nature," to lead her back to the humility, purity and heroism of apostolic times. The supreme merit of Paul III is that he listened to this manifold voice, the voice of Christian conscience, and that he did its bidding according to his means.

It suddenly became clear that the wind of change was blowing. The tenderest spot when Alessandro Farnese assumed the tiara was England. Here the affair of the royal divorce had reached the point of rupture between Henry VIII and his Catholic subjects, that is to say the point of persecution. John Fisher and Thomas More had been arrested. Paul III threatened the Tudor with interdict. He wished to obtain the intervention of the Catholic rulers against the schismatic, and carried on prolonged negotiations with this end in view. Neither France nor the Empire cared to break with an intermittent but useful ally. Besides, to withdraw Andrea Doria's fleet from the Mediterranean and send it to fight in the Thames estuary was to leave the coasts of Italy and France exposed to the Turks. Paul III, however, stood his ground. Holding fast by principle, he acted with great vigour against Henry

VIII, urging Reginald Pole to wage his campaign of protest against the faithless monarch, and no doubt having a hand in the rising of the North. In December 1538 he laid the kingdom under interdict and excommunicated the sovereign. Clement VII's policy of temporization and double dealing was a thing of the past. In France also, where the affair of the Placards had just broken out,[5] Paul III encouraged François I to employ severity; and he exhorted the Catholic princes of Germany to unite against the League of Smalkald, whose troops were defeated. Finally, in order to make it possible for the Catholic sovereigns to fight against heresy, and likewise in order to deprive the Turks of one of their trump cards in the shape of the French alliance, he managed, at the cost of immense diplomatic effort conducted with supreme skill, to reconcile François I and Charles V by the ten-year Truce of Nice (1538). The ground was now clear for the most important work of all.

Reform of the Church, the goal proclaimed by so many voices, was not in doubt; nor was the means of its accomplishment, a general council. Paul III agreed as to both, but he foresaw a danger. Might not an Assembly of the Church convoked by himself rise up against him, against his court and against the Curia which was wide open to criticism from so many points of view? The age of conciliar theories was comparatively recent, and it was necessary to avoid at any cost resuscitation of the conflict. The very stature to which the Papacy had attained during the past hundred years made him unwilling to put himself in tow of a council. The only thing to do then was to start by reforming the head of the Church, as Adrian VI had tried unsuccessfully to do; that is to say, he must first restore order in Rome and the papal *entourage.* That would be the first stage. Then would come the second, the meeting of the Council, which would now be easier to direct and to control. Finally there would be a third and much more remote stage, at which Paul III clearly foresaw the Papacy, reformed and purified, applying the conciliar decrees. The courageous pontiff who intended to undertake this enormous task would never come near to witnessing its completion, but he has the singular merit of having conceived it as a whole.

---

5. See *A Religious Revolution: The Protestant Reformation*, Volume 2, Chapter VI, p. 481.

 Paul III set to work in the early months of his pontificate. The consistories of October and November 1534 afforded him an opportunity of admonishing with firm moderation the cardinals who were present: their manner of life must be less ostentatious; they must keep an eye on their households; and they were requested to resume ecclesiastical dress, for which some of them affected great disdain. Two new Congregations were created and placed under the direction of cardinals whose reputation was irreproachable: one to supervise the conduct of the Roman clergy, the other to inquire into the administration of the Papal States. In this climate even the appointment of two "nephews" to the Sacred College was more easily explicable; perhaps it was nothing less than a supreme act of cunning, for the two lads, having been raised to the purple, were afterwards replaced in their posts at the Apostolic Camera and Chancellery by vicars who gradually brought those two important services under the Pope's direct control.

Above all, however, the pontiff's purpose and the steps he meant to take towards its realization become manifest when we consider his appointments to the Sacred College from 1535 onwards. Excepting one—Jean du Bellay, Bishop of Paris, whose red hat was a mark of favour to the King of France—all those whom Paul III raised to the purple were convinced reformers, men of integrity and ardent soul—pillars in the future work of reconstruction, as was said of them by the Polish bishop Stanislaus Hosius (himself made cardinal in 1560). In order to judge this pope one cannot do better than take a look at the counsellors whom he chose. We need in fact only cite the names of these men if we would understand the significance of Paul III's choice: St. John Fisher, a prisoner of Henry VIII, who would soon lay his head upon the block through loyalty to the Catholic faith; his friend Reginald Pole; the wise and peace-loving Sadolet; the energetic Giovanni Pietro Carafa, co-founder of the Theatines and afterwards Pope Paul IV; Michele Cervini, who was destined to precede the latter for a few days on the apostolic throne as Marcellus II. Among these batches of cardinals there were such great diplomats as Schomberg and Caracciolo, such eminent administrators as Guinucci, and such noted canonists as Simonetta. There were also some outstanding humanists, such as Aleandro and

Gaspard Contarini; the latter was a layman but one of the leading protagonists of Catholic reform, and he was elevated straightway to the rank of cardinal. Paul III even thought of conferring the red hat upon Erasmus, but the aged scholar gracefully declined.

From this brilliant company the Pope then chose the members of a "commission of reform," whose business it was to study the problem as a whole and to propose solutions. At its head were Sadolet, Pole, Contarini and Carafa. The Bull *Sublimis Deus* gave it, in addition to unlimited rights of inquiry, powers of sanction and coercion that extended even to members of the Curia. These saintly commissioners were guaranteed the fullest liberty, which they did not fail to use; their report of January 1538 was a model indictment, perfectly objective but sparing no one, even in the papal household. The regulations attached to this report by way of conclusion were given the force of law. They laid down the moral and intellectual qualifications needed for admission to Holy Orders; they imposed upon all clerics, from the humblest curate to the most exalted member of the Sacred College, a manner of life suitable to the duties of their state; and they even concerned themselves with the maintenance of buildings intended for divine worship. But were these regulations enforced? Did not their very rigour place them in jeopardy? It is hard to say whether this internal reform was any more effective than that envisaged by the Lateran Council; history shows that abuses of long standing "are proof against official remedies, and need to be dealt with in a new setting."[6] But at all events they forestalled the criticism which some members of the Council might have directed against Rome, and their most relevant clauses were embodied in the decrees of Trent.

It was not, however, to the Commission *de emendanda* alone that Paul III entrusted this indispensable task. His energy and foresight were expressed in many other ways. It is hardly necessary to recall that he granted canonical recognition to the Society of Jesus in 1540, at a time when

6. Thus Orestes Ferrara, in his splendid work *Le XVIe Siècle vu par les Ambassadeurs Vénitiens*, throws doubt upon the effectiveness of the regulations drawn up by the Commission *De Emendanda Ecclesia*.

the Commission entertained some doubt as to this new enterprise; that he authorized the foundation of the Somaschi; that he encouraged the Barnabites and Theatines; and that it was due to him that the Ursulines became in 1544 the great teaching Order that we know today. Even in 1542, when the newly established institute of the Capuchins was faced with the grave crisis brought about by the apostasy of Bernardino Ochino, Paul III's indignation yielded to his understanding that it would be absurd to destroy so useful an instrument.

Two organisms of capital importance in the subsequent history of the Church likewise owed their existence to this far-sighted occupant of Peter's throne. One was the Inquisition, an old medieval institution which had fallen into virtual desuetude everywhere except in Spain, where it had been reorganized in 1478 and had become to all intents and purposes a weapon of kingly government. Everywhere in fact the struggle against heretical doctrine had been left in the hands of careless, dissolute, and even suspect ecclesiastical courts. On the advice of Carafa, and also perhaps of St. Ignatius, Paul III resolved in 1542 to re-establish a Roman organism whose duty it would be to fight "against all those who had departed from or who attacked the Catholic faith, and to unmask such persons as were suspected of heresy." Accordingly, the Bull *Licet ab initio* erected the "Holy Office." It consisted of six (later of ten) cardinals, twenty-seven counsellors and three theologians. Carafa himself was appointed president, a fact which indicated from the start that there would be no half-hearted measures. The tribunals of the Holy Office were entrusted once again to the Dominicans. Although the jurisdiction of the new Inquisition was not clearly stated it seemed to include the whole of Christendom. A new weapon had been forged for use in the conflicts that lay ahead.

Another innovation of Paul III was the Index. Fully aware of the part played by books in the propagation of heresy, he deployed his forces likewise in this field. He had invited Cardinals Contarini and Aleandro to write a work that would instruct preachers in the proper method of expounding Christian doctrine to the various classes of society. But it was necessary also to prevent the spread of false teaching. Lists (indexes) of harmful works were compiled in several dioceses, and in 1543 stern penalties, including fines and even banishment, were imposed on those who sold condemned books. Such was the origin of the Congregation of the Index, which received its official status in 1557 during the pontificate of Paul IV.

This vast and remarkable activity enabled Paul III to clear the first stage of his grand design. The ground had been prepared; the Holy See's authority could no longer be disputed; weapons and troops were at the Papacy's disposal for the completion of its task. It was now possible to embark upon the second stage by summoning a council. But in this matter words were easier than deeds.

3. THE DIFFICULTY OF SUMMONING A COUNCIL

In order to assess the merit of Pope Paul III we must take account of the formidable obstacles which he had to surmount. Many interests were ready to combine against him. He encountered opposition first from his own *entourage*, among the officials of the Curia who had bought their places and were vexed when the news of an impending reform lowered the value of their acquisitions; among his advisers, who warned him that any interference with the system of annates, expectancies and other Roman privileges would ruin the Apostolic See; and even among very pious folk—of the type, for example, which frequented the Oratory of Divine Love—who insisted that he was putting the cart before the horse in seeking to bring about an official reform while the interior and only efficacious revolution had not yet borne its fruits.

Then he had to reckon with the Protestants, who could not be ignored even though they subsequently stood aside. They too were demanding a council: long ago, on November 28, 1518, Luther had declared his appeal to the Assembly of the Church against Rome's sentence of excommunication. But the council which they wanted was of a particular kind, in which their pastors would rank as equals of the bishops, in which the tradition of the Church (especially the Bulls and decretals of the popes) would have been regarded as null and void, the "pure Gospel" being alone sufficient to solve all problems. The "presbyterian" council was altogether unacceptable; meeting on those bases the assembly would have ended by throwing the whole Church into the Germanic chaos.

Could Paul hope for support among the temporal rulers? Certainly not from Henry VIII, erstwhile Defender of the Faith and now excommunicated. François I was playing a double game, loudly declaring himself a partisan of the council, but in fact alarmed by the prospect that the Gallican Church might be forced to relax its privileges; besides, he had allied himself with the Lutheran princes in the League of Smalkald. No, François would not readily dispatch his bishops to a council. As regards Charles V, his attitude was still more ambiguous. As King of Spain he was an eager reformer and in favour of a council; but as emperor he desired above all to reconcile his subjects, and therefore did not much like the idea of an assembly which would condemn Protestantism. Failing an imperial diet, which he would have preferred, he dreamed of a Germanic council in which his word would have been law, and upon which he would most probably have imposed a formula analogous to the subsequent Interim.[7]

We see then that Paul III had to steer St. Peter's barque among some dangerous reefs. But that was not all. Suppose them safely negotiated and the council actually in session: one delicate and very serious question would have to be answered: in what spirit would the assembly go to work? For indeed among those reformers who were most sincerely anxious for the welfare of the Church there were two currents more or less antagonistic. Speaking comprehensively and in frankly anachronistic terms, we may say that there were "modernists" and "integrists." On one side were the Christian humanists, friends and disciples of Erasmus. These included Sadolet, Reginald Pole, Contarini and other kindred spirits who, though determined on reform, laid emphasis upon the spiritual life, but favoured gentleness,

7. See *A Religious Revolution: The Protestant Reformation*, Volume 2, Chapter V, p. 440. Charles's principal counsellor, the Franche-Comtois Granvelle, was so much opposed to a council that he spread a rumour everywhere that the Pope himself was of the same opinion and "dreaded it like fire."

temporization and conciliatory formulae in the dogmatic sphere. Some of them (e.g., Erasmus himself and the Dominican John Faber) extolled the idea that the decisions of the council, before being approved by the full assembly, should be submitted to a kind of "superior council" of cognizances (i.e., to themselves). The other current ran in the direction of severity, of categorical measures, of the Inquisition and repression. At its head was Cardinal Carafa; and it was favoured by circumstances, for it is a constant of history that in moments of great peril the rigorists carry the day. Was not the Pope, in choosing one or other method, likely to alienate the rest of the assembly? It is not difficult therefore to understand that, as he himself wrote, "amid all that turbulence of heresy, dispute and war, amid all those storms which were the most terrible that had ever threatened the barque of Peter," Paul III experienced a cold sweat of anguish and begged the Lord to "comfort him and arm his spirit with strength and constancy, his intellect with the gift of wisdom."

The courageous pontiff would have singular need of constancy and strength, for it took him no less than nine years of uninterrupted effort to reach his goal. On June 2, 1536, having sounded Charles V and having sent his nuncio Vergerio to seek approbation in Germany, he summoned a council to meet at Mantua in May 1537. In fact, however, no one was altogether willing to attend. François I was directing his ambassador, Guillaume du Bellay, to inform his Lutheran friends that they need have no fears, even while the diplomat's brother, Cardinal Jean du Bellay, was assuring Paul III that his sovereign was well disposed. Charles V, furious at the choice of an Italian city, where he would not speak as master, vociferated to such good effect that the Duke of Mantua, alarmed or pretending to be so, declared that he could not answer for the security of the members of the council. A large majority of the cardinals therefore decided to stay at home.

The Pope then altered his choice in favour of Vicenza and postponed the meeting to May 1, 1538. He was now more hopeful; the Truce of Nice was on the point of reconciling those two great enemies, the King of France and the Emperor Charles. But too many interests were still opposed to the meeting of the council. When the papal legates reached Vicenza they found a total of five bishops, who seemed very surprised to be there at all.

There followed a multitude of negotiations and conferences, in which the elector Joachim of Brandenburg and Ferdinand of Austria played a prominent part, with a view to eliminating the obstacles. There was much talk and much discussion, and Paul III realized that this policy of conferences was intended as nothing less than a substitute for the council; under pretext of reconciling Catholic and Protestant theologians (which in any case was impossible), the grave questions touching the reform of the Church and the problems of faith would be ignored. Charles V was clearly behind this maneuver, which had been devised by Granvelle. Futile meetings were held[8] at Speyer, Worms and Ratisbon. It seemed that plans for a council were being deliberately set aside. Reacting firmly, however, Paul III again proposed that the assembly should take place. Vicenza was no longer available because the Venetians refused to make it so. What about Piacenza or Bologna or even Cambrai? Ferdinand of Austria suggested Trent, a small city in the Tyrol, Italian by race and language but subject to the emperor. Charles V could not but bow before a choice that seemed to flatter him, and on May 22, the tireless Pope once more convoked the council. But another three years would pass before it actually met.

War was resumed between François I and Charles V, and the former forbade his prelates to travel to the imperial city. As for the emperor, he protested to the Pope because the Bull of summons had included, immediately after his Imperial Majesty, among the "principal upholders and supporters of the Christian name the contemptible King of France, an ally of the Turks." So the question of a council had to be postponed until the Peace of Crespy-en-Valois had reconciled the adversaries (September 17, 1544). Then, however, the aged Paul flung himself into the affair, feeling that now was his last chance. François I and Charles V were both pressed to agree; negotiations were opened even with the Turks, who, being preoccupied

8. See *A Religious Revolution: The Protestant Reformation*, Volume 2, Chapter V, section: "Lutheranism Becomes a Political Force."

with the Persians, undertook not to molest northern Italy. The Bull *Laetare Jerusalem* (November 19) summoned the council for March 15, Laetare Sunday—a symbolic coincidence.

Would things be any better this time? No. Once again the legates, Cardinals del Monte, Cervini and Pole, arrived to find such a small attendance that they hurried back to Rome and asked the Pope to postpone the meeting until December. The whole summer was needed in order to send nuncios to round up the members. The Pope's grandson, young Cardinal Farnese, made another call on Charles V, who seemed more favourably disposed. But the French and Spaniards argued that Trent was too far away; the English and Scandinavians had passed to schism or heresy; and of course no German Lutheran would agree to come. At long last, on December 13, 1545, in the choir of Trent cathedral, Cardinal del Monte was able to celebrate the Mass of the Holy Spirit and declare the first session of the Council open. There were four cardinals (including the legates), four archbishops, twenty-one bishops, five generals of orders, and some fifty theologians and canonists. The number was small, but at least its end had been attained in principle. As for practical results, they were not forthcoming for another eighteen years.

4. DIFFICULTIES AND VICISSITUDES OF THE COUNCIL OF TRENT

"WE shall see the end of this Council in a few weeks," wrote one Italian bishop on arrival in the little city of Trent with its crowded mass of prelates, definitors, consultors and secretaries. Was not everyone agreed on principles? In actual fact an endless succession of obstacles lay ahead. "Christendom," both as an ideal and as a reality, was dead; and even in the sphere of the most urgent spiritual questions all sorts of private interests, enmities and appetites were at loggerheads.

There was certainly no lack of goodwill or of a sense of responsibility. Any member of the Council might have uttered the brave words spoken by the Cardinal of Lorraine in one of the final sessions: "Whom shall we accuse, my fellow bishops? Whom shall we declare to be the authors of such great misfortune? Ourselves; we must admit that much, with shame and with repentance for our past lives. Storm and tempest have arisen on our account, my brethren, and because of this let us cast ourselves into the sea. Let judgment begin with the House of God; let those who bear the sacred instruments of the Lord be purged and reformed!" Among these new Jonases there was not one who was not determined to do what was right. But they were still men, and the cyclone which shook this vessel of the Church was so violent that none could immediately distinguish what course to take in order to round the cape.

Motives of conflict were only too numerous. Some arose from differences in character, inevitable in so large an assembly of men, and they led sometimes to farcical incidents. Some prelates hurled abuse at one of the legates disputing the nobility of his birth; a Neapolitan bishop, having been described by a Greek bishop as "ignorant and perverse," rushed at him, seized his beard and shook it so violently that he tore out a handful of hair. But behind such personal animosities there almost always lay national antagonisms. Among these princes of the Church there were very few who were able to forget their loyalty to some temporal prince and, while serving the supreme interests of Catholicism, to refrain from upholding those of their own countries. The haughty Spaniards posed as sole defenders of faith and morality, but were reminded of the fact that in Spain the Church was curiously subject to the civil power; and one day, when one of them was talking too loud he was interrupted with a shout: "Are we at the Council of Toledo?" The French, whose doctrine was viewed by some with grave suspicion, made vigorous answer to their critics. A French bishop was interrupted during a discourse on the necessity of reforming the Curia with these sarcastic words: "My, my, listen how well the cock crows!" To which he retorted: "Yes, and at cock-crow St. Peter roused himself and wept." A tactful observation! As for the Italians, whenever there was an important vote to be taken, they profited by the comparative nearness of Trent to dispatch whole swarms of bishops; and this caused one member to observe: "The Holy Spirit arrives in Rome's baggage."

These clashes were not in themselves particularly serious, and the history of the Council is by no means reducible to incidents of this kind. A great majority of members, though of widely differing temperament, worked together in a noble cause, impelled by longing to do aright, by devotion to their lofty task and by the certainty that their labours were of paramount importance for the welfare of the Church.

Among the presiding legates, all passionately loyal to the Apostolic See, were del Monte, Crescenzi, Gonzaga, Morone, Cervini (afterwards Pope Marcellus II) and Reginald Pole, a man of truly ecumenical learning and judgment. The numerous theologians from various religious Orders, who drew up reports and prepared theses, included the Jesuits Le Jay, Laynez and Salmeron, the Augustinian Seripando, Musso, a Franciscan, and Bernardin of Asti, a Capuchin; Cano and Soto were two of the outstanding Dominican representatives. We can imagine them busy, not only at plenary sessions in the cathedral of St. Vigilius, but also in working groups at the smaller church of Santa Maria Maggiore, on various committees in the halls of the palace, or in convent cells where specialists wrote their refutation of heresies and drafted the decrees that would rebuild the Church.

If the Fathers of the Council had been left alone to look after the interests of the Church, without political obtrusion, their work might have been soon accomplished. The sovereigns, however, and one in particular, claimed the right to interfere in the business of the Assembly, and long made real progress impossible. Charles V was mainly responsible for these complications; extremely distrustful of the Papacy, which he always dreaded seeing predominant in Italy, he was equally anxious to avoid breaking with the German Protestants and thus prevent trouble in his dominions. He thought that the Council should be a friendly meeting-ground between Catholics and heretics, whereas the popes and the Church as a whole considered it rather as the occasion for a show-down which had become necessary even at the cost of rupture. These opposite views were long maintained, and in all sorts of circumstances. For example, it was asked whether definition of dogma or reform of discipline should be given priority. Charles V replied through his representatives: "Discipline first," in order to avoid irrevocable condemnation of the Lutheran theses. "Dogma," said the rigorist party who understood the menace of heresy; even Campeggio's suggested compromise, that the two matters be studied *pari passu*, gave rise to some heated debates. On the other hand, it is beyond doubt that in spite of their meritorious efforts to make the Council a success, several popes failed to take a firm stand apart from and above politics, and that all or nearly all laid themselves open to attack on the purely temporal plane. These facts explain the extraordinary duration of the Council of Trent, which was four times interrupted, suspended for nearly ten years, and did not reach its goal until the general situation freed Rome from political entanglement.

Meeting first, as we have seen, in December 1545, and relatively weak in numbers, the Fathers of the Council held eight sessions in a period of six months. Methods of procedure were carefully worked out so as to avoid recurrence of those demagogic tendencies which had appeared long ago at Basel and Constance. Strangely, though perhaps not altogether by chance, a plan was adopted similar to (and maybe as a reply to) that of the Confession of Augsburg, whereby some excellent results were obtained at the doctrinal level on the role of Holy Scripture as the rule of faith, on the doctrine of original sin, on justification and on the sacraments. A serious beginning was also made in the field of disciplinary reform by laying down the duties of bishops. But when Charles V learned the content of the dogmatic decrees, he gave vent to ominous rage, and ordered the Council to proceed no further on this road. It was a cruel setback. Notwithstanding the efforts of the cardinal-legate del Monte, many bishops felt a slackening of their zeal now that the emperor spoke so loud. At that moment too, about mid-May, Trent and its guests found themselves in the grip of an epidemic, a sort of lethal influenza which was nicknamed "lentil sickness" because the victim's skin was covered with tiny round disks. One, two, four, then ten, then twelve Fathers of the Council betook themselves to more salubrious neighbourhoods. The Council had to be transferred to Bologna (February 1548), where two insignificant sessions were attended by the Italians alone. The Imperial and Spanish members remained at Trent by order of Charles V, and there was nothing for it but to suspend the Council.

Just then, however, there occurred an unfortunate incident. Paul III, yielding once more to family feeling, had detached the duchies of Parma and Piacenza from the Papal States and conferred them on his own son, Pierluigi Farnese. Cardinal Gonzaga had protested. "Marvellous!" he had declared in presence of the pontiff. "A new prince springing up like a mushroom overnight!" The emperor also had been very displeased, and had retorted by appointing as Governor of the Milanese another Gonzaga, Ferrante, a bitter enemy of Pierluigi. Tension had grown throughout the years 1545 and 1546 until September in the latter year, when Pierluigi was assassinated. His body, riddled with dagger wounds, was thrown from a window of his castle, while Gonzaga hurried to occupy Piacenza in the name of His Imperial Majesty. Though he made a great show of innocence, Charles V was strongly suspected of complicity in this crime. Distraught and terribly worried that the event might herald another attack upon Italy in the manner of 1527, Paul III, while negotiating with the emperor to suspend the Council (September 17, 1549), was actively preparing a Holy League against him with the support of France, Switzerland and many Italian cities; and he was even proposing to hurl the Turks against Vienna when he died, on November 10, 1549, at the age of eighty-two, having most gloriously laid the foundations of reform, but still far from having achieved his purpose and full of anxiety for the future.

There was indeed good cause for anxiety. The last months of the pontificate had witnessed Charles V take a step whose consequences none could foresee. Partly with authority from Rome, and partly on his own account, he had signed the *Interim* of Augsburg[9] on May 15, 1548, thus strengthening the Protestant hand by entitling married priests to continue their ministry and granting the laity communion in two kinds.[10] The future was undeniably obscure.

The danger of the situation was abundantly clear when the Conclave met to choose Paul's successor. The cardinals assembled late in November,

9. See *A Religious Revolution: The Protestant Reformation*, Volume 2, Chapter VII, p. 638.
10. Paul III's curious indulgence is again explained by nepotism; he had obtained consolatory favours for Ottavio Farnese, who had become the emperor's son-in-law.

 but did not make up their minds to elect a pope until February 8, 1550. This Conclave, one of the longest in the history of the Church, was the scene of open conflict between the French and imperial factions, and could not reach a decision until the two young leaders of the opposing parties, Cardinal de Lorraine and Cardinal Farnese, reached agreement on a candidate.

The choice fell upon Cardinal del Monte, a former president of the Council. He was a man of personal respectability, although perhaps a little too much inclined towards earthly pleasures and works of art; and he was surrounded, like his predecessor, by greedy relations. In memory of Julius II, among whose domestic prelates he had been, he took the name Julius III (1550–1555). This pope has been harshly judged; it has even been written that "he said nothing and did nothing to reform the Church." That is not true. Friend and confidant of Paul III, very well aware of the Farnese pontiff's grand designs, he was firmly resolved to resume the Council's mighty task, as all the members of the Conclave had sworn to do. But he was not a man of very strong character; besides, though still in his sixties, he was prematurely aged, suffered from gout and was scared of Charles V. It is therefore not surprising that he preferred negotiation to a fight. His nepotism also, if less scandalous than that of his predecessor, was none the less notorious; nor did the business of Parma and Piacenza, which continued to give trouble and even to provoke armed hostilities, allow him a free hand. His undeniable goodwill was seriously impeded.

On December 1, 1550, the Council was summoned to reassemble at Trent on the following May 1. The emperor, who had given his consent and promised to send his bishops, was in no particular hurry to help them on their way. As for the French, they had been forbidden by Henri II to leave the kingdom, first because war with Charles V was again on the point of breaking out, and second because relations between the Louvre and the Curia were so bad as to be on the verge of rupture. The ambassador Amyot informed the Pope that France, "pure from all heresy," had no need of a General Council, and that she could quite well hold a national synod. Nevertheless a handful of bishops, meeting at Trent with the legate Crescenzi and Bishop Lippomano of Verona as presidents, did substantial work in the course of four sessions upon dogmatic decrees dealing with the sacraments. They were gradually joined by others, and even witnessed the arrival of a Protestant delegation, which they were obliged to admit upon the express demand of Charles V and which submitted two declarations of the German Lutheran faith.

Political factors once again intervened. Ottavio Farnese refused to surrender Parma to the emperor as the Pope had promised. He was supported by Henri II, who had been offended by the Holy See's policy in the matter of benefices, and who openly criticized Julius III and his Council. Turkish galleys, invited by the Most Christian King, were cruising off the shores of the Papal States; and but for the restraining hand of Cardinal de Lorraine, Henri might even have drifted into schism. His troops occupied Siena, which Montluc subsequently defended against the Imperialists with heroic vigour. The whole of Central Italy was prey to fire and sword, ravaged by the partisans of Ottavio Farnese, and behind it all the hand of Charles was evidently still at work. News suddenly reached the Council that Maurice of Saxony, in rebellion against the emperor, had just invaded Tyrol, had nearly succeeded in capturing his overlord at Innsbruck, and was preparing to march upon Trent. Confusion reigned, and on April 28, 1552, it was decided to adjourn the Assembly at once for two years.

At the end of that period Julius III had not the courage to resume his task. Disheartened by so much intrigue and opposition, increasingly sick and weary, he had taken refuge in the stately villa he had built outside the Porta del Popolo, and seemed no longer interested save in the beautiful gardens with which he had surrounded his new home. Only his silent and solitary death suggested that his conscience was not quite at ease. Many throughout the Christian world were beginning to ask themselves whether a council was really the best means of solving the Church's problems, whether such gatherings were not likely to produce an overdose of controversy, and whether an individual acting on his own might not achieve better results. This last idea was about to find its way into the mind of Pope Paul IV.

5. POPE PAUL IV

ON Ascension Day (May 23) 1555 the Church was thrilled by news of the papal election. The Conclave had chosen one who, by styling himself Paul IV, showed clearly that he meant to follow in the footsteps of Farnese. Another pope had just vanished from the scene, Marcellus II (immediate successor of Julius III), of whom it has been said that "he was shown rather than given to the Church." This man of God, this living image of reform, was one who, as Cardinal Cervini, had presided over the Council. He had been taken seriously ill less than a fortnight after his election, and had died ten days later. Palestrina had not had time to complete the wonderful Mass he was writing for the coronation. The unexpected death of Marcellus, an active man still in his fifties, had given rise to anxiety in many minds; and that anxiety was not completely removed by the election of his successor. The Dean of the Sacred College would naturally be on the side of reform; but Marcellus II had hoped to accomplish the work in a spirit of peace and by gentler methods, thinking rather to appease than to condemn. Would the new successor of St. Peter take the same line? He had been chosen by the Conclave for tactical reasons, in order to exclude both the Cardinal of Ferrara, who was too much involved in Italian politics, and Reginald Pole, who was suspected of intending to hurl the Church against the English monarchy. The new Pope was none other than the terrible Cardinal Carafa.

This grand old man remained as impetuous and imperious at the age of almost eighty years as he had been in the flower of his youth at Naples, where he had scoffed at the Spanish authorities even while he dreamed of restoring to the Church her sanctity. Slender, lean, taut and with glowing eyes, he was, says a contemporary, "like an arrow, ever ready to strike home on its target." His speech was said to be "volcanic," and his outbursts "as unpredictable as those of Vesuvius." The gentleness of his friend St. Cajetan of Tiene, with whom he had founded the Theatine Order,[11] had not influenced him in the least. Being also intelligent, refined, learned in theology, deeply pious

11. See above, Chapter I, p. 27.

and of a retiring disposition, he undoubtedly possessed the highest virtues, although the violence of his temperament sometimes interfered with their rightful employment. His lofty notion of the dignity attaching to the Holy See, together with his personal pride, led him to a theocratic concept whose anachronism he does not appear to have understood: kings, emperors and peoples must kneel before the Pope; there must be no nations, only large groups absolutely subject to the Vicar of Christ. It was unfortunate that he lived in the sixteenth century and not in the days of Innocent III.

The brief pontificate of Paul IV (1555–1559) therefore marked a pause in the labours of the Council; it was indeed more than a pause, it was a change of orientation. A man of his calibre would hardly be anxious to leave the taking of necessary decisions to an assembly not subject to his control. He would be able of his own accord to carry out the work of reform through the medium of arbitrary Bulls and decretals; this empty theological chatter was utterly fruitless. Six days after his election he held his first consistory, but said nothing about the Council—although he, with his fellow conclavists, had sworn to resume it. The cardinals looked at one another: they had understood.

It cannot be denied that Paul IV's personal efforts at reform proceeded from the best of intentions and even produced some excellent results. A number of peremptory decrees recalled bishops to the duties of their state; forbade any dispensation from the rule that fixed the minimum age for their appointment; strictly forbade the alienation of ecclesiastical goods upon any pretext whatever; reorganized the principal Vatican offices, notably the Dataria, in order to prevent simony in that quarter; abandoned such revenues of the Apostolic See as might be thought open to question; and in short clearly demonstrated that a real change had been effected in the Church. Certain cardinals whom the Pope adjudged worldly heard themselves publicly rebuked; and he of Ferrara, the ostentatious Ippolito d'Este, was overtly distributing gold with a view to his future election when he received orders to quit the Papal States without delay.

This watchful solicitude was extended to as many areas as possible. A trustworthy cardinal was appointed for each country, whose duty it would be to keep the authorities informed of all papal directions. Bishops were given increased powers, together with detailed instructions for the supervision of their clergy. Superiors of congregations were firmly requested to put their houses in order, even if this necessitated calling in the secular arm.

One picturesque episode in this campaign is worth recording here. At Rome, as indeed in all the great cities of Christendom, there were large numbers of "gyrovague" monks wandering about in defiance of the law of enclosure. Their lives were generally far from edifying, and a papal Bull ordered them to return to their monasteries or incur the penalty of excommunication. One month later the gates of the Eternal City were closed, and the pontifical police began hunting down their prey. Several hundred were rounded up, of whom two hundred were imprisoned or sent to the galleys. No pope had ever been known to employ measures of this kind.

Paul IV's chief instrument of reform, however, was the Inquisition, in charge of which Carafa had himself been placed at the time of its re-establishment by Paul III; and it was now "the apple of his eye, the favourite of his heart." The Venetian ambassador at Rome wrote: "The Pope's violence is always great, but in the matter of the Inquisition it is really indescribable. On Thursday, the day appointed for its meetings, nothing on earth could prevent him from attending. I remember the day when the Spaniards occupied Anagni: all Rome was running to arms, trembling for its life and property; but Paul IV calmly went off to preside over the Holy Office, dealing point by point with the agenda, just as though there were no enemy at the gate." Controlled thus by the Pope's iron hand, and entrusted by him to Ghislieri,[12] a Dominican prior no less rigid than himself, the Inquisition acquired formidable authority, receiving extraordinary and almost unlimited powers. It was ordered to prosecute even the semblance of heresy, "in no case to employ gentleness," never to hesitate in making an example even of the highest dignitaries. All suspects—pedlars of unorthodox books, Jews and Moors—were arrested and brought before the stern Dominican tribunals.

12. Afterwards St. Pius V.

Reviving and giving legal form to another of Paul III's ideas, Carafa established the official catalogue of forbidden books, the Index (1558), which was soon afterwards entrusted to a special Roman Congregation. Sixty-one works came under the ban.

The Inquisition was quite impartial, and had no respect of persons. The Patriarch of Aquilea, for instance, had excused a Lenten preacher who had spoken too lightly of predestination. He was summoned to appear, and, though exonerated, lost the Red Hat he had been promised. Cardinal Morone, the famous diplomat, who ventured to remark that violence in the sphere of religion had never borne good fruit, was imprisoned in the castle of Sant' Angelo. Cardinal Pole, being guilty of the same offence, was deprived of his position as legate in England and summoned to Rome, whither his sovereign, Mary Tudor, wisely prevented him from travelling. Every Catholic State was requested to provide facilities for the Inquisition. France declined, but Spain, where it had long been powerful, joyfully agreed; and it was at this period that all suspected of Lutheranism, Erasmianism or Illuminism were subjected to the fiery persecution which has earned the Spanish Inquisition so vile a reputation. Beautiful writings, such as John of Avila's *Audi Filia*, were condemned. St. Teresa herself fell under suspicion. Thousands, nay, tens of thousands of works were consigned to the flames. At the instigation of his fellow Dominican Melchior Cano, "who could smell heresy at a distance of ten leagues," Archbishop Carranza of Toledo was arrested because of a commentary on the catechism which had been declared suspect. This appalling reign of terror, though justified to some extent by the perilous situation in which the Church then stood, was surely going too far; such at least was the opinion expressed in many quarters.

Moreover Paul IV, an upright pope, determined to place the welfare of the Church above all temporal interests, became involved in political affairs of which the least that can be said is that they added nothing to his glory. A Neapolitan, whose family had suffered under Spanish rule, he detested everything to do with Spain, and was fond of saying that no such evil man as Charles V had been born on earth for a thousand years. Like Julius II, he dreamed of expelling the "Barbarians" from Italy and of reconstituting the peninsula as a fourfold entity, with Venice, Naples and Milan unquestionably subject to the Apostolic See. Urged by his nephew, Carlo Carafa, and more or less supported by the King of France, he hurled his troops against Naples; but the Duke of Alba brushed aside the attack. Simultaneously the terrible defeat of France at Saint-Quentin (August 10, 1557) obliged François de Guise to return in haste and oppose the invaders of his country. The collapse of the papal armies was complete. Rome was humiliated, and to crown her misfortunes the Tiber overflowed its banks to such a depth that it was possible to row a boat in the piazza of St. Peter's. Amid this desolation Alba made his entry, coming with scornful humility to pay his respects to the common Father of the faithful.

The political sovereign of the Papal States had been taught a harsh lesson; but worse was to come, this time from the hand of Providence through the medium of Carlo Carafa, his much too well-beloved nephew, a young soldier of fortune whom he had raised to the Sacred College and appointed Secretary of State. Carlo was a man devoid of morality, who, though governor of the Milanese and general of the Empire, had defected to the French from the lowest motives of self-interest, and whose private life and intrigues were a permanent scandal. Paul IV, however, thought the world of him. Around this young adventurer a whole family clique, including the Duke of Palliano and the Marquis of Montebello, was busily engaged, while a network of dispensations and privileges brought in handsome profits. A day came at last when rumours of the scandal reached the pontiff's ears, perhaps through the good offices of a Florentine agent. The aged Pope was greatly upset and ordered Padre Isackino, a saintly Theatine, to investigate. His report was far from satisfactory, and Paul IV now showed admirable strength of soul. Mastering his grief he held a secret consistory (January 1559) at which he delivered an astonishing address. He admitted his fault in having trusted unworthy men, and announced that three of his nephews—Cardinal Carlo, Palliano and Montebello—were dismissed from all their ecclesiastical offices and banished from Rome. Young Cardinal Alphonso, who alone had done no wrong and therefore remained at his post, was forbidden ever again to speak of the exiles. Six cardinals vainly besought the

Pope to mitigate the rigour of the sentence. Disconsolate as he was, he grimly refused to yield—"a splendid example," says Massaretti, "of honesty and true magnanimity."

The old man had nevertheless been broken by this tragic event. While multiplying his own fasts and other penances, as if to expiate the fault which his conscience would not forgive, he redoubled his intransigence in the work of reform, hurling terrible invective at bishops who lived at Rome instead of residing in their dioceses, referring the slightest peccadillo[13] to the Inquisition, and having his police spy on the private morals of Rome, just as Calvin did at Geneva. He died a holy death o August 18, 1559, and that evening there was serious rioting by the Roman mob, which had lately honoured him with a statue for having reduced taxation. The Dominican convent and the offices of the Inquisition were sacked; heretic prisoners were freed; insult was heaped upon the dead Pope's memory; and the famous statue overturned.

In the church of the Minerva at Rome, above the heavy sarcophagus of marble framed in gold, the image of Pope Paul IV raises its right hand in everlasting benediction—or everlasting menace.

6. PIUS IV BRINGS THE COUNCIL TO A SUCCESSFUL CONCLUSION

IF one thought may be said to have been uppermost during the arduous Conclave which opened at the beginning of September 1559 and lasted for more than three months, it was determination not to subject the Church to another ruler as harsh and authoritarian as the dead Carafa. Except for this, however, the cardinals were in almost total disagreement. Divided as they were into three groups, "Spanish," "French" and "Carafist,"[14] they took a long time finding the candidate who would satisfy them all. As

13. For example, violation of Friday abstinence, which was punished with imprisonment.
14. Constituting those who had been admitted to the Sacred College by Paul IV.

generally happens in such cases, they ended by choosing a "back-bencher" of whom no one had hitherto spoken much good nor yet much evil, and who had never held very high office. This man was Cardinal Giovanni Angelo Medici, Archbishop of Ragusa and a native of Milan. His supporters claimed him to be descended from the illustrious Florentine family of that name, but the wags called him *Il Medichino*, "the pocket Medici." He belonged in fact to that middle-class society which had its sons educated at the best schools and was not averse from seeing them hold office in the Church.

Medici was a sexagenarian, of stoutish build, but vigorous, full of high spirits and astute simplicity. Panvinius, a witness of his election, has left this portrait which there is every reason to accept as truthful: "Wide forehead, blue eyes, sideways glance, prominent red nose, scanty beard and fullness of figure. His features, and above all his gait, were somewhat lacking in dignity: a stoop and mincing steps invited laughter rather than respect." With such characteristics he was obviously a very different man from his fiery predecessor; but it could at least be hoped that the well-known law of alternation, which appeared to operate almost invariably in the field of papal elections, might produce a moral contrast no less profound than the physical dissimilarity which was plain for all to see. Modest, moderate, careful to break nothing and even to repair what had been broken, the new Pope took the auspicious name of Pius IV. His reign, which lasted until 1565, followed paths very different from those of his predecessor.

It was possible to breathe once more, but an all-important question remained: would he encourage the reform? If so would he straightway reassemble the Council? He had sworn in writing to do so at the Conclave, where he had given every sign of readiness to fulfil that undertaking. Not that he himself was altogether beyond reproach, for three illegimate children bore witness that he had paid handsome tribute to the disorderly spirit of the age. But when all was said and done, he had managed to preserve discretion; he had never caused scandal; and, as Panvinius notes with perhaps a touch of irony, "he had distinguished himself by his bearing and reputation" in the various secondary posts which he had occupied.

Sanctity then was not the principal characteristic of this man, to whom would belong the credit of having resumed and finally accomplished the indispensable work of reform, both with vigour and with greater ability than his forerunner. Here indeed we have one of the more surprising episodes in this amazing story: for the performance of so manifestly a providential task, God makes use of such instruments as Paul III, Paul IV and Pius IV.

The first acts of the new pontificate did not seem to indicate a firm resolve to break with the deplorable errors of that age. Many were sullied by the most obvious nepotism. Among the issue of his four brothers and five sisters Pius IV had many nephews, and this hungry horde descended upon him in full cry immediately after his coronation. But for all his apparent simple-mindedness, *Il Medichino* had a crafty eye and was no bad judge of men. Those of his nephews who came begging received offices and honours galore, but in such sort that they were kept at a safe distance from Rome and could exert no real influence. There lived at Milan another young nephew of the Pope, who asked for nothing. This was the son of his sister Margaret, wife of Ghiberto Borromeo; a brilliant student at the University of Pavia, he was also known to lead a blameless life amid the dissipations of his youthful contemporaries. Pius IV, with whom he was a great favourite, summoned him to Rome, and a few weeks later not only gave him the Red Hat but also appointed him Secretary of State. The fortunate lad was barely twenty-two years of age. Here indeed was an act of nepotism if ever there was one; but Heaven must have had a hand in this choice, and the Pope must have been a first-class judge of men, for the young cardinal turned out to be one of the greatest saints of the age, "the Pope's right eye" in the labour of reform. He is known to history as St. Charles Borromeo.

With the aid of this peerless collaborator, whose temperament, though firm as a rock, bore no trace of violence, Pius IV was able to retain but at the same time to modify the system introduced by his predecessor. So far from suppressing the Inquisition, for which he had no liking, he was at pains to emphasize that in doctrinal matters its authority remained universal and absolute: it had the right, nay the duty, to proceed against anyone, even a bishop or a cardinal, who yielded to the lure of heresy. He was careful, however, to insist that it must not intrude elsewhere; simoniacs, blasphemers, ill-behaved clerics and sodomites were outside its jurisdiction. In several cases the new Pope inclined to mildness. For example, the unfortunate Bishop of Aquilea, who had been haled before the Inquisition for having merely excused a suspect preacher, was allowed to submit his writings for examination by a more lenient authority, and was completely exonerated. The terrible Index of Paul IV, so brutal that St. Peter Canisius called it a "stumbling-block," was revised and curtailed. For instance, it no longer included the complete works of Erasmus, which had been condemned *in odium auctoris*; only certain treatises were expressly named. There was thus a change of climate; the aims of Paul IV were not abandoned, but the means thereto were altered.

In one case alone Pius IV showed himself implacable, almost to the point of ferocity. It was a mysterious business of nightmare quality, reminiscent of a Shakespearian tragedy—the affair of the Carafas. The late Pope's nephews had countless enemies, whom they had offended in the days of their power and who were determined on revenge: Colonna, Sforza, Gonzaga, Pallantieri and others. These men considered that Cardinal Carlo had escaped too easily from the punishment due to his scandalous conduct; besides, he had imprudently returned to Rome and was behaving with all his old swagger. A shocking piece of news made it possible to reopen the dossier. The Duke of Palliano, alias Giovanni Carafa, suspecting his wife Violaine of adultery, assumed judicial functions and accused her, together with her alleged accomplice, before a court presided over by himself and two of his relations. By means of torture he secured a full confession from the young man, whom he promptly stabbed with his own hand, leaving him dead with no fewer than twenty-seven gaping wounds. Then, with the approval of the unhappy woman's own brother, Violaine was declared an adulteress and, though seven months pregnant, suffered a hideous death by strangulation with a cord. The crime had been committed while Paul lay on his death-bed, leaving vacant the Apostolic See; but reports reached Rome, there were angry protests on all sides, and those who hated the Carafa clique immediately broke loose.

A formidable record was drawn up; it filled eight chests and constituted an overwhelming indictment of the family of Paul IV. Even young Cardinal Alphonso, by far the best of them, was charged with abuse of confidence and extortion. Arrested and tried by a consistory that knew no mercy, while Rome was put in a state of siege to avoid any possible demonstration, the Carafas were found guilty, despite the intervention of the King of Spain. The three murderers of Violaine were hanged, as was only right; so also was Cardinal Carlo, the justice of whose execution is open to doubt.[15] Alphonso alone was acquitted, but was ordered to take up residence in his diocese and not to leave it during the remainder of his life. As for the Duke of Montebello, another Carafa of ill repute, he managed to escape in time to avoid arrest. Was the inflexibility of Pius IV on this occasion due to pressure of public opinion? Or did he seek to prove that he had broken with the habits of his predecessor? Or again, was he reminding the clans, and even the cardinals, that in spite of his apparent good nature he was more than capable of wielding authority? It was at about this time that he made a quaint remark which caused much mirth in Italy: "I have four great worries, all beginning with a C." The four C's were Carafa, Colonna, Cardinals and Council.

The last of these worries was by no means the least. It had undoubtedly weighed upon the mind of Pius ever since he had assumed the tiara, and he was working patiently for the fulfilment of his plan. The personal initiative of Paul IV had evidently failed, and a return must be made to the Council. Those insurmountable difficulties which had prevented the success of the Council some fifteen years earlier had lately been removed. Charles V, who had retired to the monastery of Yuste in 1557, died there on November 21, 1558. His vast dominions were now shared between two empires, Spain under Philip II and Germany under Ferdinand, neither of whom dreamed of reviving the pretence of a Holy Roman and Germanic Empire. Henri II died in 1559, shortly before Paul IV. Since the disappearance of the two

15. A revision of the case, ordered by St. Pius V, proved that a number of documents produced against him at the trial were forgeries.

 great adversaries the climate had improved, and with the return of political peace it had become easier to work for the reform of the Church.

Pius IV saw that the occasion was propitious. He acted accordingly and opened negotiations with the great rulers. Philip II was in principle very much on the side of reform, but he was thinking of marriage with the Protestant Elizabeth of England. Ferdinand, whom the Sovereign Pontiff hoped to win over by conferring upon him the imperial crown, showed himself less favourable to a council than to a series of simple "conferences" at which his Catholic and Protestant subjects might in the end agree. Catherine dei Medici, regent of France, still preferred a policy of *rapprochement*, temporization and "conferences"; the breakdown of the Conference of Poissy in August 1561, and the famous "Massacre of Vassy" in the following year, had not wholly sufficed to convince her that chances of reaching agreement were remote. Difficulties notwithstanding, the Pope remained firm, and his Bull *Ad Ecclesiae Regimen* summoned members to Trent for Easter Sunday 1561. Complications did not cease for all that, and many months of involved negotiation were necessary before the Council could resume. Happily for Pius IV, he was aided in this most difficult task by a remarkable collaborator, who was perhaps the ablest diplomat of his time—Cardinal Morone, whom his terrible predecessor had flung into prison on suspicion of heresy, and whom the Roman lampoons treated as an "enemy of the Blessed Virgin and the saints." Formerly nuncio to Ferdinand, who called him his friend, Morone succeeded in persuading the emperor that his true interest lay in supporting the Council. At the same time Catherine dei Medici discovered that Protestantism in France might prove a very real threat to her power, while some judicious promises of gold helped the waverers to make up their minds.

That fair weather lay ahead became apparent as, week by week, the little Alpine city welcomed an increasing number of bishops, theologians and other dignitaries. Whereas the early sessions of the Council, long ago, had been attended by no more than sixty to eighty members, the final meetings took the votes of more than two hundred fifty delegates in presence of a large audience. Titian's famous picture in the Louvre gives some idea of the grandeur of these plenary sessions. Seated before the altar of Santa Maria Maggiore, the four legates presided over a sea of white mitres watched by the accredited representatives of every Catholic nation. The streets, squares, palaces and convents, and even the humblest dwelling-houses, were literally packed.

Reassembled at last in January 1562 under the direction of Cardinals Ercole Gonzaga,[16] Stanislaus Hosius, Girolamo Seripando and Luigi Simonetta as legates, the Council set to work in good earnest, bent upon obtaining solid results with the least possible delay. Nine sessions were held in the space of three months; and although personal conflicts were not entirely absent, they were not envenomed by political differences, nor were they so bitter or so violent as before. There were a few awkward moments, as when Catherine dei Medici, furious at seeing the Council resolved to curtail princely privileges, ordered her ambassadors to leave Trent; but on the whole everything ran smoothly.

Most of the great dogmatic and disciplinary problems then facing the Church were studied one by one. The Eucharist, the Mass, the cult of saints and Purgatory were the subject of dogmatic decrees; others regulated the residence of bishops, the morality of the clergy and the rights of princes. "No Council in the history of the Church," says Cardinal Hergenrother, "has determined so many questions, established so many points of doctrine or made so many laws." It was an immense achievement: after so much delay and opposition the Church managed to formulate with extraordinary vigour and absolute precision answers to the heretical theses as well as to the criticism directed against herself. Before long the Missal and Catechism, approved by the Council and compiled by some of its members, would disseminate this teaching among the great mass of the faithful. Before long the seminaries advocated by the Council would provide the Church with an altogether new type of clergy, ready for the labour of reconquest. And before long the Papacy—which, in spite of all its faults, must be credited, in the persons of Paul IV and Pius IV respectively, with having initiated the Council and brought it

16. His place was afterwards taken by Morone.

to a successful conclusion—would devote itself under St. Pius V to the task of injecting the reform into the blood and marrow of the Church.

"I cannot describe," wrote an eye-witness, Paleotti, "the spiritual joy of all, their gratitude to God, their act of thanksgiving when the Council sat for the last time. I myself saw many of the most solemn prelates weep for joy, and those who had the very day before treated one another almost as strangers embrace with deep emotion. An astonishing outburst of cheers for the Pope marked this final gathering." The date was December 4, 1563. The decrees were solemnly signed by four legates, three patriarchs, twenty-five archbishops, one hundred sixty-nine bishops, seven abbots, seven Generals of Orders, ten episcopal procurators and the ambassadors of all the Catholic powers. Confined to his palace, old and sick, suffering from asthma and rheumatism, but receiving daily reports on the progress of the Council, Pius IV might well be proud to have been the instrument of this imposing and decisive work. Yet when his two intimate friends, Charles Borromeo and Philip Neri (both future saints), congratulated him upon his success, he replied simply: "All was done by God's inspiration."

7. THE COUNCIL OF TRENT AND THE DEFINITION OF DOGMA

A tree is judged by its fruit, and in order to appreciate the importance of Trent one need only consider its results. These are immeasurable, and such that no other council in the whole history of the Church has been of equal consequence. The decisions made in the course of its troubled sessions established the Catholic faith in such a way that it has never since been questioned. "I ask you," says Bossuet, "to show me a single Catholic author, a single bishop, a single priest, a single man whatever he be, who thinks he can remain in the Catholic Church and say that he does not accept the faith of Trent, or that the faith of Trent is open to doubt. That will never be." In this passage the great orator is referring exclusively to the doctrinal work of the Council, although its achievement in respect of morality and administration, if less conclusive,[17] was equally significant from an historical point of view. Whereas each of the dogmatic decrees included a "canon" (i.e., a short clause anathematizing those who deny the doctrine set forth), the disciplinary decrees, whose purpose was to reform the Church, contained no censures. All, however, dogmatic and disciplinary alike, were adopted according to no predetermined plan or logical order, but with so broad a vision of the problems confronting Holy Church that together they fill fourteen quarto volumes of the official edition begun in 1901 and still incomplete.

The dogmatic work of the Council of Trent is a monument of wisdom and exactitude. The faith of the Church, based upon Scripture and Tradition, is formulated with a clarity, force and inclusiveness which she had never previously enjoyed. We feel the passage of a mighty wind; we observe at the same time and at every step the firmness of those theological notions which were the fruit of immense labour extending over more than a thousand years. Here is no system sprung, like the doctrines of Luther and Calvin, from a single brain; here indeed is expressed the collective conscience of the Church, not only at that date, but in the past and in the future. Catholicism was no longer destitute of theologians as in the early days of the Lutheran attack. A great majority of the Fathers of the Council were men of outstanding ability, well acquainted with theology, patristics, canon law and Scripture.[18] Above all, they "felt with the Church" so deeply that they naturally followed the surest line of tradition even in matters upon which they were not thoroughly informed, and every detail of their conclusions is today in full accord with the demands of historical criticism. The *rota scripta*, reports drawn up by the consultors, amaze us with their erudition, and still provide ample material for dictionaries and handbooks of doctrinal history. It was

17. On the dogmatic plane the decisions of the Council are binding on all Catholics: to reject them is heresy. In the field of discipline, on the other hand, he who disputes or refuses to subscribe them is rash or rebellious, even schismatic, but does not thereby put himself outside the Church.
18. Less well with the history of dogma; but the reformers themselves were no better off in this respect.

 not in vain that there had occurred half a century earlier that revival of theology which has been described as one of the glories of the Catholic Renascence.[19] As the Council set forth the dogmas of the Church, there hung over it a cloud of witnesses: Cajetan (1468–1534), the great Dominican cardinal and theologian of the Trinity, whom the Papacy had sent against Luther[20]; Ambrose Catharin (1487–1553), an authority on Grace; Francesco Vittoria, the renewer of Thomism; many controversialists who, from Johann Eck to John Fisher, from Clichtove to Tapper, had fought with such determination against heresy; and the splendid figure of St. Ignatius who was represented there by several members of his Society. Among those present at the sessions, and playing a decisive part therein, were the Dominicans Melchior Cano and Dominic Soto, disciples of Vittoria, to whom modern theology is heavily indebted. It was the manifold effort of all these thinkers which ultimately led to the stupendous edifice of the "canons."

Here we must frankly acknowledge the historical (or dialectical) function of Protestantism in the evolution of these principles. The part played in the great debate by Luther, Calvin and the rest was exactly that recognized long since by St. Paul, in a celebrated passage to the Corinthians,[21] as belonging to heretics. On the strictly spiritual plane the Catholic revival, as represented, for example, by Cajetan of Tiene, Zaccaria, Giberti and Ignatius of Loyola, owed nothing to anti-Protestant endeavours; but on the doctrinal level the blows delivered by the heretics led the Church to discern more clearly those points of her structure which were threatened and to reinforce them accordingly. Every one of the great Protestant theses was surveyed by the Council, which opposed to it the Catholic truth, especially the three fundamentals bearing upon revelation and the bases of doctrine, upon the role of faith, works and grace, and upon the sacraments with particular reference to the Eucharist.

---

19. Fr. Cayré, *Manuel de Patrologie.*
20. See *A Religious Revolution: The Protestant Reformation,* Volume 2, Chapter V, pp. 377–78.
21. "For there must also be heresies, that they also who are approved may be made manifest among you" (1 Cor.11:19).

Protestants claim that every Christian must discover Revelation in direct contact with God by means of the inspired Book, which is the expression of His Word. To read and meditate the Bible is sufficient to establish genuine Christianity solidly upon its bases; the teaching of the Church contributes nothing to knowledge of the truth. The Council replies that "the teaching mission of the Church is to guard the perfect integrity of Holy Scripture and Tradition,[22] the two sources of our faith." These twin sources are equally necessary to the life of the Church. The first of them is indicated with absolute precision: the Council establishes the Canon of Scripture[23] and declares that all the books which constitute the Bible were written "at the dictation of the Holy Spirit." The text as at present approved is that of the Latin *Vulgate*, St. Jerome's illustrious work, the definitive edition of which was begun immediately the Council ended and was published in 1592. No one, however, may interpret the sacred books in his own way; no one must "in matters concerning faith and morals attribute to Scripture a meaning other than that which the Church has given and does give to it." Tradition also is expressly attributed to "the dictation of the Holy Spirit." What then is Tradition? The Council does not define this word dogmatically; but its content is revealed by reference to the Fathers and Doctors, to the decrees of recognized councils, to papal decisions, and to the intentions and consent of the universal Church. Thus a communal notion is opposed to Protestant individualism, the principle of authority to anarchism. It is the Church that enables her children to derive from Holy Scripture whatever fruits they can expect therefrom; she it is who teaches them what they must believe and what not believe. A complete exposition of all this doctrine was provided by the *Catechism* of the Council of Trent, published in 1566.

There is another point, besides the sources of faith, at which Protestants diverge from traditional teaching; I mean the role of faith in man's supernatural destiny. Luther won many followers by his doctrine of justification

22. The Council always uses the plural "traditions"; but it is now established custom to speak of "Tradition," a rather less comprehensive term than the former.
23. This is the "canon" followed in all Catholic Bibles. It makes no distinction between what we call the "protocanonical" and "deuterocanonical" books.

by faith, even while Calvin preached the terrible thesis of predestination in the cathedral of St. Peter at Geneva. Against these theories the Council took its stand, perfectly aware, however, that their success was due to certain deep-seated aspirations of the age, to an anxious search for the true laws of Christianity, to a hungry longing for salvation. It is remarkable that the Assembly of the Catholic Church, without yielding to the temptations of pagan humanism, remains infinitely closer than its adversaries to humanism properly so called. It does not despise man, it does not belittle him as do the vehement prophets of heresy; the decrees of the Council bear witness to that optimism which St. Augustine, St. Bernard and St. Thomas have made part and parcel of Catholicism. Luther and Calvin place no confidence in man. The Council of Trent has such confidence, because man bears within himself an ineffable likeness, which no defilement can erase. This is not to say that he is unscathed; original sin is there sure enough and is minutely defined in five canons. But, darkened as it is by sin, human nature is not irremediably affected. Reason and will are damaged, but it is not true that they are without clear-sightedness, integrity and energy. What God asks of man is that he should co-operate fully in the work of his salvation, certain meanwhile that his effort is vain without grace, but equally assured that grace will not be refused to him so long as he remains faithful. Works therefore are necessary; faith alone is not enough. A Christian guilty of mortal sin is deprived of grace and condemned, even though he believes. Considerable stress is laid upon this double role of faith and works in the decrees of the sixth session (thirty-three canons in sixteen chapters), which are due in large measure to the saintly Cardinal Cervini, afterwards Pope Marcellus II. Justification is not secured by faith alone, still less by Luther's "conviction" of being justified. It requires human effort *as well as* the operation of God's mercy. Our Lord's sacrifice, the merits of God made Man, save each one of us from the consequence of sin, from the intolerable burden of his wretchedness; they touch the depth of his conscience, at the innermost point of his freedom, and lead him to the presence of eternal light. Man's free will is offset by the infinite goodness of God. It is of course, as the Council emphasizes, "with fear and trembling" that man must work out his salvation; but it is not true to say that God, as a whimsical tyrant, calls some to heaven and dooms others to hell by virtue of an incomprehensible act of predestination. The central dogma of Catholicism is *not* the Fall, the terror of eternal chastisement consequent upon sin; it is the Redemption, the charity of our Lord Jesus Christ, His love of our unhappy race.

The sovereign favour of Christ is not limited to one period or to one set of circumstances; it is for ever active in the sacraments, where the ineffable operation of grace joins with the faith, the transport and the effort of a faithful soul to lead it to salvation. On this point also the Council takes a firm stand against the tenets of Protestantism. It imposes, under pain of anathema, belief in the seven traditional sacraments, upholding their divine origin upon the strength of Holy Scripture. It defines their essence and their mode of operation. The function of the sacraments is not, as Luther taught, to nourish faith; they are not, as Zwingli maintained, "signs of Christianity"; they really contain the grace which they signify, and they confer it upon those who do not oppose it with evil dispositions. Baptism is indispensable to salvation; but it is false to maintain that salvation cannot be lost except by loss of faith, as if baptism itself exempted man from the duty of co-operation. Confirmation, rejected by heretics as "injurious to the Holy Ghost," is declared to be man's free and unqualified undertaking to play his bounden part in the work of salvation. Penance and Extreme Unction, condemned or misrepresented by the Protestants, who consider the essential of forgiveness to reside in the merit of Christ, are declared holy, sacred and necessary. In absolving the sins confessed by a penitent, the priest performs a supernatural "judicial act" in the name of Christ, who has delegated His powers to him; and the act of contrition is an integral part of that self-conquest which is a *sine qua non* of salvation. Holy Orders, likewise rejected by the heretics, are vouched for with the utmost solemnity. Their scriptural origin is declared; the power of consecrating and offering the Body of Christ belongs exclusively to those who have been rightly ordained. Against those who uphold the theory that marriage is simply a contract, and who therefore maintain the validity of divorce, the Council firmly asserts marriage to be a sacrament, instituted by Christ Himself, who has willed that it shall be indissoluble.

126 Finally, in the thirteenth, twenty-first and twenty-second sessions, the sacrament of the Eucharist was defined with such vigour and precision as had never yet been accorded it in any official document of the Church. Eight chapters and eleven canons are set against the multiple and contradictory interpretations of the reformers. They assert the *real* presence of Christ in the host, His *substantial* presence (not virtual, as Calvin said), and His *entire* presence under each species; and they teach *transubstantiation* as opposed to the Lutheran doctrine of impanation. In practice, for traditional reasons, communion in both kinds is reserved to priests. The Council emphasizes the moral and spiritual dispositions with which the faithful should receive the sacrament, having first confessed their sins in order to be in the state of grace. The Eucharist, however, is something more than a sacrament offered to men for their salvation; it is also and above all a sacrifice offered to God (which the Protestants unanimously refuse to admit), a sacrifice which re-enacts that of Calvary, and continually applies the merits thereof. The supernatural framework within which this sacrifice is offered is the Mass, whose central place in the work of redemption is declared.

Thus on all essential points of difference between Catholic tradition and heretical doctrine the Council speaks and resolutely determines what is to be believed. Its achievement is of capital importance, assuring to the Church stability of her foundations, removing revealed truth from the arena of debate, establishing rules which none henceforward can reject without thereby lapsing into error. It must also be observed that this immense doctrinal undertaking was not limited to urgent problems. In fact there was no current question, great or small, upon which the Assembly did not touch and provide a solution. The cult of saints, for example, was declared lawful within certain limits which would avoid abuses. As regards indulgences, they are linked with the power given by Christ to His Church to "bind and loose"; they must never be abused, but are recognized as perfectly legitimate. On several other doctrinal points the Council avoided anything in the nature of dogmatic definition, but laid down certain principles which would guide the Church in subsequent decisions. Thus the first official statement of Our Lady's Immaculate Conception is contained in a decree of Trent, which formally declares her exempt from the otherwise universal taint of original sin.

8. THE COUNCIL OF TRENT AND THE REFORM OF DISCIPLINE

BY including all dogmas within an almost complete system the Council of Trent established the Catholic faith as an indivisible whole, against which heretical error would be powerless. But this all-important work could not endure so long as the human society entrusted with the deposit of faith remained open to attack at many points. Disciplinary reform was therefore a necessary appendage of the doctrinal task. Besides, the two elements frequently interlock. It is, for example, upon the theology of the Church conceived not only as the spiritual assembly of the elect, but also as a human society possessing its own laws, organization and hierarchy, that depend such decrees of the Council as are intended to clarify those laws, to substantiate that organization, and to place that hierarchy on more secure foundations. It was of course upon their own theology of the Church that Luther, Bucer and Calvin had relied in their assault upon Rome and her priesthood.

The most pressing need, after so many years of fruitless endeavour, was to eliminate certain deplorable customs which dishonoured the Church and justified the criticism directed against her. An impressive body of decrees, interweaving and completing one another, laid down rules governing the whole hierarchy of persons from the Supreme Pontiff to the least of the faithful. *In capite et in membris*: the words had been so often repeated; the necessary reform must operate both in the head and in the members.

Not much is said about the head; it is indeed one of the few points upon which the Council saw no need to define and expatiate. There is no decree relating to the Pope as others do to episcopal residence and the power of secular princes. There is mention of the Sovereign Pontiff in Session XXV, where it is said that "nothing new in the Church can be decided without consulting him." Infallibility, though put forward by the Jesuit theologians, was not included. On the other hand, the Pope is declared "universal Pastor having full power to rule the universal Church." This is repeated several times, and he is reminded in terms reminiscent of St. Bernard's *De Consideratione* that he is "bound by the sacred duties of his office to watch over the universal Church," to extirpate abuses and to keep a watchful eye upon negligent pastors, "because Jesus Christ will call him to account for those shepherds whose evil government has shed the blood of their flocks." He is implored, in a pathetic adjuration, to choose as cardinals none but those worthy of their exalted dignity; and here no doubt is the reason for the Council's reserve in respect of the Papacy, whose past faults it wisely abstained from criticizing. Only let the Pope create good cardinals, selected from all parts of the Christian world, and there would be no more bad popes on the throne of Peter. Reform properly speaking takes place at a lower level.

The cardinals themselves were treated less gently. It is curious, and incidentally strong evidence of the freedom reigning in the Catholic Church, to find members of the Council—some of them bishops, others mere theologians—adopting a strongly critical attitude towards the Sacred College. The saintly Archbishop Bartholomew of Braga, for instance, threw this neat little dart at the *porporati*: "It is my opinion that their illustrious Lordships are in sore need of illustrious reform." The Council itself took this view; it bade the Princes of the Church to lead exemplary lives, to be frugal and to despise worldly vanities: "Since their duty is to assist the Sovereign Pontiff in the government of Holy Church, it is only right and proper that they should possess such outstanding virtue and regulate their conduct in such a way as to serve as models for the rest of mankind." That familiar figure of the dissolute cardinal, the red-hatted brigand, henceforward stood condemned.

The Council showed immense solicitude for every detail relative to the episcopal order, whose duties were the concern of no fewer than twelve sessions. They are the king-pin of the whole structure: *Ecclesia in episcopo.* The most important duty of which they are reminded is that of residence, to which the Council returns several times. Ancient penalties were revived and new ones enacted against those who neglect the souls committed to their care. A bishop must never be absent from his diocese for more than

three months, never during Advent and Lent. The obligation of residence
automatically prevented accumulation of benefices, which is forbidden by another decree; it was impossible to live at one and the same time at Mainz, Speyer, Trier and other places. Residing in his diocese the bishop would also be better able to fulfil the functions of his office. What were those functions? The Council enumerates them with rather more detail than method; but taken together its admonitions present a fine picture of the bishop: attentive to the needs of his clergy and flock, careful not to confer Holy Orders upon any but worthy subjects, visiting all the churches in his diocese at least once a year, preaching without fail every Sunday and feast day, keeping himself aloof from politics, financial interests and family ties. The type thus represented was a little too perfect to allow of its immediate realization; but it set an example which ultimately took effect, and continues to be a powerful influence.

The Council also devoted a good deal of attention to priests, and its work in this respect proved to be among the most fruitful of its undertakings. The ideal is similar to that proposed for bishops: "Those who handle the Lord's vessels must be purified in order to serve as examples; those who are to be initiated into the sacred ministry must be trained in the practice of every virtue." The Council repeats itself in this key over and over again. The familiar figure of the worthy and venerable parish priest, living modestly in his presbytery, charitable to the unfortunate and devoted to his people, can be traced in the decrees of Trent. He will be unmarried; the Council absolutely refused to follow the Protestants on this point, imperial entreaties notwithstanding. He must, like his bishop, keep residence and preach, explaining to his flock the Holy Scriptures, the sacraments and the liturgy. Will he be capable of doing so? Indeed yes. For the Council, taking its cue from such contemporary educationists as the Jesuits and even Calvin, proposed the establishment of seminaries, schools for the training of young clerics. In these special colleges the future priest would receive solid intellectual grounding in the liberal arts; a religious education in Scripture, patristics, hagiography and everything necessary for the proper administration of the sacraments, particularly that of Penance; and a moral formation which would fit him for his lofty mission. Rich and poor alike were to be admitted to these colleges; the Council even shows some preference for the poor, and every bishop is urged to have a seminary in his diocese. All this was a splendid initiative of vital importance for the future of the Catholic Church.

As for the regular clergy, the Council did not overlook their need of improvement. In the time of Paul III the Commission of Reform had proposed a drastic remedy in the shape of suppression of all existing Orders. The Fathers of Trent did not accept this radical measure, for many definitors and counsellors were themselves religious. But they did create a repository of regulations binding upon the regulars: age and conditions of admission, material organization of convents, election of superiors, etc. Nothing was omitted from the code, strict application of which was entrusted to the bishops. The Council also attempted to put an end to the scandal of *commendam* by prohibiting the grant of abbeys to persons who were not regulars.

Thus the whole hierarchy was covered: the teaching Church and her clergy would have no excuse for misconduct. Moreover these "moral" decrees properly so called were accompanied by others intended likewise to restore religion to its full dignity, to revive the deepest Christian loyalties in the field of worship, to safeguard the principles of unity and authority within the Church. The use of Latin, for example, the traditional language of the liturgy, was upheld against the heretics by the Council, which unanimously rejected that of vernacular,[24] and also upheld the custom of pronouncing in a low voice the most sacred words of the Mass, viz. part of the Canon and the formulae of Consecration. The vernacular, however, is not forbidden in certain well-defined cases (e.g., in private reading of the Bible, where its use is likely to be more profitable to the faithful). Strict rules are also laid down governing the duration of Mass as well as the respect and solemnity with which it must always be celebrated.

The Church, however, includes not only clerics; the mass of the faithful are of even greater importance, since it is in the last resort on their behalf and with a view to their salvation that all the foregoing measures are prescribed.

24. See a discussion of this question by A. Michel in *L'Ami du Clergé*, January 15, 1953.

The Council does not forget them, and the eighteenth session obliges them to hear Mass on Sundays and holidays of obligation. Other decrees forbid duelling and fix the minimum age for marriage. All the same, it is a little surprising that not one of the numerous sessions was devoted entirely to a portrayal of the true Christian layman, of the faithful Catholic inspired by the spirit of reform. This may be because the Catechism, which had been ordered by the Council and upon which a special commission was busily engaged, would provide the laity with all the necessary rules.

There remained one very serious problem, in one sense the most difficult if reform was to be achieved: how to prevent interference in ecclesiastical affairs by the secular rulers, who were in large part responsible for abuses. On this point the Council was visibly hesitant, and did not come to grips with it until the twenty-fifth session. It may have felt that its advice would fall on deaf ears, that its orders would prove ineffective. In the closing sessions there is a distinct advance towards freedom from secular interference, but some members were still too closely allied with the sovereigns. There was tremendous uproar when the project for "reform of princes," in forty-two chapters, was duly submitted to the ambassadors attending the Council. Those of France and Spain were for once in agreement, and joined forces in an indignant protest. The Fathers were not disheartened, and prepared a new scheme; but to everyone's amazement the Archbishop of Prague, acting in the emperor's name, demanded its withdrawal. After prolonged negotiations a number of decrees were passed forbidding princes to interfere in ecclesiastical matters, requiring them to apply the conciliar canons in their several States, and calling upon them to respect the rights and property of the Church.

These difficulties showed the Council, and indeed the Church as a whole, that one final problem had yet to be solved: the problem of enforcement. Decrees, canons and censures had been plentiful enough in the past: the last Council, some fifty years earlier, had paved the Lateran with good intentions; but what was left of them? "Unarmed laws fall into contempt," said Cardinal de Retz a hundred years later. The question now was whether Holy Church possessed weapons wherewith to enforce the wise laws she had just made. The Fathers of Trent were wide awake to the difficulty, and that is why, in submitting their decisions to Pope Pius IV,[25] they requested him to set up a "Congregation of the Council," whose duty it would be to carry out the decrees and, when necessary, decide the manner of their application.[26] But this was hardly sufficient. It was abundantly clear that such energetic measures of reform hurt too many interests, and not only those of secular princes. It was therefore necessary that the Council, itself the fruit of a great reawakening in the Christian soul, should extend its work by transmitting its own courageous spirit to the whole of Christendom. This was to be mainly the task of the saints; but it would also be necessary to establish an authority of sufficient dignity and strength to address appropriate language to vested interests. Italy, the Empire, Portugal and Poland were willing to "welcome" the decrees as bidden; but who would overcome the hesitation of Spain, the touchiness of the Low Countries, the cantankerous Gallicanism of France? The Council had accomplished its task. It was now the turn of the popes; and Providence, which had enabled the Church to take the decisive step, willed that the pontiffs who took over from the Assembly should understand their duty and be qualified to fulfil it.

9. ST. PIUS V

THE pope upon whose shoulders was placed the formidable burden of proving to the world that the decisions of the Council of Trent were no mere *flatus vocis* turned out to be at once a man of consummate ability and a saint. At the first consistory after his election he delivered an allocution whose import was summed up in two sentences: "We shall not paralyse the advance of heresy except by an operation proceeding from the heart of God. It is we, the light of the world, the salt of the earth, who must enlighten

25. He ratified them by the Bull *Benedictus Dei* on January 26, 1564.

26. Henceforward too anyone receiving an ecclesiastical benefice had to sign a formal declaration that he submitted to the decrees of the Council.

men's minds, enliven their hearts by the example of our holiness and our virtues." He himself practised these principles in striking fashion. Rome soon learned that the new pontiff lived in a monastic cell, drinking only water, spending hours in prayer and meditation on the Passion of Christ, weeping prostrate before the Blessed Sacrament or reciting the decades of his Rosary. It soon became clear also that there would be no more splendid processions of lordly cardinals through the city streets, no more prelates driving in their carriages with pretty women. There was no longer talk of galas and scandalous feasts; on the contrary, charitable undertakings received generous donations and a new impetus was given to works of public utility. Admiration reached its zenith when the Vicar of Christ was seen going barefoot, carrying the monstrance or visiting the basilicas as a humble pilgrim. Such a thing had not been witnessed for centuries. The citizens were thrilled, and wished to erect a statue to this undoubtedly great pope, but he refused.

The new occupant of Peter's chair was a lean figure of a man, with heavily lined features, wide forehead and the prominent cheek-bones of a Ligurian peasant. His keen, deep-set eyes seemed fixed immovably on their appointed goal. Behind the heavy moustache and long white beard an unsmiling mouth proclaimed a will of iron, inflexible resolution. His effigy on the noble medallion struck in 1570 is vaguely reminiscent of Calvin. "He is no laughing matter," wrote a Venetian ambassador; and that was indeed the least that could be said. Does one laugh at the Inquisition, with which formidable institution he had identified himself? Michele Ghislieri had for many years, ever since he joined the Dominicans at the age of fourteen, lived so austere and devout a life that Cardinal Carafa took a liking to him, made him his associate in the direction of the Holy Office, and finally, when he became pope, appointed him head of that institution. Under Pius IV the Grand Inquisitor had dared to protest loudly against all misdeeds, even when the Pope himself was at fault. He was indignant, for example, at the elevation to the purple of a thirteen-year-old Medici, as well as of an Este who was no more than twenty-two; but his prestige was so high that no one had been able to bring him down. The laborious Conclave following the death of Pius IV hesitated for some time between the rather disturbing character of Morone, the scholarly but insignificant Sirlet, and the colourless Montepulciano. The electors ultimately agreed, though not without some trepidation, upon the Prefect of the Holy Office. Cardinal Charles Borromeo, a nephew of Pius IV, did much to further this triumphal choice, perceiving in Ghislieri the mark of the Holy Spirit. The new Pope assured those who trembled at seeing Carafa's heir, the Inquisition incarnate, upon the papal throne: "I will act in such a way that Rome will regret my death more than my accession"; and he kept his word. When asked under what name he wished to rule, he showed himself to be without malice and anxious only to serve the Church. He would not take that of his master and model, Paul IV, but chose to be called after his immediate predecessor, whose work he was going to continue. He would be known as Pius V (1566–1572).

The cause of reform was certainly in good hands. Immediately after his election he proceeded to carry out the disciplinary decrees of Trent. Bishops were forthwith ordered back to their dioceses under pain of imprisonment in the castle of Sant' Angelo. The canons of St. Peter's were called to heel: their ancient privileges were no longer valid. The parish priests of the city were reproved for allowing their congregations to laugh and joke in church: they were informed that this must cease, and several of them were arrested. Ormaneto, a stern priest from Verona and formerly Vicar-General to St. Charles Borromeo, was directed to reorganize the Curia upon strict principles. Simony, traffic in favours, nepotism, everything of the kind must be at once abolished—an undertaking rather too comprehensive to be of lasting effect. Some disgruntled voices were heard to complain that the Pope himself had set a poor example by appointing his nephew Michele Bonnelli cardinal secretary of state. True the young Dominican was no more than twenty-five years old; but his conduct was beyond criticism, and his uncle never overlooked his slightest fault. The cardinals created by Pius V were men of outstanding virtue—Souchier, abbot-general of the Cistercians, for example, and the saintly Burali. Other members of the Sacred College, together with the bishops, were visited with an unwelcome flood of reproach, admonition and more dangerous invective. A wind of austerity was beginning to blow through the Church; it had already reached gale force at Rome. Here the papal police swept the streets clean of prostitutes. Horse-races akin to the Sienese "Palio" had long been staged in front of St. Peter's; these were now banished to a remote quarter of the city, and soon became obsolete. The uncompromising pontiff would also have liked to suppress the Roman Carnival. Since this was impossible, short of provoking revolution, he instituted the Forty Hours' Prayer as atonement for the licentiousness of those days, and himself withdrew to Santa Sabina where he spent the time in penitential exercises. One of his most spectacular and most questionable acts was to clear the papal palaces of as many pagan nudities as he was able, a gesture of which the city of Rome took advantage by founding the Capitoline Museum.

Together with such coercive and punitive measures Pius V adopted others of a more constructive kind. Once again in obedience to the decrees of Trent, he concerned himself with the editing and publication of those books which the Council had held to be indispensable. It was not sufficient to exclude harmful works, which were named in the revised Index; he must give the faithful that wholesome nourishment for which their souls hungered. Accordingly there were published in succession four books that were to be absolutely fundamental: the *Catechism*, the *Breviary*, the *Missal* and the *Summa* of St. Thomas Aquinas.

Preparation of the Catechism had been begun during the last weeks of the Council by a commission under the presidency of Cardinal Seripando. After the dissolution of the Assembly the work was continued by Cardinal Borromeo assisted by three Dominican theologians. It was not until September 1566 that the Catechism appeared, after five years of unremitting effort; but the result was a magnificent achievement, setting forth in precise terms all that a Catholic may and must believe as regards the Creed, the sacraments, Christian morality and the spiritual life. Quickly translated into all languages and distributed throughout the world, this compendious volume was destined to be the code and charter of Catholics, and it remains in constant use.

The Breviary, wherewith the clergy (and pious layfolk too) follow the "canonical hours," had existed for a very long time. The most popular version was known as that of the Minors and dated from 1277. It had received numerous additions in the course of centuries, and had become much too bulky. In the time of Leo X someone had conceived the unfortunate idea of introducing mythological hymns and other pretty things which were dear to the humanists[27] but far removed from true Christian tradition. Clement VII had set up a commission to correct these abuses, and the Spanish cardinal Quinones had compiled another breviary, called after Santa Croce, which had proved unsatisfactory. Pius IV established a commission for the reform of the Breviary in 1564, but little was accomplished. It was Pius V who took the business in hand with his accustomed energy; he entrusted it to a commission of cardinals, brought it to a successful conclusion, and finally (1568) published a new breviary that was shorter, more firmly centred on the principal office and relieved of many superfluous feasts. Only a very few Churches (e.g., Milan, Lyons and Toledo) refused to adopt it.[28]

Reform of the Breviary presupposed that of the Missal, which was carried out in the same spirit of uniformity. Hitherto the Western Church had celebrated Mass according to four rites: Roman, Milanese or Ambrosian, Gallican and Mozarabic. The commission of cardinals which had just remodeled the Breviary prepared a new missal; it was published in 1570 and eliminated the differences, which were considered unsuitable for public worship. Certain new features were also established, such as the *Introibo* and *Confiteor* at the beginning of Mass, the beautiful prayer *Suscipe Santa Trinitas* at the Offertory, and St. John's prologue as the "last gospel."[29] Excepting some very small details to which a few Churches[30] and Orders[31] remained faithful, the Missal of St. Pius V was adopted by the whole Catholic world, and remains in use almost unchanged today.

---

27. Our Lady, for example, was described as "blessed goddess" and the Trinity as "threefold visage of Olympus"!
28. See an article "Les Réformes du Bréviaire au XVIe siècle: rôle de l'Espagne," in *L'Ami du Clergé* (May 20, 1954), p. 305.
29. See Daniel-Rops, *Missa est.*
30. For example, Lyons and Milan.
31. For example, the Carthusians and Dominicans.

Lastly, there was a fourth publication, which, though perhaps less well known than the other three, exerted an enormous influence on the subsequent history of the Church. Pius V, himself a Dominican, had been familiar with St. Thomas from youth upwards, and he considered Aquinas's thought as the firmest possible foundation upon which to rebuild the Church, "a solid barrier against the storm." In 1567 he proclaimed St. Thomas a Doctor of the Church, placing him alongside Ambrose, Augustine, Jerome and Gregory the Great. Next he instructed two theologians of his Order, Giustiniani and Manrique, to prepare from the Vatican manuscripts a definitive edition of the *Summa Theologica*, the cost of which he himself defrayed. The universities were directed to teach only Thomism, which was adopted soon afterwards by the Jesuits.

All this activity in the fields of doctrine and discipline was far from sufficient to occupy the days of Pius, who strove at every level for a return to Christian loyalties, for unity and for good government. Secular princes, without exception, were requested in no uncertain terms to further the designs of the Church by promoting reform among their subjects and by employing all their forces in the struggle against heresy. The Bull *In Coena Domini* reminded them of their duties. Not all submitted with an obedience proportionate to the Holy Father's urgency. But that lean old figure in the Vatican, never abandoning his principles, and despising the customary means of diplomacy, advanced at every point, speaking forthrightly, threatening whenever necessary, and supported by the incorruptible agents of the Inquisition.

Orthodoxy launched a huge offensive on so many fronts that we can scarcely grasp it as a whole. In Germany, the land *par excellence* of heresy, Maximilian II appeared to be making dangerous concessions; but he was checked by a threat of excommunication, just as the Diets of Augsburg (1566) and Speyer (1568) were about to place Catholics and Protestants on an equal footing. In England, where Elizabeth I was erecting her State Church, Pius V spoke up regardless of the fatal consequences that must and did ensue[32]: he excommunicated the heretical queen and released her

32. See Volume 2, p. 267.

 subjects from their allegiance. The Duke of Alba, who was fighting the Protestants in the Low Countries, received encouragement and blessing.[33] In Poland the Pope did all he could to assist the efforts of King Sigismund II, who, despite the insecurity of his own position, was trying to bring back his country to the Roman faith. But when Queen Catherine Jagellon of Sweden, a faithful Catholic, agreed at the insistence of her husband to communicate in both kinds, she quickly received a Bull of excommunication. It need hardly be said that reaction was more severe in a country where the pontiff's influence was capable of immediate exercise. The Italian princes, cowed or convinced, rallied to his side without a moment's delay. A few executions were sufficient to exclude any risk of Protestantism obtaining a hold upon Florence and Venice. At Mantua the Dominican Casanova made a sensational swoop, seized the Protestant minister Celaria, and delivered him to the judges of the Inquisition, who burned him at the stake. The imperial ambassador protested, but was quickly snubbed by Pius V. In Spain an even warmer welcome awaited the radical measures recommended by the Pope. Philip II (1558–1589), an austere and taciturn but earnest monarch, was by no means willing to submit without question to the least wish of Rome; but in this matter he adopted of his own accord a policy of repression. From the depths of the Escorial, where he spent his days between work and prayer, there issued a stream of Draconian orders for the hunting down of heresy, free-thinking and the faintest scent of Protestant sympathies.[34] The Inquisitors appointed by him displayed a sombre zeal. Prisons were crowded, and the smoke of many an *auto da fé* rose into the sky. Tons of books and hundreds of men perished in the flames. As for France, in the Machiavellian hands of Catherine dei Medici, she began by offering passive resistance, endeavouring to protect her suspect bishops (among them Cardinal de Châtillon) from the hammer-blows of Rome. But when the Parliament of Paris resolved to take arms against the Protestants, Pius V dispatched a strong contingent of reliable troops to assist

33. See Volume 2, Chapter IV, p. 246.
34. See below, Chapter III, p. 194.

in this holy task.[35] His ceaseless activity left nothing undone that might secure the triumph of Catholicism, and he actually thought of negotiating the conversion of Russia under Ivan the Terrible!

In the mind of this Pope, whose outlook was still so largely medieval, the policies of loyalty and Christianity were identical. To him, as Vicar of Christ and guardian of the deposit of faith, belonged the right and duty to teach men what Christianity required of them, to dispose of earthly crowns in the interests of the Church and her faith, to direct the necessary struggle everywhere. The climax of his vast activity, in which he seemed truly to be blessed by heaven, was the thrilling victory of Christendom over the Infidel, for which he was ultimately responsible. Profiting by the incompetence of the new sultan, Selim, unworthy son of Solyman the Magnificent, Pius V's anachronistic genius revived the idea of a crusade. Nuncios were sent to the various courts, and, wonderful to relate, obtained more than empty promises. The Pope himself provided money and ships. Commanded by Philip II's twenty-four-year-old half-brother Don Juan of Austria, who was assisted by an experienced Catalan seaman, Luis de Requescens, the international fleet of Christendom set sail against the Muslims. On October 7, 1571, Christ's warriors, chanting the psalms, gave battle in the Gulf of Lepanto. It was a terrible engagement, full of surprises and anxiety. Don Juan himself stood on the prow of his flagship, holding a crucifix. When evening fell over the glorious bay, the smoke of burning Turkish galleys spread a reek of timber and corpses. The entire enemy fleet had been destroyed or captured, and aboard the *Marquera* a wounded soldier named Miguel de Cervantes, whose arm had been shattered in the fight, joined in the *Te Deum.* When Pius V received the news he cried out in reference to the youthful victor: "There was a man sent from God, whose name was John!" It seemed that the loss of Constantinople was avenged; and when the aged pontiff died (May 1, 1572), this brilliant triumph appeared as the crown of all his efforts, the pledge of his permanent success.

The facts, however, were not quite so straightforward. Lepanto was

35. See below, Chapter III, p. 219.

 indeed a glorious episode, but without a morrow. The manifold policies of Pius V were by no means fruitful of lasting results, and immediately after his death religious passions once again broke loose, more violent and confused than heretofore. Pius V was a very great pope, notwithstanding his unbridled precipitateness, and his enduring title to posterity's gratitude and admiration is summarized by Cardinal Grente in these words: "The decisions of the Council of Trent would become reality; the ardent labours of Catholicism would receive fresh impetus."[36] Nevertheless it has to be admitted that so enormous a task could scarcely have been fulfilled in a pontificate of only six years had there not existed at the same time a galaxy of saints who strove with all their might to reanimate, reorganize and invigorate the Catholic Church, men and women no less venerated[37] and perhaps better loved than Ghislieri: St. Charles Borromeo, St. Teresa of Avila, St. John of the Cross and St. Philip Neri.

10. EPISCOPAL REFORMERS: ST. CHARLES BORROMEO

THE Council of Trent had laid down the necessary principles of Catholic reform. The Holy See, in the person of St. Pius V, had shown its firm determination that they should not become a dead letter. But it was necessary to inject the new spirit deep into the Christian conscience, even in the remotest parishes.

Once again the honour and the burden of this undertaking lay first of all with the bishops, of whom the Council had drawn so noble a portrait in reminding them of their duties. Would they be capable of understanding what the Church required of them? One might expect that they would,

36. *Saint Pie V*, 1914, *ad fin.*

37. Five hundred years had passed since a pope (Gregory VII) had been canonized in 1085. Four hundred more elapsed before the canonization of another (Pius X). Clement X, a Dominican, beatified Pius V in 1672; Clement XI canonized him in 1711.

especially when it was recalled[38] that godly men had effected wonderful transformations in many a diocese long before Rome took official charge of the reform. Their series had never been interrupted: the line had remained unbroken from early to late, from the precursors of reform to those who must execute its decrees.[39] The solicitude and courage exhibited by Giberti at Verona, by St. Thomas of Villanova at Valencia, and even (with some mistakes) by Guillaume Briçonnet at Meaux, would be found no whit the less in numerous other prelates. Among them stands one particularly radiant figure: St. Charles Borromeo (1538–1583), Archbishop of Milan.

On January 30, 1560, Pope Pius IV had created three new cardinals. One of these was his nephew,[40] Carlo Borromeo, son of his sister Margarita. A few weeks later he appointed Carlo his Secretary of State, and subsequently poured out upon him a wealth of lordly titles: Archbishop of Milan; Protector of Portugal and Lower Germany; Legate at Bologna; Protector of the Carmelites, of the Canons of Coimbra, of all the Franciscans and of the Order of Christ; Archpriest of Santa Maria Maggiore and Grand Penitentiary. In addition, Borromeo received a host of rich benefices which brought him an income of more than one hundred million francs. The citizens of Rome, who delighted in treating all Vatican business with a measure of sarcasm, laughed heartily. They had seen a fair number of papal nephews loaded by their uncles with honours and prebends, without exactly benefiting the Church. Here was one more of them. The new pope would do no better than his predecessors.

The wits of the Piazza Navona were mistaken. The young cardinal, summoned at one stroke to such exalted responsibilities, was more than adequate to the burden. He was only twenty-two years old, but his experience of life, his wisdom and intelligence were far beyond what is normal in a youth who has scarcely emerged from adolescence. It might indeed have been asked whether he had ever been a child. At the age of five, little

38. See above, Chapter I, section 3.

39. Thus Ormaneto of Verona, trained in the school of Giberti, became Vicar-General to St. Charles Borromeo.

40. Another was a young Medici aged seventeen.

Carlettino's favourite game was to build altars and play at liturgical ceremonies. He received the tonsure when no more than eight years old, and at twelve became abbot of a monastery. In this last capacity he took so important a view of his office that he actually determined to reform his monks! During seven years at the University of Padua he distinguished himself by his inexhaustible charity towards misfortune of whatever kind, as well as by his gaiety and devotion to study. He was a tall, lean fellow, with a long aquiline nose and unattractive looks, but he gave an impression of calm inflexibility, of efficiency and cool courage. On the death of his elder brother he afforded striking proof of his vocation: instead of asking his uncle for permission to return to the world and take his place as head of the family,[41] he made haste to have himself ordained priest.

God had indeed marked Borromeo with His seal, and his austere manner of life quickly gave the lie to those who scoffed at his elevation as an act of nepotism. "Of wealth," said the preacher of his funeral oration, "Charles possessed no more than a dog receives from its master: water, bread and straw." He had no sooner taken residence with his uncle than he showed himself in his true light, and he would have been the same in whatever situation Providence might have chosen to place him. A tenacious worker, spending much time also in prayer and meditation according to the *Spiritual Exercises* of St. Ignatius, his only recreations were an occasional hunting party to keep himself in form, and those little gatherings of a few friends for serious discussion, which he laughingly called his "Vatican nights." Was it possible then to be the Pope's nephew, Cardinal Secretary of State and holder of innumerable benefices, and yet to be a saint? The Roman people and the Curia yielded to the evidence. So did the Sacred College, which, having seen him at work as an administrator preparatory to and during the Council of Trent, thought for a moment of offering him the tiara on the death of his uncle, and followed his advice when he unexpectedly put forward the name of Cardinal Ghislieri. Charles Borromeo was now aged twenty-eight; he stood on the threshold of an astonishing career.

41. Although a cardinal he was still only a subdeacon.

The Council had completed its work, a new pope had been elected, and the former Secretary of State considered that his principal duty now was to set an example by removing to the archdiocese of Milan in obedience to the decree of episcopal residence. It was an enormous province, covering not only the Milanese but also parts of Venetian territory and the Swiss Alps; no fewer than fifteen suffragans were subject to his jurisdiction. So long as important ecclesiastical business detained him in Rome or at Trent, he had been obliged to leave its government in the hands of Ormaneto, that virtuous and talented priest whom Pius V summoned to Rome in order to reform the Curia. The situation in the archdiocese of Milan was certainly deplorable. Its priests were devoid of zeal, and so ignorant that most of them could not pronounce the words of absolution in Latin; some of its empty churches were used as barns, while the monasteries were fallen so low that their parlours and refectories were the scene of balls, weddings and banquets. A formidable task confronted Charles Borromeo, and to it he devoted the remainder of his life.

He made his solemn entry into Milan on September 23, 1565, and forthwith assembled a provincial council, which all his suffragans were ordered to attend for the purpose of enacting the decrees of Trent and receiving his instructions. Next he gathered around him all who seemed likely coadjutors: Jesuits, Theatines, Barnabites and clerics of the Oratory lately founded by St. Philip Neri. A vast, centralized reform of administration restored order in eight hundred parishes. These were henceforward grouped in deaneries or *pieri* under *vicars forane*, subject to regular visitation by special inspectors and even by the archbishop himself. It was also arranged that provincial councils would meet at stated intervals to study problems common to all the dioceses, each of which was to hold an annual synod. Following the directions of Trent, large seminaries were established, among them the famous Collegio Borromeo at Pavia (whose noble porticoes still preserve the founder's memory), the Swiss College at Milan and the seminary at Ascona on Lago di Maggiore. Discipline was everywhere restored. Lax priests found themselves invited to make a "pilgrimage" to the archiepiscopal residence, whence they were courteously but firmly conducted to a house of retreat, not to emerge until they had done penance and amended their lives. The monasteries too were brought back to better ways. There were to be no more ballrooms, no more junketings; and nuns received orders to cover their windows with grilles solid enough to keep the gallants out. One can hardly imagine a more rigorous application of the Tridentine decrees.

Knowing well the importance of his work, Borromeo preserved every one of his mandates and pastoral letters, every one of the ordinances resulting from the deliberations of his provincial councils. All this material was collected and published, thus providing reformers the world over with a detailed interpretation of the ideas of Trent. Valieri of Verona aptly described Charles Borromeo as "the Doctor of Bishops."

It would be idle to pretend that activity of this kind was to everybody's liking. When Charles Borromeo set out upon his chosen path he had enemies secret and avowed. The Spanish governors of Milan had too many personal or national interests in the affairs of the Church to accept without opposition the austere independence of the archbishop. His many conflicts with them went as far as excommunication, and Rome dismissed all appeals against his sentence. There were also the "Humiliati," a degenerate offshoot of what was in effect a Benedictine third order. These pseudo-monks numbered about two hundred; they had made huge profits from the wool trade, and lived in scandalous luxury. When Borromeo sought to curb their excesses they were so angry and made such an outcry that he was obliged to threaten them with severe penalties; one of their members, Farina, learning what was afoot, shot and slightly wounded the archbishop during Mass. Yet another source of opposition were the canons of La Scala, who claimed to possess some ancient privilege exempting them from visitation by their hierarchical superior. More secret but no less dangerous was a minor war which seems to have been waged by the Jesuits. It was not that they failed to agree upon ends and means, but they wished that the Society might benefit by their efforts and obtain for itself all the best subjects. Charles Borromeo, thinking of his own seminaries, could not allow this; while admiring the sons of St. Ignatius, and helping them to erect colleges, it was no doubt in order to resist their pious encroachment that he founded the Oblates of St. Ambrose, a kind of secular missionaries under his immediate control.

Such a man could not but make a deep impression by his wonderful determination, his sanctity and his example. The people, to whom he gave all his goods, held him in veneration. His hospitals and hospices were full. His Schools of Christian Doctrine gave religious instruction to thousands of children. He was even excused for having regulated the Carnival and forbidden masked fêtes. His influence extended far beyond his archdiocese, even to Lucerne, where his arrival seriously alarmed the Protestants of Switzerland; and to him the famous Golden League of the Catholic cantons, sometimes called the "Borromean League," owed its existence. His glory attained its zenith in 1576, when there broke out at Milan one of the most horrible plagues of the century. No one dared risk trying to relieve the sick, who were shut away in the lazar houses to die of cold and hunger as well as of the epidemic. Their archbishop, however, was not afraid to visit them, celebrate Mass for them and give them holy *viaticum*, meanwhile exhorting his clergy and people in letters of sublime charity to organize collective aid. He had sold all that belonged to him, including his furniture and bedclothes. "He has nothing left upon which to live," said a contemporary, "but it might be said that he raises the dead by his presence."

Exhausted by all this incredible effort, Charles Borromeo died in 1584, at the age of forty-eight, leaving to the Church that model of a bishop which was later reproduced in St. Francis of Sales, Cardinal Bérulle and many others. Three churches at Rome were dedicated to him, whereas St. Francis of Assisi and St. Dominic have only one each. "It was a long time," writes Fléchier, "since the Church had beheld anything so great as a cardinal, an archbishop, a nephew of the Pope, descend from riches to become poorest of the poor in his diocese."

What St. Charles Borromeo did with such brilliance at Milan was accomplished on a more modest scale, but often with striking courage and enthusiasm, by many other bishops in all the four corners of Christendom. Certain of them were remembered with such affection by their people that in several dioceses these bishops of the Catholic Reformation are

146 venerated somewhat after the manner of those who, amid the chaos of the "Dark Ages," were the self-appointed guardians of the city and defenders of the faith. Here we may recall the picturesque Archbishop of Braga, Bartholomew of the Martyrs, who had taken a notable part in the deliberations of Trent and who founded the first Portuguese seminary; Alessandro Sauli, apostle of Corsica, the heroic reformer of a people in sore need of reformation, and who even tried to abolish the "vendetta"; Cardinal Hosius, Bishop of Chlom in Poland and of Ermeland, one of the presidents of the Council, who did much to bring his country back to Catholicism by means of his personal endeavour as well as by the catechism which he edited; and also Cardinal Lorraine, who, though his life had not always been exemplary before the Council, thereafter chose the road of reform and in 1567 founded at Rheims the first French seminary.[42] There were indeed many more: Paleotti at Bologna, Burali at Piacenza, Guerrero at Granada, Ribera at Valencia, Ludovico de Torres at Monreale and so on. Twenty years after the closing of the Council the Church possessed a body of first-rate bishops, prepared to hold the course set for her by the Fathers of Trent.

11. REFORM OF THE OLD ORDERS: ST. TERESA AND ST. JOHN OF THE CROSS

THE same spirit of revival which had found its way into the religious congregations and institutes during the last half-century was henceforth greatly strengthened and increased under the official auspices and guidance of the Church. The old Orders, in competition with the more recent formations of clerks regular, perceived that nothing less than a determined effort of reform would enable them to survive. And so, while other foundations (e.g., the Oratory) continued to appear, the better elements of the older institutions pulled themselves together and gradually returned to their ancient discipline. This movement lasted far into the seventeenth century.

42. He afterwards degenerated, so that his work must be considered rather as a false start.

Among the Benedictines reform, as we have seen, had already made considerable headway at Bursfeld, Montserrat, Padua and Monte Cassino. It now won Germany under the leadership of Fulda, and Austria, where Abbot Gaspar Hoffman of Melte provided the necessary inspiration. In Lorraine, Didier de la Tour, a young monk of Saint-Vannes near Verdun, started a movement which was joined by forty abbeys. Many of these were in France, including Saint-Pierre at Jumièges; and in 1621 there sprang from this reformed branch the famous Congregation of Saint-Maur. Among the sons of St. Bernard, the white-cowled Cistercians, the most important reform was that brought about in 1573 by Jean de la Barrière, commendatory abbot of Feuillant near Toulouse, who had been converted to the strict observance and imposed it on his monks. The "Feuillants" became very numerous in France and Italy; their monastery at Paris, which became celebrated during the Revolution (for reasons far from religious), was founded in 1588. Reform of the Premonstratensians was accomplished almost simultaneously in Spain by Abbot Didace de Mendieta of Trevino, and in Lorraine first by Daniel Picard, abbot of Sainte-Marie au Bois, then by his successor Gervais de Laruelle. The congregation of Lorraine favoured "the ancient rigour" and lasted until the Revolution. Meanwhile, among other canons regular, those of the Augustinian tradition, there began a notable movement led by St. Peter Fourier (1565–1640), which was to go far beyond the limits of a monastic reform.[43] The Mendicants, who had for long, if somewhat sporadically, set an example of return to good traditions, were everywhere in the grip of reforming zeal. In Spain and Portugal the influence of St. Peter of Alcantara (1499–1562)—an ascetic who practised the most terrible austerities, who was among the first to recognize the vocation of St. Teresa, and who died just as the Council drew to its close—exercised a deep posthumous influence on the whole Franciscan Order. At about the same time the Capuchins, now separated from the Observants and formally recognized as "true sons of St. Francis," underwent enormous expansion, reaching a total of eighteen thousand members. One of the most active and

43. Volume 2, Chapter VI, p. 475.

 most efficient Orders of the time, they were joined by some remarkable men with various titles to fame: St. Felix of Cantalice, St. Laurence of Brindisi, St. Felix of Sigmaringen, who was martyred by the Calvinists, and Joseph Le Clerc du Tremblay, afterwards celebrated as Richelieu's "Grey Eminence." Nor did the reforming spirit fail to penetrate even the Augustinians, who had been so severely tried by the apostasy of Luther and many of his brethren. They made considerable advances in Spain through the influence of St. Thomas of Villanova, in Lorraine through that of François Hamel, while in France, where they were known as "Little Fathers," they were extremely popular. Thus a gigantic movement towards better things stirred the old Orders during the half-century following the Council of Trent, a movement in which the female branches also shared, and one of such complexity that no adequate account of it can be given in two short pages. Nowhere does it assume more impressive and more sublime characteristics than in the ancient Order of Carmel, where there appeared at this time two of the richest personalities that the Church has ever produced: St. Teresa of Avila and St. John of the Cross.[44]

In the last days of August 1562, while the Fathers of Trent in their twenty-second session were preparing to discuss the "decree on the life befitting clerics," there took place in a little city of far-away Old Castile an event of apparent insignificance, but one which was to become an example and a symbol in the great work of Catholic reform. Huddled inside her rust-red walls, swept in winter by the cold north winds of the high plateaus, with her network of narrow streets and irregular squares, Avila already contained so many convents, chapels and churches that the foundation of one more hardly called for comment. At angelus time it was by hundreds, and even thousands, that the celestial voice of bells bore over the sierra the multitudinous prayer of a people for whom their faith had ever been the most important business of life. Avila of the loyal, Avila of saints and knights, was one huge monastery. What difference could it make that the tolling of one more little

44. They will be studied here only as reformers; for their mysticism see Volume 2, Chapter VI, pp. 458–62.

bell would rise to the dark blue sky of Spain from the new convent of St. Joseph situated in the northern and most populous quarter of the city?

In actual fact, however, this tiny convent[45] was intended by its foundress to be very different from the rest, especially from the great convent of the Incarnation with which everyone was familiar as a daily resort for gossip with the religious. In this new convent the walls were unplastered; a double grille of closely intersecting rods stretched right across the choir and completely hid the nuns. It was said that those who joined the community would never again emerge; that they would devote the whole of their days to prayer, fasting and the discipline; that they would wear habits of material so rough as to recall the camel-hair of the ancient hermits, and that they would go barefoot. "Mitigation" of the primitive rule[46] had been accepted and confirmed by Pope Eugenius IV in 1482. Since then, the Carmelites thanked heaven, wiser practices had prevailed. Abstinence from meat had been reduced to three days a week; the uncouth habit had given place to broadcloth, which was better suited to the distinguished members of the Order; and as for solitude and silence, they had found a substitute in a pleasant régime of visits to the parlour, where the conversation of such godly persons could not but exert the best of influences upon their guests. The convents of women were specially devoted to this form of apostolate, and it sometimes happened that a pretty young Carmelite would carry her zeal so far as to prolong such a conversation far into the night, outside the enclosure. It was precisely against these usages and customs, to which no sensible person objected, that La Madre took her stand, and in leaving the Incarnation to found her shabby little monastery she was considered to be out of her wits. Her name was Teresa de Cepeda, she was of "pure blood," belonged to the ancient nobility and was at this time aged forty-seven.[47]

45. The nuns' choir was only about ten yards long.
46. It had been given about 1220 by the patriarch Albert of Jerusalem to the rugged solitaries who claimed to be heirs of the prophet Elijah.
47. One of twelve children, she was born in 1515, a few months before the accession of Charles V, on the threshold of that golden age of Spain to which she herself would contribute so much brilliance.

150 Seeing her twenty-five years earlier walking in the street, slender and gracious, her figure neatly arrayed in velvet petticoat, swinging at every step an enormous skirt of orange taffeta striped with black, who could have foretold that the daughter of Don Alonso and Doña Beatrix de Ahumada would one day become the "austere, fanatical reformer," as she was later called by her erstwhile companions? Fanatical she most certainly was not, nor yet austere in the sense used by malicious tongues. This middle-aged spinster, a little stout, but with rosy cheeks, still youthful looks and plump red mouth, loved to sing and dance and laugh, and would often tell sanctimonious hypocrites that she "disliked gloomy saints." In her rather prominent dark eyes there shone by turns rapture and tenderness, a touch of merriment and high intelligence. Her father was a man of stern piety, and she had been inured from early youth to long periods of prayer, daily rosary, silence and compunction; but despite this harsh upbringing she had never lost her faith, her virtue or her happy disposition. In that strong soul of manly intellect and courage, but of feminine tact and intuition, grace had found a soil marvelously prepared for the accomplishment of God's work.

On August 24, 1562, when she founded her quaint little convent of St. Joseph, Madre Teresa was obeying an order from on high. It would not be untrue to say that she had long lent a somewhat inattentive ear to the summons of her Lord; but we shall perhaps better represent the development in her of that sublime love which she would one day prefer before all else if we speak of the "intermittent reactions of her heart." An initial impulse had driven her to the cloister at the age of twenty; but the impulse had derived additional strength from the bitter ponderings of adolescence, which, having left the enchanted gardens of childhood, discovers life with its tares, suffering and misery, and asks whether all is not vanity of vanities. She had become a Carmelite as others contract a marriage of convenience, from disgust and uneasiness. All the same she was a faithful and even fervent Carmelite, as far as it was possible to be so in the company of one hundred eighty more or less worldly religious. Her youthful decision, however, her "determination" as she liked to call it, had linked her more closely than she suspected with her true destiny. Because she had "great firmness and constancy in the pursuit," even while continuing to live as a Carmelite of the "mitigated" observance, with one foot in the convent and the other in the city, she had advanced along her road, nursing the most repugnant cases in the infirmary and spending long hours in prayer. She never allowed "Christ with His Cross" to fall.

Then the great crisis had come upon her, a twin crisis of body and soul. During the years 1537 and 1538 she had been the victim of nervous disorders, fainting, vomiting and partial paralysis, symptoms in which the irreverence of modern psychiatry claims to recognize religious hysteria. Her condition was so grave that on one occasion she was thought to be dead, and came near to being laid in her coffin. These terrible sufferings passed away for the time being, only to be succeeded by another crisis which Teresa herself afterwards considered to have been even more serious. This was "the period of infidelity." For a long time she wearied of the choral office, prayed only with her lips, discussed embroidery with her sisters, and romances of chivalry with kindly folk who visited the parlour. Yet even while she did so she rebuked herself for her infidelity to what a silent voice in the depths of her heart repeatedly assured her to be the true Carmelite rule. In her wonderful autobiography she speaks of "that soul which so often destroyed itself." No, that soul was never destroyed, but it was gravely imperilled. In 1543 the cruel shock of her father's death had momentarily torn her from herself—"God's first knock upon the door." The advice of a strict Dominican confessor had helped her to recover her balance, though not for long and quite inadequately. She was able once again to pray, but did not yet completely renounce the world: for ten more years she attempted to reconcile the irreconcilable and continued uncertain of herself.

God, however, lay in wait for her. One day in the year 1553 He struck and spoke. We must leave Teresa herself to describe the scene. As she was passing through the chapel she came face to face with a bust of the *Ecce Homo* which had recently been placed there. "It was so striking a representation of Christ covered with wounds that at first glance I was overwhelmed with feeling for His sufferings on our behalf. My heart was shattered as I thought of my ingratitude for His wounds. I threw myself on my knees before Him, and begged Him to give me strength once and for all, that I might never again offend Him." This was the decisive shock, the ray of light similar to that which long ago had stricken Saul on the road to Damascus. Having recovered possession of herself, clear-eyed now and resolute, Teresa the worldly Carmelite understood that she was henceforth "Teresa of Jesus." While her Jesuit confessors gave her firm guidance and restored her to full strength through the discipline of fervent communion, Christ Himself came upon the scene with slow mysterious tread. Strange phenomena occurred in her, around her and by her agency. A mystical link was forged between her and the God of ineffable espousals. She experienced such feverish ecstasies that she emerged from them haggard and speechless, but her countenance shone with unearthly radiance. Sometimes the nuns and other worshippers in the chapel of the Incarnation saw her raised several feet above the ground, although she clung with all her strength to the grille. Certain people were deeply troubled by these fantastic happenings, wondering whether they might not proceed from Hell. No, replied the visionary with her charming laugh, she "cocked a snook at the demons." That was also the opinion of two of the greatest saints then living, Peter of Alcantara and Francis Borgia, to whom the matter had been referred. Filled with such mystical graces as few in this world have known, walking firmly in the unitive way, Teresa of Jesus might have penetrated the realm of inconceivable happiness and forgotten the world. But no; the great ecstatic was a woman of flesh and blood, a true daughter of the Spanish highlands, filled with the sense of reality and well aware that she was called to something other than escape into the empyrean. Was it her astonishing combination of solid realism and spiritual energy that had caused the Sovereign Master to choose her from among all others? A day came when the Presence, who was her almost constant companion, showed her that she had been sent as a witness and a guide. In order to "compensate" Our Lord for the sufferings which Luther and other heretics were causing Him, and for all wicked religious, she would found a convent of perpetual prayer and unrelenting penance, in accordance with those principles whose requirements had been stated in the *Book of the Institution of the First Monks* (1507). The example of the sublime Franciscan, Peter of

Alcantara, had proved that such a life was by no means impossible. Thus was born Teresa's decision to found the convent of St. Joseph of Avila, the first house of the Carmelite reform.

St. Joseph's, a mustard grain, was the tiny seed of what was to become a mighty tree. In that small community,[48] robed with the white mantle of Our Lady, there was set on foot a spiritual venture whose riches would be discovered in the results that flowed from it. Teresa herself had already taken wings and learnt the royal flight of infinite space. What of the others? Must she "drag these souls with a tow-rope" or handle them "with great gentleness for their greater good"? This first convent at Avila, for which she felt a peculiar tenderness throughout the remainder of her life, was a testing ground where she learnt how to lead souls to a higher life by the right admixture of sweetness and compulsion. With what loving cogency she would address the sisters, begging them to "yield entirely to the dramatic truth of the Incarnation, Passion and Redemption." With what terror in her voice she would paint for them "the world on fire," Catholicism threatened both from within and from without. Teresa would have her daughters "solitary, silent, disdainful of the body and its demands, but gay as children; humble, but never forgetting the dignity of their souls; submissive, but to the Holy Spirit; in love, but in love with Christ; stripped of everything, but queens of the world."[49] This little convent was "a heaven on earth if ever there was one"; it became the model for sixteen other houses of women founded by the indefatigable Teresa in a space of twenty years, not to mention those friaries which would follow her example.

Five years passed, five years of ripening in seclusion. Then Teresa, led through prayer into the region of activity, and free in the freedom of the Spirit, set out upon the appalling roads of Castile, which were quagmires in winter and carpets of dust in summer. For fifteen years she was continually on the move, herald of God's commandments, revolutionary of Christ, opposed to all the easy-going morality of her age, a permanent invalid who

48. At the beginning it consisted of no more than five or six nuns.

49. Marcelle Auclair, *Sainte Thérèse* (Paris, 1950).

seemed to be made of iron, at once the victim of love and the shrewdest of organizers. The same soul whence sprang, with cries of exaltation and anguish, the burning pages of the *Interior Castle* and *Thoughts on the Canticle*, gave birth also to three concise codes: the *Constitutions*, the *Book of Foundations* and the *Visitation of Monasteries.* Both groups of works were written in the same cramped script, without punctuation and obviously thrown off in feverish haste. They form a singular blend of reason and passion, of austerity and childlike gaiety, of the most impetuous spiritual elation and the most down-to-earth realism, which is so characteristic of this extraordinary saint and which Bergson rightly advances as proof of those solid mundane qualities which are usually found in the great mystics.

The first man to understand Teresa, and to see at a glance what she could do for the Order, was Fr. Rubeo, Prior-General of the Carmelites and a native of Ravenna, who happened to be making a visitation at Avila. Reform was already in progress elsewhere, notably at Brussels, where the example of St. John Soreth survived, and at Venice, where the austere Audet had done good work. The measures proposed by this holy nun were therefore of sound lineage, and he gave her every encouragement. Duly authorized to found convents according to the strict rule (the original rule of Carmel) which she applied at St. Joseph's, and even to establish monasteries of men if she was able to do so, Teresa set to work without delay. Her first campaign lasted from 1567 to 1571, during which period she made seven foundations, at Medina del Campo, Malagona, Valladolid, Toledo, Pastrana, Salamanca and Alba de Tormes. The heavenly Spouse gave visible aid to His beloved on earth, and her steps must have been guided by the angel who had long ago transfixed her heart with a fiery javelin. The proof is in her meeting at Medina with a man who was indeed sent by God and of whom she had need if her work for the male element of the Order was to be accomplished. This man is known to history as St. John of the Cross.

A little slip of a fellow, agile, furtive and emaciated, he was not quite five feet tall; but you scarcely noticed the fact when you met the penetrating and almost unendurable gaze of those dark feverish eyes. Born in 1542, he was not yet twenty-five, and could have been Teresa's son; but young as he was, he had already led a hard life. His father was dead, "abhorred" by his relations for having married a very poor girl, whom he had left with three infant boys. The widow Catalina worked at a hand-loom in order to support herself and her sons. Little Juan had had to make trial of various trades on the noisy fairground at Medina; but the pure race of the Spanish hidalgos was visible in his features and his conduct. His intelligence was as a flame of fire. At the time of his meeting with Teresa he had managed to study at the Jesuit college, earning his daily bread meanwhile as a hospital attendant. Then, at the age of twenty, he had joined the Carmelites and had been sent to do his theology at Salamanca. Turning his back, however, upon worldly ambition, despising the doctoral cap and ring, he had returned to his monastery with the intention of living that life of renunciation, the life of Carmel in days gone by, which was the centre of his dreams. If his superiors would not let him do so, he would join the Carthusians. Teresa and John were well suited to understand one another. The reformer, who possessed a marvelous gift of insight, and the enthusiastic little friar "were in perfect accord from the very first words they exchanged." Teresa invited the young man to put away all ideas of the Charterhouse and to collaborate in her great work. He was thrilled, but added with all the impetuosity of youth: "On one condition—that I won't have to wait too long."

There would be no waiting. John of St. Mathias, as he was then called, donned the new habit of the Discalced Carmelites which Teresa herself had tailored: the tunic of rough serge, the scapular, the leather girdle three fingers wide and the white mantle of Our Lady. And now straightway to work! After the foundation of the first male Carmelite house, at Duruelo in 1568, monasteries of the reform quickly multiplied. The authority and fervour of the Discalced attracted many first-rate subjects, for the austere grandeur of the new Observance made a deep impression. Fray Juan himself, preaching by example and practising the most terrible asceticism, went so far beyond the requirements of the primitive Rule that on one occasion he scourged himself to blood for having taken a morsel of food before the community's dinner time, because he felt faint. The custom of Perpetual Adoration, introduced by him, spread throughout Spain. Thanks to the simultaneous and combined activity of these two fiery souls the reforming movement made triumphant progress. The convent of the Incarnation at Avila, which Teresa had left, witnessed her return as prioress by order of the Apostolic Visitor, together with her spiritual companion John, whom she brought as confessor. She was determined to reform the Incarnation, and by dint of patience, tact, charity and love she won admission for the new ideas. Having fulfilled that task, she embarked on her second campaign, in course of which she founded convents at Segovia, Beas, Seville and Caravanca, and once again drew to herself innumerable souls. It seemed that her efforts were irresistible.

Teresa had yet to discover one of the secret laws of Providence, that nothing durable is achieved in this world except through resistance and combat. She met this inevitable opposition for the first time at Seville, in the person of a shabby little nun who was green with envy and accused her of the most shameful conduct. The famous Jesuit Rodrigo Alvarez came down on Teresa's side; but the gale had been let loose, the decisive storm from which few can escape who are called to a great destiny. The ensuing struggle is known as the "War of the Mitigated." One can indeed understand those feeble religious, those pampered nuns, who thought they were doing no great wrong in offering a few sops to the world and yet were so fiercely castigated by the example (and sometimes by the speeches) of Teresa and her daughters, and even more fiercely by the voice of public opinion. It was all too easy to compare the heroic efforts of the Discalced with the easy-going routine of the Mitigated. Again, here were the apostolic visitors sent by Pius V to make known the decrees and wishes of Trent, overriding the General's instructions and lending full support to the reform. There were angry murmurings. A general chapter at Piacenza took steps to counter the "excessives," which shows how difficult it was for the Church, even under the ablest of popes, to give effect to the new spirit everywhere. When the nuns of the Incarnation assembled to elect a prioress, the voting was rigged and Teresa ousted in favour of a *mitigata.*[50] But her very fame protected her from serious hurt: King Philip II himself

50. The fifty-five religious who had voted for Teresa were declared "excommunicated and accursed." The rest, by choice or compulsion, rallied to the cause of the "Mitigated."

had made her acquaintance, while no less a person than the Grand Inquisitor, who had carefully examined her autobiography, professed to hold her in the greatest esteem. The enemy therefore rounded upon John, her friend and collaborator. He was seized by night, chained like a criminal and carried off to the house of the *mitigati* at Toledo, where he was doomed to long months of suffering. Every day, in the refectory, he was subjected to the discipline, each friar administering a stroke; and what strokes those were, accompanied with insult and mockery. Next they tried to seduce him: let him only renounce his follies, and he would be appointed prior somewhere. He refused, and more ill treatment followed. Was he not an *alumbrado*, one of those detestable Illuminati whom the Inquisition was hunting down? Calm, supernaturally calm in his dungeon, John employed his pen; and from that darkness leaped the flame of his *Spiritual Canticle.*[51] At length, after seven months of captivity, he managed to escape; and at the same time Teresa won a glorious victory. She had moved heaven and earth, petitioned the king, used every measure of diplomacy and caused Rome to intervene. The Pope upheld the Discalced: his Brief of 1580 erected them into an autonomous province subject to the wide direction of the General of the Order.

It remained to be seen whether this victory was decisive. John, who since his imprisonment had adopted the name John of the Cross, might at one time have thought it was. He had been made prior of the beautiful Carmel at Granada; and there in his cell, from which he had a magnificent view of the Alhambra, the Generalife and the plain of the Genil, he wrote the *Ascent of Mount Carmel*, the *Dark Night* and the *Living Flame of Love.* The same might have been thought by Teresa, the last act of whose astonishing career closed with a scene of triumph. "Old and weary, but always young in her desires," she took the road more than ever "God's wandering lady." In spite of sickness, which was undermining her strength, and the exhaustion caused by her austerities; despite the hazards and perils of the way, she set out for a third time, travelling from city to city and founding convents at

51. By a curious coincidence El Greco was then at Toledo painting his famous picture, *The Division of the Seamless Robe.*

 Villanova de la Xara, Palancia, Seria, Granada, Burgos. Seventeen houses of women and fifteen of men: what a noble harvest! The final picture of herself bequeathed to posterity is that of an aged nun, crouched beneath the awning of an uncomfortable wagon, wrapped in her great white mantle and with lowered veil, moving along the roads of Castile to the merry music of jangling mule-bells. One can name few examples of such sublime power used with such simplicity.

On October 4, 1582, her forces were spent, and she was obliged to halt at Alba de Tormes. It was the feaṣt of St. Francis, and Teresa had always loved the Poverello. Was he coming to gather her to heaven? She believed her work to be finished: the chapter at Alcala had approved the Constitutions of the reform, and everything seemed in good order. She herself could do no more. "I have not a good bone left in me," she would murmur; and then, carried along by that mysterious strength derived from the mystical marriage, she would add with a radiant smile: "Now it is time to see one another, my love, my Lord." She remained in full possession of her faculties to the very end, continuing to advise on the government of the house in which she lay and guiding its young steps. Her final moments were wonderfully peaceful; the old lady's wrinkles seemed to have disappeared, her countenance was pale, "the colour of full moon," but gave forth a certain luminosity. With her last breath she recited the psalm: "Reject not, O Lord, a penitent heart...." Of what need she repent after all her heroism and mortification? But in the eyes of the saints there is no limit to humility.

Left alone on earth, deprived of her support, Teresa's spiritual son John continued the task she had begun. So many and such terrible difficulties, however, beset his path that it seemed Providence intended to lead him to the pinnacle of sanctity by way of suffering. At that time the reformed Carmelites experienced a crisis similar to that through which the Franciscan Order passed on the morrow of the Poverello's death. Fr. Nicholas Doria was a man of "angular features, commanding look, devoid of feeling and possessed of iron determination."[52] He belonged to the proud Genoese

52. Fr. Bruno, *St. John of the Cross* (1929).

family which had produced the famous admiral Andrea Doria, and in temperament was utterly different from St. John of the Cross. The age of the mystics was succeeded by that of the organizers. These were years of confused antagonism and of episodes that were often painful to a degree. The factions clashed at various points, both of course appealing to the lessons of "good Mother Teresa." She had always said that the mystical experience should find its fulfilment in apostolic endeavour, that the contemplative must not pray and practise mortification for himself alone. This, however, was not exactly Doria's view; he improved upon the asceticism of the primitive Rule and objected to the Carmelites taking up missionary work. Those who attempted to oppose this formidable man—he was known as the "Lion of Carmel"—met with pitiless retribution, and hundreds of regulations were added to the articles of the Rule.

St. John of the Cross obeyed in silence for some years. Then he expressed his disapproval, and the new heads of the Order directed their fury against him. Deprived of his dignities and offices, he was forced to retire to the desert of Penuela, where he continued peacefully to lead that life in God which had always enabled him to endure earthly trials with equanimity. His mystical experience became still more exalted, still more intense, a continuous dialogue of his soul with Christ Himself. When it became clear that he was a very sick man at the end of his strength, with his feet and then a large part of his body covered with ulcers, he was carried to the convent of San Salvador at Ubeda, a bleak Moorish fortress scourged by the high winds of the plateaus. There he died in 1591, having passed so far beyond the regions of the world that he suffered neither in his poor body, which was devoured by ulcers, nor mentally at the sight of his work and that of Teresa thus undone.[53]

In fact, however, the crisis did not end, as it had done with the Franciscans, in permanent division among the Discalced Carmelites. In 1587

53. He was beatified in 1675, canonized in 1726, and in 1926 proclaimed a Doctor of the Universal Church. The canonization of St. Teresa is described in the closing pages of Volume 2 of this work.

Sixtus V authorized them to have their Vicar General. In 1593 Clement VIII made them totally independent of the "great Carmelites," that is, of the Mitigated, and formed them into an autonomous congregation with its own General. In 1611 the Constitutions received their definitive form. This was a triumph for the spirit of St. Teresa and St. John of the Cross, its lofty mystical demands and its apostolic realism. With Thomas of Jesus the Carmelites, who were primarily contemplatives, formally linked themselves to the ancient eremitical tradition, to the "Holy Desert," where it would be lawful for those who felt themselves called to the mixed life to work for the glory of God by preaching, works of charity and public worship, more or less as did the sons of St. Francis.

The reform of Carmel quickly spread to large parts of the Christian world. It subsequently proved to have been one of the most important events in the history of the Church, and countless souls would drink at the well-springs reopened by the two great mystics. Today the Carmelites in their silent cloisters bear witness that the spirit of St. Teresa and St. John of the Cross is not dead, that God promised the two heroic founders a teeming progeny. It was their spirit which in recent times became incarnate among us in the sublime figure of St. Thérèse of Lisieux.

12. ST. PHILIP NERI AND THE FOUNDATION OF THE ORATORY

THE riches of the Catholic Reformation become evident when we consider that the Church produced in that single period saints so different as Pius V and Ignatius of Loyola, Francis Borgia and Cajetan of Tiene, Charles Borromeo and Teresa of Avila, not to mention Francis Xavier and Peter Canisius. We must emphasize and be grateful for these very differences, which appear in both character and conduct. It might seem at first glance that to reform the Church by recalling the Curia, the religious Orders, the secular clergy and the laity to the better observance of Gospel principles would be a humdrum business, carried out according to a given set of rules and with unvarying success. This idea is very far from the truth; all those leaders of the Catholic Reformation, in their united effort to advance God's cause, show differences amounting sometimes almost to contraries. No two of them, whether popes, bishops, abbots or religious founders, were hewn to the same pattern.

Such is the liberty of God's children, and of that liberty no saint in all the history of the Church has given more striking testimony than St. Philip Neri (1515–1595), founder of the Oratory. About 1590 you might have seen in the streets of Rome an odd-looking fellow with bald head, bushy beard and tall ungainly body. Gesticulating wildly, he would talk and laugh with anyone he happened to meet. The least one can say is that he showed no trace of affectation. He enjoyed nothing so much as dropping a witty remark, a popular joke and even raising a laugh against himself. You might have said he was determined you should not take him seriously; but it is just this kind of humility, this mingling of ease and playfulness, which appeals to men. If rebuked for his shabby clothes, he would appear next day clad in the richest furs, and walk more solemnly than a cardinal in procession. If applauded at the end of a spiritual discourse, he would act the clown, tottering down the altar steps like a drunkard, and then break into a fantastic dance. His disciples were vastly entertained. They seemed to delight in his broad humour, and scarcely a day passed without their beloved Pepo doing one of these turns of which he alone knew the secret; but a close look made it clear that each conveyed a lesson. Here are two overdressed young dandies following in the train of his companions: as they pass the gallows on the Ponte Sant' Angelo the saint grasps them by the shoulders and invites them to step up amid loud jeers from the crowd. Here is a solemn citizen who has never learnt that heavenly joy is also human simplicity: the saint hands him a little dog and orders him to carry it for several hours. One day a pretty girl joined his circle out of mere curiosity. Philip clapped his spectacles on her nose and burst into peals of laughter. "Come, you dunce, you great fathead, you brute beast!" he would roar at someone whom he had caught in the act of sinning, at the same time pulling the man's ear, his beard or his jacket. But all was done with such simplicity that no one except a fool would dream of showing resentment. His "continual hilarity of mind" was infectious, and his humour, which he scarcely ever put aside, lay on the borderline of tenderness and irony, of moral counsel and facetiousness, just at that point where Christian liberty finds vent in joy.

At the same time, however, this curious and in many ways alarming individual possessed a soul of spotless purity. He was also a very great mystic and Heaven loaded him with visible graces and charismata. It was said that Christ Our Lord had hallowed him in a mysterious encounter, of which Philip never spoke but which was unquestionably a determining influence in his life. The story goes that at that moment his fleshly heart became too small to contain the ocean of his supernatural love, that it swelled and swelled until the curvature of his ribs increased to make room for the dilated organ.[54] We are told also that when he prayed he belonged no more to this earth, that he escaped into heaven whither he stretched his thin and almost transparent hands. In the sick-room, one of his most favoured spots, it was plain that God used him to effect miraculous cures. In the chapel where he said Mass, what were those cries, those songs and mysterious dialogues, which lasted for hours at a time? Scarcely a marvel has been left unrelated of him. He had only to look at a cardinal to know whether his purple would one day turn white, his red hat become a triple crown. His penitents had no need to recite their sins, for the saint, like the Curé d'Ars nearly three hundred years later, could read their hearts better than could they themselves. If anyone ventured to ask him "How do you know, Father, that I have committed this fault?" he would burst out laughing and reply: "By the colour of your skin."

Such was Philip, a saint far removed from the new model created by St. Ignatius. He was born into a family of poor shopkeepers at Florence in 1515, the fateful year in which St. Teresa first saw the light of day, and his sweet ways won for him in early childhood the nickname *Pepo buono*, "good little Philip." Towards the end of his sixteenth year he was sent to learn the secrets of business with one of his uncles, but suddenly enlisted in the service

54. An autopsy performed after his death showed that his heart was in fact abnormally large, and ribs raised. Aneurism, anatomists will say.

of Christ. For years he lived in wretched conditions, sleeping in churches or their porches, carrying his food in the hood of his cloak. At the same time he took a share in the lay apostolate, a rather hirsute messenger of the Word, member of a class inconceivable today, but common enough at that time. He preached in the open air to eager groups in all parts of Rome, even in the most disreputable quarters, and effected some astonishing conversions. He was often seen in the catacombs praying before the tomb of some martyr, and regularly made the pilgrimage to the "seven churches," the most famous and most venerable basilicas in the Eternal City. The Brotherhood of Charity, whose members were drawn from all classes of society, had no more devoted servant than this odd layman whose lips were filled with God.

A small nucleus of the faithful gathered gradually around him as if by chance. They were recruited among those whom he had challenged in the streets with his famous cry: "Ah, brother, is it today that we're going to do good?" For reasons which are not very clear, and under influences no less obscure, he agreed to become a priest, although he seems never to have taken a regular theological course. Theologians and theology, however, are not indispensable to the working of God's Spirit, and it was most certainly that Spirit which spoke through Philip's mouth.

In the little church of S. Girolamo della Carità, or rather in the crypt of that church, he used to receive his friends, who met together as fervent souls in quest of truth and virtue. This little group was known as the Oratory,[55] one of the most singular institutions (at least in its beginnings) ever recognized by the Catholic Church. With characteristic spontaneity Philip gave rise to a new method of spiritual exercises entirely different from that of St. Ignatius. A free verbal commentary, it was called *Oratorio*, and gave its name to one of the most beautiful forms of religious music. One of the brethren began by reading a passage from some edifying book. Another explained and commented upon this text. A third asked questions, put forward objections and elucidated such points as were still obscure. But one must never

55. The name had been applied somewhat earlier to other small bodies of a like sort, from which it must be carefully distinguished. (See above, Chapter I, p. 7.)

remain too long upon the dizzy heights of speculation; so another member would narrate an episode of ecclesiastical history, while another recalled day by day the events of Our Lord's life. Philip presided; at every stage he would interject some remark or observation; and it was always he who rounded off the discussion. After this the meeting broke up, hurried down the steps of the church and started in procession through the streets. Then they all went to pray in the catacombs, or perhaps from St. Peter's to St. John Lateran, from San Lorenzo to the basilica of Santa Croce, which preserves the memory of the crusaders. As they walked they sang with alternate voice those splendid antiphons which had lately been set to glorious music by a brilliant composer named Palestrina.

It is quite certain that Philip had at this time no idea whatever of founding an Order. He would have been astonished to learn that he was in fact doing so; he would doubtless have answered with a smile that there were quite enough Orders as it was: all those ancient bodies which were in process of reform and all those which had been established during the past thirty years—Theatines, Barnabites, Somaschi and the Oblates of St. Charles Borromeo, not to mention the most active of all, the Jesuits, whose new General, Francis Borgia, was leading them to glory. There were also numerous Orders of women. What need then of yet another congregation? This, however, is exactly what resulted from his anarchical exertions. A brotherhood was created from the many princes and religious, artisans and aristocrats, who took part in the daily *Oratorio.* Some of them, in their various ways, contributed work of prime importance to its foundation. Among these were the little Florentine tailor Parigi, who served Philip for thirty years at San Girolamo; Cacciaguerra, an ex-merchant, who became a lofty mystic; the elegant Tarugi, a papal chamberlain, whose grand velvet suits rubbed shoulders quite happily with the fustian of his brethren; and Baronio, a homely student from the Abruzzi, who was afterwards celebrated as the great historian Cardinal Baronius. The Oratory now began to hold its meetings in the larger church of Santa Maria in Valicella. Crowds were attending the exercises, and the Florentines invited their fellow countryman to take charge of the church and parish of St. John which they maintained at Rome. But the nucleus from which all this proceeded was very small, perhaps no more than fifteen members. Later they were obliged to dissolve and give more regular shape to the movement, which would otherwise have run into trouble. During the last years of his pontificate, indeed, Paul IV expressed his disapproval, and even Pius V let it be seen that he did not altogether trust them.

Thus, in spite of Philip's hesitation and resistance, the Oratory came into being, and groups were established at such places as Naples, Milan, Lucca, Fermo and Bologna. At Naples the institution was well organized, at Lucca and Fermo hardly at all; in no case was there more than the slenderest link with that of Rome. Nor was it until 1575, by express order of the Pope, that Philip allowed his free movement to become a congregation. The new congregation, however, was unique: clerics and pious laymen were to pray and work in common, subject to a very simple rule which imposed no external discipline or strict regulations. It was to be a republic controlled by Love, wholly different from the Society of Jesus. The one and only tie acknowledged and proclaimed was "that born of mutual affection and daily intercourse"; and when Philip was asked what was the sum total of his Rule, he answered quite simply, grave yet smiling: "Nothing but charity."

Nevertheless this first Oratory, whimsical and unorganized though it was, exerted considerable influence and produced many men who distinguished themselves in the great struggles of that age. The idea was of such spiritual strength that it became even more widespread than did the institution properly so called. In France, during the next century, Cardinal de Bérulle used it to found an Order somewhat different in appearance, though in spirit fairly close to that of the sublime vagabond of the Roman streets, whose initial impulse passed later still to the Oratory of Gratry.[56] In his own day and country Philip's example took effect among the clergy. To his "school of sanctity and Christian gaiety" the priests of Italy were to owe

56. Other congregations of clerks regular came into being at this time: the Clerks Regular of the Mother of God, founded at Lucca by St. John Leonardi for preaching and the struggle against Protestantism; the Clerks Regular of the Pious Schools, founded at Rome by the Spaniard St. Joseph Calasanctius mainly for the rescue of abandoned and delinquent children. The example of St. Philip Neri's Oratory was later imitated by St. Francis of Sales, St. Vincent de Paul and others.

 those most attractive characteristics of simplicity and graciousness which we find among them even today.

The holy founder himself, confined to his room by sickness and old age, died in a manner worthy of his life. Having obtained the privilege of saying Mass at home, even in private, he took advantage of it to spend several hours in offering the Holy Sacrifice. Feeble and emaciated, resembling a fine candle or a sheet of old parchment, he continued until the last a victim of the same joyous fever, the same supernatural flame. To everyone who came to see him he would repeat the precept he had made his own since adolescence: "Live in God and die to self." He was now an octogenarian, but the doctors solemnly assured him that he was in perfect health and would live to be ninety. Philip, however, by way of a final jest, decided to give them all the slip. Only a few beheld his passing: a pale hand was raised in blessing, a light murmur hovered on his lips and God's fool slept in Christ (1595).

13. A NEW CHURCH OR A NEW LOOK?

WHEN we consider the history of the Church at that decisive turning point in the sixteenth century, we cannot but fix an admiring gaze upon the popes who summoned the Council and gave effect to its decrees, upon the Fathers responsible for those decrees, upon the bishops who applied them throughout the Catholic world, and upon all those saints, both men and women, who expended whole treasuries of courage and faith in the reform of ecclesiastical institutions and of souls. The results of their manifold effort were immense, and we continue to profit by them. They are summarized as follows by a "neutral" historian: "The work of unification was at the same time a work of purification and rejuvenation. There was indeed, in 1563, a new Catholic Church, more sure of her dogma, more worthy to govern souls, more conscious of her function and of her duties."[57]

57. H. Hauser, *La Prépondérance espagnole*, p. 7, being volume 9 of the series *Peuples et civilisations.*

We may, however, question the accuracy of this phrase, "a new Catholic Church." It deserves careful consideration, because such expressions are common and are used even among Catholics. The question is, whether the religion of Trent is identical with that of the medieval period and with that of the early Christian ages. Here is an example of the kind of thing one meets in the writings of authoritative commentators: "Since times had changed, the popes, bishops and theologians who led the resistance to the new men and their ideas were obliged to establish a new religion in the shape of Tridentine Catholicism, which we have by no means defined until we have done something more than study its dogmas."[58] In some Protestant circles, too, it is commonly maintained that Protestantism alone brought about a return to genuine Christianity, to the pure evangelism of the primitive Church, and that Tridentine Catholicism is a fabrication, half Italian and half Spanish, far removed from the true faith.

This interpretation of events is equally untrue in respect of both Catholicism and Protestantism. The equation "Reform = Return to the primitive Church" is the expression of a myth propagated by the enemies of traditional Christianity but contradicted by historical facts. "'Reform' and 'Primitive Church' are convenient terms wherewith to hide from their own eyes the rashness of their secret desires. What they really wanted was not restoration but innovation."[59] As had already been observed,[60] the objective judgment of history considers the "Protestant Reformation" as a revolution cutting short the development of Christianity. No less objectively, the Catholic Reformation can be traced back in unbroken line to Christian origins, both as regards the manner of its operation and in respect of the principles to which it adhered. Bossuet proved as much in his penetrating reply to a letter addressed to him by Leibniz, in which that great philosopher explained the Protestant objections to the Council of Trent.[61] His arguments remain valid.

58. L. Febvre: "Une question mal posée: Les origines de la Réforme française et le problème général des causes de la Réforme," in *La Revue historique*, CLXI (1929), p. 76.

59. Ibid., p. 60.

60. See above, p. 1ff.

61. The letter and reply are in Lachat's edition of Bossuet's *Works*, vol. 18, pp. 198–210.

There is no measure adopted by the Council, or by the popes of that time, whose origin cannot be detected in the earlier principles and organization of the Church. There is no article of faith proclaimed by the Assembly which is not solidly based upon Scripture and Tradition. Nor are those articles in fact so very numerous as they may seem; they are all reducible to five or six central notions. "If the Church was obliged to multiply them," says Bossuet, "it was because those whom she condemned by their means had stirred a proportionate amount of mud." It is also true that at some points the decrees of Trent appear to go beyond what had hitherto been taught. But it has always been agreed in the Church that she has an unquestionable right and duty, as the depository of faith, to make ever more explicit what is implicit in Revelation. That has been the essential function of the Councils ever since Nicaea, which might with as much justice be accused of having "innovated" upon the letter of the Gospels. It is quite natural that a religion which is to endure and develop through the centuries should not remain imprisoned within the limited framework of its origins. "A growing tree is never the same, and yet it is always the same."[62] The changes brought about by Trent did not constitute a "new religion"; they were necessary steps taken to preserve the old. It is precisely this balance between absolute fidelity to revealed truth and the evolution of formulae and customs dictated by the passage of time that has characterized the Catholic and Roman Church throughout her history. Therein lies the full significance of what she understands by Tradition.

We are not dealing then with "a new religion." But is it possible to maintain that on the morrow of the Council of Trent the Catholic Church was exactly such as she had been in the age of the cathedrals and crusades? Certainly not. New features appeared, others became less marked, while others again completely vanished. A new spirit emerged, of which it has been rightly said that "we have by no means defined it until we have done something more than study its dogmas"; a spirit whose elements it is not

62. L. Cristiani, *L'Église à l'époque du concile de Trente* (1948), being vol. 17 of Fliche and Martin's *Histoire de l'église.*

easy to determine—inviolability of principles, increased sense of unity, strengthening of discipline—but which borrowed ideas from the circumstances attending its emergence, and which, as it penetrated human groups and their mental habits, took on a variety of colours while remaining substantially the same. The spirit of the Council of Trent is found in devotional practices as well as in architectural forms, in the liturgy as well as in music.

One more phenomenon is likewise familiar to history. The Christian religion, though permanent and faithful to itself in the unchanging certitude of Revelation, assumes manifestly different aspects as it makes its way during the course of centuries into the most varied forms of society. The Church of the "Dark Ages" is not in all respects identical with that of the Roman Empire under Constantine any more than with that of Byzantium; and the Church of St. Bernard and St. Louis appears in many ways original. Similarly today the Church in the United States, while holding the same dogmas and subject to the infallible authority of the Pope, wears a look very different from that of the Church in France, in Italy or in Spain. Because she is human as well as divine, the Church inscribes her destiny in the register of history, of geography and of sociology. Thus her one and only self reveals a variety of facets; and it was just such a new look that she presented on the morrow of Trent.

We must now review the fundamental characteristics of the Tridentine spirit, in order to obtain a proper idea of this "new look." Undoubtedly the most striking feature is that the dogmas of the Church, being now clearly defined, are found to be more solid and inviolable. The indignant Leibniz, in his letter to Bossuet, is fully aware of this fact: "Henceforward one cannot without heresy call in question the authenticity of a single book or any part of Holy Scripture; one can no longer doubt that justification is effected by an inherent quality, or that the justifying end is distinct from confidence in divine mercy; or that there are seven sacraments; or that the Body and Blood of Christ are present in the Eucharist together with His divinity; or the matter, form and minister of the sacraments, or the indissolubility of marriage." He was perfectly correct, and herein is the primary contribution of the decrees of Trent, whose effects would be transmitted to the faithful by way of the Catechism and Missal. From now onwards it would be impossible to dispute and call into doubt truths upon which the Church had pronounced judgment in the most solemn and definitive terms. Those truths had been too fiercely assailed to allow of their being left without a protective wall. The Tridentine Church is first and foremost *orthodox*, concerned above all with the security of doctrine and loyalty to dogmas; and this characteristic has remained prominent ever since.

Here is a second and no less striking feature: the Church's new look represents a religion infinitely more worthy, more grave and at the same time more mystical, seeking to satisfy the anxious pursuit of souls hungry for the Absolute. I say first more worthy; this is an aspect to which we, the heirs of Trent, are so accustomed that we find it almost impossible to imagine a Church which allowed dogs to disport themselves in buildings dedicated for public worship, and permitted gentlemen to go there "carrying their hawks, like half-witted buffoons," joking at the tops of their voices during holy Mass. It is likewise impossible for us to understand those entertainments, held even in the sacred edifice as well as in the streets, at which clerics joined the common folk in every kind of tomfoolery. The Council put an end to all this kind of behaviour, which had been common enough as late as 1540.

The very type of the Christian was henceforward changed. Reception of the sacraments and more frequent communion transformed the better sort of men. Faith at this period was perhaps no greater nor more ardent than in the Middle Ages, but it tended to give daily life a more deeply religious rhythm.[63] Morality also benefited, although its progress, particularly in the domain of sex, was rather slow. A wave of mysticism, however, caught up the loftiest and most ardent souls, whom we find in the Oratories of St. Philip Neri no less than in the austere Carmelite houses of Spain; and that

63. Certainly among the spiritual élite. As regards others, was there not a risk that this grave and solemn countenance of religion might separate religion itself from the rest of life? Was it not the origin of the modern divorce between the two halves of man's existence, between the fulfilment of his duty to God and everything else, in which God scarcely features at all?

wave continued to roll throughout the following century. A regenerate clergy also made its appearance. It was better trained, thanks to the seminaries, and the great majority was free from those shortcomings for which it had been erstwhile and justly criticized.[64] At the head of this clergy we see the gradual disappearance of pleasure-seeking, political or warlike popes, giving place to wise and respectable pontiffs, many of whom were prudent administrators or fervent mystics.

We come lastly to the third feature of the "new look." It was around a regenerate Papacy that the Catholic world became more strongly unified. The Church of the Council of Trent is a more centralized Church, more highly organized than in the Middle Ages. The prestige of the "Bishop of the Universal Church," having grown considerably since the happy ending of the Schism and the conciliar crisis, emerged still greater from this half-century during which the Papacy had both directed and approved the Council's work. To the democratic and anarchical tendencies of Protestantism there was opposed a monarchical system, which continued to increase until its coronation three hundred years later with the dogma of Papal Infallibility. Ever more widely recognized as supreme head of the hierarchy, the Pope came also to be looked upon as competent to exercise control over all that the Church thinks, believes, wills and does. Moreover he now had at his free disposal the Society of Jesus, a body comparable to a regiment of picked troops. Discussion as to the principle of authority became steadily less frequent. The principle of unity was still a matter of doubt; but while some Catholics long continued to protest against "ultramontanism," the ultimate acceptance (explicit or tacit) by all States of the Tridentine decrees and papal decisions proved that the authority of the Holy See was no longer in question. The Council of Trent abruptly halted an evident inclination on the part of monarchs to establish national Churches; and although this tendency might still give rise to such crises as that of Gallicanism in the seventeenth century, those responsible never had the least intention of destroying Christian unity.

64. Ecclesiastical dress underwent a change. It differed increasingly from secular costume and black, which had been approved by St. Charles Borromeo, became the fashion.

But admiration for the results obtained in the Tridentine period must not blind us to certain shadows in the portrait as a whole. The Church's new look included some less attractive features to which attention has been rightly drawn by adversaries of the Council and its work; these, however, have not escaped the notice of sound historians on the Catholic side.[65] In so far as it was a genuine return to life-giving sources, an act of heroic obedience to the demands of faith, the Catholic Reformation is beyond disparagement. But it was accomplished in an atmosphere of often tragic strife, for the Church had forcibly to defend herself against the theories and encroachments of heretics. The result was a certain hardening, an inevitable rigidity, even a certain narrowness; and in so far as the Tridentine reform was obliged to become a "counter-reformation" it developed characteristics which we cannot overlook if the truth is to be told.

The Church of the "new look" was a fighting Church. The Fathers of Trent alone pronounced more condemnations than all previous councils together; they could not have done otherwise when confronted with a swarm of propositions hostile to her teaching, and when they saw the advance against Mother Church of adversaries who, under pretext of strengthening her walls, would have irretrievably destroyed her. All the same, Trent most certainly hallowed a final breach with the Protestants. As things stood when the Council ended its work, this rupture was not only desirable: it was quite indispensable. Protestantism was no longer an affair of wavering on the part of Luther, or of tentative agreement on that of Melanchthon; Calvinism had forged a block of steel which was nothing less than a well-organized counter-Church. Invitations to discuss points of difference were bound to prove illusory and deceptive, so that the only possible reply was a categorical "*Non possumus*." This was clearly understood by those theologians of the Council, particularly the Jesuits, who had laboured to prevent any sort of compromise; and the same fact explains the attitude of Laynez, second General of the Society, at the Conference of Poissy, where he seems to have done all he could to

65. See, for example, G. Bardy, "L'Église catholique, moyen âge et temps modernes," in *Année theologique* (1949), fasc. iv, a model of intelligence and probity.

make a settlement impossible. Many historians have blamed the Church of Trent for this "intransigence." But the charge is of its very nature mere "lay" or "Protestant" reaction; the Church, as guardian of Christ's deposit, could have no truck with error. Neither the Fathers of the Council nor the popes, however well disposed they might have been, could have recognized the character of truth in the vagaries of Luther, Zwingli, Henry VIII and Calvin. A Catholic, if he desires to remain an orthodox Catholic, is bound in conscience unreservedly to subscribe the anathemas of Trent. It remains, however, none the less true, on the historical as distinct from the theological plane, that this hardening and stiffening, concomitant with a similar process in the Protestant camp, did much to involve the whole of Christendom in the bloody discords which marked the end of the sixteenth century, and from which the Church of Christ as a whole would emerge exhausted, and maybe for ever mutilated.

Within the closed circle of Catholicism also we discover certain features which appear to have altered the ancient visage of the Church. "Because they were fighting a heresy, the Sovereign Pontiffs and the Fathers of the Council gave their definitions such heavy outlines that one can easily lose sight of those positive riches with which they were not called upon to deal. Formulae devised for the condemnation of error are always partial, throwing light upon only one aspect of the truth; but we must not forget that revealed truth is richer and more fruitful than can be expressed by definitions. The unhappy crisis of the sixteenth century led the Catholic Church, or at least a fair number of her theologians, to thrust into the background some essential factors of her doctrine and life. The thesis of justification by faith is affirmed by St. Paul, repeated by St. Augustine and taught by the councils of Milevis and Orange."[66] It may therefore be asked whether the anathemas, indispensable though they most assuredly were, did not result in a narrowing of Christian thought.

Some critics have detected the same phenomenon in the composition of the Catholic community. It is quite certain that a greater degree of unity and more centralization were necessary if anarchy was to be avoided; but

66. G. Bardy, ibid.

 Protestants have argued that the result was a kind of militarism, a system of absolute uniformity, and that the Church has been impoverished by the disappearance of that astonishing diversity which is so noticeable, for example, in St. Jerome's violent clash with St. John Chrysostom. The criticism is hardly justified. One need only consider such exact contemporaries as St. Philip Neri and St. John of the Cross, or their immediate junior St. Francis of Sales, to see that differences of character and vocation were by no means impossible within the strict hierarchical setting which had now become the rule. Besides, the very succession of popes and the diversity of their characters ensured an opportunity for discussion, arbitration and improvement.

More evident is another feature which cannot fail to impress the historian. "In order effectively to oppose the Protestant doctrines concerning the invisible character of the spiritual Church, emphasis was laid almost exclusively upon the visible Church regarded as an institution, a system of government, an organism. The tract *De Ecclesia* developed along these lines, in the margin as it were of theology properly so called, one party viewing it as a thesis of Apologetics, the other as a part of Canon Law.... They ended by virtually forgetting the interior aspect of the life of the Church as Mystical Body of the Saviour and habitual dispenser of Grace"[67]; and it is one of Pope Pius XII's most outstanding titles to fame that he stressed the need for a theology of the Mystical Body, without which Catholics become mere members of a society and, eventually, of a party. Nevertheless it cannot be denied that the Council of Trent, by placing so much emphasis upon the visible Church, did much to give her the characteristics of a social force, characteristics which the triumphs of a renascent art, under papal direction, endowed with such imposing (though sometimes disconcerting) magnificence. Of the two inseparable elements which constitute the divine majesty of Christ, it is His Glory rather than His Cross that seems in profane eyes to be exalted by the Tridentine Church. True Catholics alone know that the one implies the other, and even the marbles of St. Peter's somehow reflect the presence of Him who is God of the poor in spirit.

67. G. Bardy, ibid.

Such then is the "new look" presented to history by the Church. When the Council ended, and when Pius V died, the terrible crisis which had shaken the Christian world for half a century was far from ended: it had still to reach its bloody culmination, but at least the barque of Peter had been secured against shipwreck. Catholicism had confronted heresy. By reforming herself she deprived her adversaries of their most powerful means of propaganda, and defined her teaching with such force and clarity that souls in quest of the Absolute would no longer need to ask Luther and Calvin for the fulfilment of their ancient hopes, but would obtain it through St. Teresa or St. John of the Cross. She also managed to graft into her own thought whatever was acceptable in humanism, all the creative intellect which that movement had given to the world; and she had revealed that living synthesis through the medium of her saints—through Ignatius of Loyola, for instance, as she would do later through St. Francis of Sales. Meanwhile, as if to compensate for the losses of people and territories inflicted upon her by Protestantism, she sent other saints in the wake of Francis Xavier[68] to win for her a world. Indeed the Tridentine Church with her new look is no less great, no less admirable, than her predecessors. She had cleared a decisive stage on the dark and difficult road by which redeemed humanity has striven for nearly two thousand years towards the light. 175

14. IN THE MIRROR OF ART

THE new countenance of Holy Church is so reflected in the mirror of art that the spirit of the Council of Trent is perhaps nowhere so fully manifested as in the achievements of architecture, painting, sculpture and music which flowered in its climate.[69] These were very numerous in the half-century

68. See Volume 2, Chapter V.
69. Before dealing with this subject we must pay tribute to Émile Mâle, who has shed so much light upon its every facet. To follow the chapters of his great work, *L'Art religieux après le concile de Trente* (1932), is to understand completely the spirit of the Council of Trent.

 between the death of Leo X (1522) and that of Pius V (1572), during which the Tridentine reform took shape in men's mind, found expression in the conciliar canons, and at length began to pass into the manners and institutions of society. For while that reform was a movement towards austerity it was by no means systematically hostile to the arts. Exactly the opposite is true. Against the Protestant iconoclasts, who rejected painted and sculptured images, and would have nothing but bare walls in their temples, the Church encouraged veneration of artistic works which allow the faithful to strengthen their belief with beautiful forms; she continued more than ever to regard the splendour of her churches as glorifying the majesty of God. In all countries where Protestantism had failed to obtain a hold, and especially in Italy, which was almost wholly free of the taint, art continued to live the same intense life it had enjoyed in the preceding era, and the Church to fulfil her ancient role of patron and protectress.

Of the eight popes who occupied the throne of Peter during those fifty years, only one, Adrian VI of Utrecht, showed himself indifferent to the arts, except to despise and condemn the masterpieces of antiquity as pagan idols. But Clement VII, during whose pontificate the sack of Rome seemed to destroy the creative urge, took the first opportunity to do all he could to revive the tradition of his predecessors. He summoned Michelangelo to begin work in the Sistine Chapel, and took a close interest in the building of Saint-Louis-des-Français, the first window of which he had long ago erected as Cardinal Giulio dei Medici. Paul III, who first convoked the Council, was a man of encyclopedic mind and an exquisite connoisseur. Responsible for many artistic undertakings, he built the Porta Santo Spirito and the celebrated Palazzo Farnese, the young Sangallo's masterpiece which was completed by Michelangelo. He also constructed the Pauline Chapel and Sala Regale, in the Vatican, and did much to advance the work at St. Peter's. Julius III concentrated almost exclusively upon his delightful Villa del Monte; but Palestrina's masterpiece, the *Coronation Mass*, is associated with the name of Marcellus II. Paul IV continued work on St. Peter's, encouraged his niece to build the Roman College and also the Annunziata, the apse of which was afterwards richly decorated by Zuccari. He was able to recognize in Michelangelo's "Last Judgment" his own solemn and tragic faith. Pius IV, under whom the Council ended its labours, ranks as a patron with Julius II and Leo X. He laid out the Piazza of St. Peter's, created the famous Casino Medici in the Vatican gardens, rebuilt the precincts of the Sacred Palace, completed the ceiling of St. John Lateran, erected the Porta Pia and the Porta del Popolo (near which latter he built a charming villa), and had Michelangelo build the ingenious and imposing church of Santa Maria degli Angeli in the Baths of Diocletian. Other work was done by his order at Ancona, Ostia and Civitavecchia, and it was also he who assured the triumph of Oratorio. The austere St. Pius V gave more attention to works of public utility than to works of art properly so called. It is none the less to his credit that he did not impede what had already been begun, and even encouraged the widespread movement which, on the morrow of Trent, caused many bishops and all the religious Orders to restore their churches or build new ones.

Nothing is more false than to imagine a sort of hiatus between the popes of the Renaissance and those of the Tridentine era. What those of the fifteenth century had commenced was carried on by their successors in the sixteenth—in a different spirit, no doubt, but with the same determination. There is no more remarkable proof of this statement than the history of St. Peter's, of that stupendous building site the opening of which in 1499 marked the beginning of the "High Renaissance," and which never closed during a period of one hundred fifty years, notwithstanding storm and stress in the shape of war, revolt, intrigue and human weakness. Bramante, who conceived the brilliant project, had long been dead; Raphael, his successor in charge of operations, had followed him too soon into the grave, as also had his two assistants Fra Giocondo and Giulio Sangallo. Immediately after young Antonio Sangallo had taken his place, work was completely suspended by the terrible disaster of 1527. But the task was resumed as quickly as possible: once again hundreds and hundreds of workmen took over the site; once again marble and other precious materials were brought from far and wide. In 1546 Michelangelo took charge of the gigantic work so well suited to his colossal genius, and returned to Bramante's plan for a Greek cross.[70] But he decided to substitute for the cupola which was to have been modelled upon that of the Pantheon, another and even more wonderful structure inspired by Brunelleschi; and he laboured until death to realize this titanic dream which was to figure forth the greatness and incomparable majesty of the Church. The amazing history of St. Peter's is a concrete sign of the determination of Catholicism to declare itself and triumph.

It must, however, be added that this loyalty to art, of which the Tridentine Church afforded such striking proofs, went hand in hand with a profound modification of her attitude towards the very significance of art. The great humanist and patron popes had thought of it as an end in itself, destined to lend surpassing radiance to the Church and particularly to the Holy See, without trying to place it at the service of faith. The result was a large measure of ambiguity and some questionable complacency, from which even the Tridentine popes were not altogether free. Many of the works of art produced between 1522 and 1572 were secular and profane, sometimes in the least agreeable sense of this word. Certain frescoes painted in the Vatican and the Castle of Sant' Angelo for Paul III were curiously pagan in tone; and the enormous sums spent by Pius IV on his "Casino" are no less surprising. It remained to be seen whether art, under ecclesiastical patronage, would remain outside the great current which was urging it to renew and purify itself. Here also the Spirit of the Council played a part.

In the twenty-fifth and final session it was decreed that "the Holy Council forbids the placing in churches of any image which is inspired by an erroneous dogma and might lead the simple astray. It wishes that all impurity be avoided, that images be not given suggestive charm; and it forbids the erection anywhere, even in churches not subject to visitation by the Ordinary, of any unusual image unless first approved by the bishop." These words represented a new attitude of the Church towards religious iconography, which was to be pruned, corrected and purified from a moral as well as from a dogmatic point of view. Such was the negative aspect of the Council's

70. This was subsequently abandoned by Maderno. See Volume 2, beginning of Chapter VI.

aesthetic work; but before long, as fruit of the same spirit which animated the Assembly, a positive operation was set on foot tending to transmit that spirit to the realm of art, an operation whose principles were formulated by Molanus in his Latin treatise on *Painters and Sacred Images* (1570).

The first sign of the existence of a new spirit was a wave of modesty. In 1558, during the lifetime of Michelangelo, Paul IV anticipated the conciliar decisions by giving orders that the nudities of the Sistine Chapel must be covered, an undertaking completed by St. Pius V. Later, under Clement VIII, it was nearly decided to *erase* all "scandalous" frescoes. The action of Paul IV was generally approved; St. Charles Borromeo followed his example wherever possible, and Bellarmine subsequently boasted of having extracted a promise from an artist friend never to paint a nude. Some bishops were even more zealous, destroying all pictures and statues which they considered immodest. The eviction of pagan statues from the Vatican Palace by Pius V was yet another manifestation of the same spirit; and this campaign of prudery was afterwards carried to such lengths that Pope Innocent X had a charming new-born Infant Jesus, by Guercino, covered with a shirt![71]

The same attempt to correct ancient manners was pursued in all directions. It was not only nude figures that were banished from the churches, but also those of "useless" persons and "trifling" episodes, all those curiosities in fact which lent a frequently charming but none the less unchristian picturesqueness to the works of the Renaissance. Paolo Veronese was actually summoned from Venice to appear before the Holy Office on a charge of having introduced into a "Last Supper" figures unworthy of so grave a subject. He could only reply that he put them there to fill gaps in the canvas and "do good"; upon which he was ordered to retouch his picture within three months. Naturally enough everything suggestive of doctrinal error was ruthlessly condemned. In the years immediately following the Council religious censorship objected even to the apocryphal traditions, of which

---

71. Note, however, that this modesty extended only to works placed in churches. Pagan decorations, though often very free, were still accepted in private residences, even those belonging to the popes (e.g., the Palazzo Farnese).

 medieval painters had made frequent use. Some artists met with disapproval for having shown the Blessed Virgin swooning at the foot of the Cross, whereas the Gospel says that she was standing: *Stabat*. Later on a more generous attitude was adopted; but the Apocrypha had become a dead letter, and would be ignored altogether by modern artists.

A still more considerable effort on the positive side corresponded to this negative aspect. The Church of the Council of Trent, seeing the possibilities of art in the field of apologetics, resolved to employ it as a weapon against heresy and as material in the rebuilding of Christianity; and this resumption of art by the Church is one of the outstanding events of the age.[72] Whereas the Renaissance, particularly in the fifteenth century, had marked the zenith of creative individualism, the period following the Council corresponded to the flowering of a Catholic art with new and well-established characteristics, which most certainly found inspiration as well as hostility among the theologians.

This profound transformation of artistic ideals was facilitated by the fact that artists themselves were affected by the impulse of contemporary trends; an increasing number were believers. Towards the end of his life Michelangelo, under the influence of his saintly friend Vittoria Colonna and that of the Society of Jesus, whose spirit and methods he greatly admired, behaved in all respects as a Christian, grave and austere, filled with anguish at the thought of death and judgment. "Now I realize," he exclaimed, "how mistaken was the passionate illusion that made me look upon art as a sovereign idol...." The type of dilettante and pleasure-seeking artist so familiar to the Renaissance, working with equal enthusiasm and equal talent both in the religious and in the pagan sphere, vanished almost completely. It gave place

---

72. On this point especially the labours of Émile Mâle have thrown entirely new light. In the Introduction to his great book he admitted with splendid humility how much his thought had been modified in this respect. At the end of *Art religieux à la fin du moyen âge* he had written: "Henceforward there would still be Christian artists, but no more Christian art." Later studies caused him to change his mind. In all works of art produced after the Council of Trent, which he had tended to despise, his genius and patience discovered a symbolism and an apologetic in harmony with the preoccupations of that time.

to a very different type, whose members believed and practised the Catholic faith, sometimes with conspicuous piety. Among these was Guercino, who heard Mass each morning and went to pray in church every evening; Bernini, who communicated twice a week and made an annual retreat; and the devout but sugary Carlo Dolci, who made a vow never to paint a figure which could not lead souls to devotion.

"Since art had become a form of doctrine, the artist also came to consider that the subject of his pictures was an essential part thereof." In the Renaissance period the theme of a work was often a mere pretext for the joyful play of shape and colour. But from now onwards, and with growing importance throughout the seventeenth century, what mattered was the truth which an artist sought to express, or rather that which his theological advisers asked him to express. So it was that after the Council of Trent art took its place in the battlefield, where its protagonists devoted themselves to exalting all that Protestantism condemned: "The cult of Our Lady, the primacy of St. Peter, belief in the sacraments, in the efficacy of prayers for the dead and of good works, the veneration of images and relics—all these dogmas or ancient traditions were defended by art in alliance with the Church." The subjects represented during a period of more than one hundred years bear the stamp of this apologetic and combative purpose.

Art, however, took its cue not only from the thought and activity of the Tridentine Church, but also from her climate. Catholicism as regenerated by the Council was a solemn and moving religion, in which the faithful soul was invited (e.g., by the *Exercises* of St. Ignatius), to meditate the Passion of Christ and to think of life in terms of death. Art likewise assumed this character. During the Renaissance Christian art had been free to exalt the joy of living. But this new art looked farther back to the late Middle Ages, so pregnant with anguish and with terror; it no longer gave expression to repose in God, but to the terrible adventure[73] of seeking for the Absolute as experienced by the great sixteenth-century mystics. Artists no longer

73. Note, however, that St. John of the Cross repeatedly describes it as a *happy* adventure: *dichosa ventura.*

 conjured up the beauty of creation, but the tragedy of man doomed to death by sin; and some of them (e.g., Valdès Leal of Seville), carried this tendency to the point of the macabre. Funereal pomp, so dear to the Jesuits, and catafalques carved in stone were other indications of the same outlook. The masterpiece of this period[74] is the "Last Judgment" in the Sistine Chapel, Michelangelo's last great undertaking. Begun on the morrow of the sack of Rome, in the gloomy atmosphere of that appalling tragedy, and completed just as the master's interior development drew level with the spirit of Trent, it is a prodigious achievement, almost inaccessible to our human sensibility. We find in it no trace of open air or countryside to refresh the eye or give the heart repose; all is bathed in an atmosphere of molten lead and vertigo, a perfect reminder of that unimaginable "day of wrath" spoken of by the *Dies irae*, when time and space will collapse into the abyss, and when the human race, herded as in the fresco beneath the uplifted hand of its Eternal Judge, will cower in terror on the frontiers of despair.

But the reaction of a believing soul to sin and punishment were not the sole preoccupation of Tridentine art, which strove at the same time to express the glory of the Church in her new-found strength and certitude. This purpose is evident henceforth in every field, in architecture as well as in painting and sculpture. The Annunciation, Transfiguration, Ascension and Assumption, all those themes in fact which show Earth supernaturally linked to Heaven, were represented time and again in the glory of cloud and nimbus, but soon also against the magnificent spread of gold and purple hangings, symbolic of the Church Triumphant. Architecture was similarly affected. Abandoning the regular harmonies of the Renaissance (themselves copied from antiquity), flat ceilings and painted decoration, as well as the play of light and shadow so dear to the Gothic builders, it adopted a new type of church whose model was the famous Gesù at Rome, which Vignola began for the Jesuits in 1568. The type of religious edifice adopted by the Counter-Reformation, and carried to all four quarters of the world

74. Perhaps we should say one of the masterpieces, remembering the cruel "Deposition from the Cross."

by the Society of Jesus, is as far removed as it is possible to be from the Protestant temple. Among its features are a proud facade, rising tier upon tier and seemingly alien from what lies behind; purely ornamental pediments broken by statues and turrets; a nave with cylindrical vaulting and bordered by independent side chapels; and a monumental dome above the transept crossing. It is in fact a building devoid of mystery, containing so much coloured marble, stucco and gold ornament that it suggests a palace drawing-room[75] rather than the house of a lowly God.

It is difficult to say what influence these ideas exerted upon Christian art from an aesthetic point of view. For the period of their introduction followed the disappearance of the sublime architects of the High Renaissance, who were succeeded by men of great talent that sometimes amounted to brilliance, but who no longer possessed the creative power of their forerunners. The geniuses who were later inspired by the Tridentine spirit in countries beyond the Alps were either as yet unborn or had scarcely begun their work: in 1572 El Greco was twenty-five years old, and Rubens had not seen the light of day. Michelangelo alone of the race of Titans survived at Rome until 1564. In no technique do we find men of equal stature with their predecessors: Brunelleschi, Bramante and Michelangelo were unmatched by Vignola, "the modern Vitruvius," by Vasari,[76] or even by Palladio (1518–1580), to whom Vicenza owes its beauty and Venice the church of San Giorgio. In sculpture neither the clever and somewhat boastful Benvenuto Cellini (1500–1571), who was far removed from the spirit of the Catholic Reformation and spent most of his working life in France, nor Sansovino (1485–1570), who made the bronze doors for St. Mark's at Venice, could show anything to rival the masterpieces of Donatello and Verrocchio, let alone the "Moses" and "Slaves" of Michelangelo. In painting Primaticcio

75. This impression, however, which makes the Jesuit churches look like secular monuments, must not cause us to forget that these "boudoirs of God" were designed with a view to religious functions. They were meant to enable all the faithful to see the altar and follow the Holy Sacrifice, whereas the old Gothic rood-screens hid the altar from the congregation.

76. He built the Palazzo Uffizi at Florence, but is better known as the author of *Lives of the Painters, Sculptors and Architects.*

 (1504–1570), with his firm talent, happy, smiling and equal to every task imposed upon him by the King of France, could not be considered the equal of the great masters.

To this slackening as it were of creative intensity there is only one exception: Venice. In that opulent city, queen of the Adriatic, lady paramount of Cyprus, and conqueror of Lepanto, who knew not that she was already in decline and was intoxicated with her own splendour, three men continued on a level with the masters of the golden age. Titian, who died in 1576, reached the age of ninety-nine without losing anything of his power or fervour; he seemed rather to have derived from his length of years a sovereign serenity which perfected the richness of his gifts. His often refractory pupil Tintoretto (1516–1594), son of a dyer named Robuski, was a genius at once popular and aristocratic, eager to cover enormous surfaces.[77] His tireless and cunning hand decorated churches and palaces, as well as producing a whole series of retables. Paolo Cagliari of Verona, better known as Veronese (1528–1588), used delicate and splendid colours to depict blazing sun, luminous tresses and golden breast-plates. To him fell the honour of painting, in the Doge's Palace, the most glorious scene in the history of his country; and this picture, "The Triumph of Venice," would alone suffice to show posterity the magnificence of the Serenissima.

All three of these masters entered the service of the Tridentine Church, though it would be too much to claim that they did so altogether without mental reservation and regret. There are still pagan and Renaissance elements in their work, where Sacred Love, as in Titian's famous picture, is not seldom opposed by Profane Love. The conciliar canon, one feels, did little to inspire Tintoretto's dazzling "Susanna," in which the bather and her bracelets are well calculated to tempt the hungry old men lying in wait for her; and, to choose but one of many beautiful forms, Veronese's "Judith" is little more than a gorgeous Venetian courtesan. Nevertheless there are whole stretches of their work in which these illustrious masters of the city of the Doges are completely in accordance with current religious

77. His "Paradise" is the largest known picture.

trends, celebrating Holy Church in her new-found glory, indicating the return to Scripture which was so characteristic of that age, expressing the gravity of faith and the depth of the Christian drama. Titian's "Entombment," Veronese's "Calvary" and Tintoretto's fifty pictures in the Scuola di San Marco (among them a striking "Ecce Homo") bear witness to the deepening of the Christian spirit in these men's souls; just as their portraits (e.g., Titian's famous "Paul III with his Nephews") and their vast biblical scenes (e.g., Veronese's "Marriage at Cana") proclaim the solemn pride then experienced by the Church, the majesty of the popes, and the splendour of reawakened tradition.

Unfortunately the whole artistic achievement resulting from the Council of Trent was destined not to remain at this high level. Like all great creative movements, the Renaissance had hatched its own perils. The most serious of these was mannerism. Talent sought to discover the secrets of genius, and, as always happens in such cases, found only recipes. Systematic consideration of genius and its methods led to some curious excesses. The awful God of Michelangelo, having been copied over and over again by Guido Reni and Domenichino, became in due course a commonplace, just as Leonardo's Christ and Raphael's Madonnas became more and more insipid until we reach Guido's Jesus and Dolci's sentimental Virgins. The disciplinary rigour of the Council of Trent, by imposing upon artists imperious moral criteria, subject matter, and sometimes even models, produced the same sort of result, a pious conformism from which religious art would not always benefit. It cannot be doubted that here we have one of the least happy results of the Tridentine achievement. It contributed in large measure to the success of a "sacred art" in which neither the great creators of the Renaissance nor the romanesque and gothic sculptors and masons could any longer have recognized themselves.

But despite mannerism, which was the logical outcome of lessons learned from genius, and despite the sumptuous, vain-glorious and purposely theatrical features of Tridentine art, there was still a chance of improvement. The possession of superior and almost excessive technical means, the love of rich materials, the mystical glow resulting from the experience of the great ecstatics, and a certain mysterious madness which so often seizes decadent arts as if to lead them back to the innocence of their origins—all these factors combined to create a new style which would flower from 1570 onwards and produce some most alluring masterpieces. I refer of course to Baroque, the unexpected but none the less legitimate heir of the austere reformers of Trent.[78]

The visual arts were not the only ones to profit by the solicitude of the Council. Music also was reformed, nor had it, as had painting and sculpture, to await inspiration.[79] At the close of the Middle Ages religious music, like everything else, was in a sorry plight. Gregorian chant, which the Church had made peculiarly her own, was hopelessly decadent. Since the coming of *ars nova*, in the early fourteenth century, its grave homophony had been ousted by a polyphony which, though sometimes attractive, was often full of eccentric ingenuities and laden with secular, not to say vulgar, elements. Liturgical melodies served merely as themes for the rivalry of contrapuntists; and as for the liturgical text, it was very difficult to understand one word. The twenty-third session of the Council determined to abolish these vagaries. It decreed that young clerics must be taught Gregorian chant, and that the accompaniment must be kept clear of anything unseemly or lascivious; the music known as "measured" or "figured" (i.e., which was written with notes instead of the strokes used for plainsong) was just tolerated on condition that it did not interfere with the wording of the liturgy. Was this then the death of sacred polyphony? No; for it met with several great masters who thought of their art in terms of the new regulations and caused it to blossom as never before.

78. Baroque will be studied in the last chapter of Volume 2 of this work, p. 497.

79. The spirit of the Council of Trent hardly appears in secular literature; theology, mysticism and spiritual writings properly so called seem to have monopolized all the talents. The true literary masterpieces of this period are the works of St. Teresa and St. John of the Cross. Tasso's *Jerusalem Delivered*, with its brilliant setting, its picturesque episodes and its constant praise of Christian courage, corresponds in a way to the spirit that led to the victory of Lepanto; but its mediocre sentiments and its suspicious episodes leave one with the general impression of a religious veneer rather than a true religion.

The first of these masters was Costanzo Festa (*ob.* 1545), whose *Te Deum* is still in the repertory of the Sistine Choir. Next came Giovanni Animuccia (*ob.* 1571), whose *Magnificat*, hymns and motets, while remaining polyphonic, were in full accord with the new spirit; he also composed for the Oratory of St. Philip Neri those first little musical dramas of narrative songs from which Oratorio afterwards developed. But the real leader of this reform was Giovanni Pierluigi Palestrina (1526–1594), formerly choir-master at Palestrina. When the bishop of that diocese became Pope Julius III, he brought Giovanni Pierluigi to Rome, and there the young musician's bewitching and abundant genius proved to the most supercilious reformers that consonant harmony, perfection in counterpoint and the ablest use of polyphony could go hand in hand with the most genuinely religious aspirations. Himself a sincere believer and a disciple of St. Philip Neri, for whose Oratory he too composed "oratorios," he was wellnigh bound to write music of calm faith and ecstatic purity. The works of this angel of song include ninety-three Masses (of which *Papae Marcelli* is the most celebrated), six hundred motets, forty-two psalms and innumerable *ricercari*, not to mention a host of secular pieces, while his *Stabat Mater* is even today upon the lips of every Catholic. His influence still remains decisive, for he accomplished a permanent revolution in the world of music. His pupil and rival, Tomas Luis de Vittoria (1540–1611), was a Spaniard living in Rome. He was of a more mystical turn of mind than Palestrina, and his works reflect the markedly Spanish characteristics of St. Teresa; but already during the lifetime of his master he was employing the latter's technique to such an extent that he was nicknamed Palestrina's "swan"—or "ape" by some malicious tongues. 187

At Rome there is one day in every year upon which the spirit of the Tridentine Church seems to make its presence felt. This day is Good Friday, when we have only to attend the ceremonies in order to find ourselves swept right back into that atmosphere of splendour and anguish, of mystical elation and reborn dignity breathed by the Church in those years of the sixteenth century during which the great task was completed. On that holiest of commemorations the Pope himself comes to celebrate the liturgical rites in the Sistine Chapel. The cringing figures of Michelangelo's "Last Judgment" seem to have been placed there expressly to remind him of life's tragedy. But if he raises his eyes he beholds upon the ceiling, where prophets and sibyls mount pensive guard, the gesture of sovereign love whereby with outstretched hand the Almighty everlastingly gives man his being. That is the place, beneath the silent gaze of that attentive throng, in which to hear the sublime music of Palestrina's *Stabat Mater* and *Improperia*[80] soaring to the vault on voices so pure that they might belong to Cherubim and Archangels. It is then and there, as the august celebrant unveils the Cross, that the significance of the whole historic drama is suddenly revealed. Prostrate in his person before the instrument of suffering and shame, the whole Church feels herself exalted, delivered from the faults, the weakness and the misery of all those human individuals of which she is composed. Prostrate likewise, the Christian soul realizes that she is destined to a future of light and glory, because she has again renewed her loyalty to the message entrusted to her by God and sealed with His Most Precious Blood.

80. Both the exclusive property of the Sistine Choir, which supplies the music on these occasions.

CHAPTER III

The Rending of Christian Europe, Part One

1. THE AGE OF FANATICISM

ON one of the many occasions when St. Teresa of Avila was explaining to her nuns the meaning of that prayer which asks the Lord to "have pity on those who have no pity on themselves," she cried out: "My God, the world is in flames." It was true. During the last third of the sixteenth century the entire world, or at least the whole of Christendom, fell victim to fire and sword. Some kingdoms found themselves engulfed in civil war; in others terror alone had been able to establish an often precarious peace; and there was once more bloody conflict between States. Men were everywhere burned at the stake, hanged, quartered or beheaded, and all without a qualm of conscience. That impassioned century would have considered itself untrue to its vocation if the closing years had made way for mercy. Fanaticism triumphed; cruelty reigned.

Painful as it may be to a follower of the God of Love, one thing is beyond question: responsibility for this manifold tragedy must be attributed to religion. In this respect, of course, religion was faithless to the teaching of its Founder; but it had been established thus in the great majority of consciences by fifteen hundred years of strife, political contamination and ineradicable prejudice. If we are to understand the men of that period we must not judge them by our standards of "liberalism" and "tolerance"; we must, in Vacandard's phrase, make for ourselves "an ancestral soul." And this is not perhaps so difficult when we think of the depths of horror to which other fanaticisms have led in quite recent times, fanaticisms which, with their domineering social and political interests, jeopardize the whole future of man, the very meaning of life. In the sixteenth century discussion centred not upon the "death of God," but upon the manner of interpreting Christian revelation; the debate, however, was no less acrimonious.

The problem of heresy, and of the attitude to be adopted towards heretics, had confronted the Church right from her beginnings; it was already a well-worn topic in St. Augustine's day. But it had never received definitive and permanent solution. Throughout the Christian centuries some had advocated gentleness while others favoured coercion. The Church, through her Fathers and theologians, upholds *in principle* the dictum of St. Bernard that "faith is a work of persuasion, not of force; but *in fact* many of her sons, and even of her rulers, have acted just as if belief could be imposed by violence." There is even an appalling decretal of Innocent III which orders the withholding of medical attention from a sick man unless he consents to receive the sacraments, even if it involves the patient's death. Surely it is lawful to take counter-measures against those who not only reject the faith, but by degrading and perverting it lead souls into error. The Bishop of Hippo had already allowed them as a kind of prophylactic. In an age like the sixteenth century, when the terrible crisis of western society endangered the very conception of the world and of man, it was surely natural that believers should uphold the legitimacy of measures which, by demolishing adverse doctrines, would ensure the triumph of their own views. To leave a man free to choose his faith would have seemed a betrayal of those principles which were dearer than life itself; and *neither camp* would tolerate such treason.

I say "neither camp," because nothing would be more unjust than to saddle the Catholic Church alone with responsibility for a disaster that involved the Christian world in an orgy of bloodshed. Fanaticism was no one's monopoly. There are many documents to show that Protestants indulged the same cruel intransigence as their opponents, taking their stand upon those very principles by virtue of which their brethren perished at the stake. It was Luther who wrote: "If we have the power we must not tolerate

contrary doctrines in the State; and to avoid greater evils those who do not
believe must be forced to attend sermons, to hear the Decalogue explained and to obey at least externally." These were most moderate requirements; his henchman, the gentle Melanchthon, wished "the civil authority to employ the sword against abettors of new doctrines." The two Wittenbergers had in mind such men as Hoffman, Thomas Münzer and other Anabaptists; but these arch-heretics themselves thought no differently upon this point. "A man deprived of God has no right to live, for he is an obstacle to pious souls," said Thomas Münzer, in whose own case the precept was to be literally applied.[1] We know what John of Leyden did, once he had established the "Kingdom of Zion" at Münster.[2] Zwingli, another of Luther's rivals, fully agreed with him in this respect, declaring that "it is the Lord who has commanded 'Slay the wicked one who is in your midst.'" From Calvin, naturally, one could compile a rich anthology of fanatical maxims. The whole of his *Defensio Fidei*, written after the death of Servetus, repeats as a sort of *leit-motif* that "it is lawful to punish heretics, and their execution is perfectly in order." This theme was obligingly taken up by his successor Theodore Beza: "To pretend that one must not punish heretics is equivalent to saying that one should not punish parricides and matricides." We might indeed fill page after page with a monotonous series of such excerpts, but Beza himself provides the conclusion of all these maxims: "What is liberty of conscience? A diabolical dogma."[3]

It is to the honour of humanity that there were exceptions to this apparent unanimity in fanaticism. There was one man who even attempted with uncommon heroism to stem the current. In 1554 Sebastian Castellio, whom Calvin had driven from Geneva,[4] wrote a treatise to prove that Scripture

1. See *A Religious Revolution: The Protestant Reformation*, Volume 2, Chapter V, p. 396.
2. Ibid., p. 441–42.
3. Fanaticism was not peculiar to the West. In Russia the theologian Joseph of Volokolamsk, opposing the theories of Nil Sorsky, exclaims: "To kill a heretic with one's own hand and to kill him through prayer by converting him are one and the same thing. Besides, death is redemptive of heretics themselves: it diminishes their responsibility before God."
4. See *A Religious Revolution: The Protestant Reformation*, Volume 2, Chapter VI, p. 527.

provides no justification whatever for the execution of heretics. From the religious standpoint, he explained, there are two kinds of heretics: heretics in conduct, whom we ought to amend by instruction and the example of an upright life; and heretics in opinion, whom it is impossible to judge since their crime is committed deep down in the heart, beyond the estimation of man. Here are some words of his which show him to have been far in advance of his time, and suggest that he may have been satisfying a taste for paradox: "Having often sought to learn what a heretic is, I have discovered only that we consider as heretics all those who do not agree with our opinion." Elsewhere again he says: "You do not prove your faith by burning heretics, but by dying for it"—a wonderfully penetrating observation, as true today as when first uttered.

Here and there throughout Christian Europe, especially in humanist circles, there were men who thought just what Castellio had so aptly expressed in words, and some of them had the courage to say so. Such were the "Meaux Group," "those men infatuated with hope, who knew not how to hate." Such was the great Sir Thomas More, who would one day give his life for the true faith, but who wrote in *Utopia*. "Every man has the right to confess the religion of his choice, and to try to convert his neighbour by force of reasoning as well as by his friendly behaviour. But he must refrain from any show of aggressiveness towards the opinions of other people and from supporting his arguments by recourse to violence." Such also were Erasmus, Rabelais and many others in every country and of every obedience, whether Protestant or Catholic, who together formed the embryo of a "third party." Its success would be long delayed, but its sporadic existence during the whole period of the drama was consoling, more especially as these moderates were also good Christians (Catholic or Protestant as the case might be). Their tolerance must not be confused with the scepticism of, say, Jean Bodin, forerunner of Bayle and Voltaire, who advocated a natural religion having in his eyes all the appearance of Positivism. So serene an attitude, however, was out of harmony with an age that was passing through a grave crisis of conscience and regarded unbelief as even more unthinkable than reprehensible. Those who appealed to it were denounced, censured and vilified in both camps,[5] and their influence was for a very long time almost negligible. Men could not turn to them until at length Christendom, exhausted and weary of carnage, realized that the probable end of internecine warfare was mutual destruction. The Edict of Nantes would have to await the passing of another thirty years.

We know that the bloody storm, "the hideous carnage" which Erasmus prophesied, had begun to rage long before the 1560s; why then, one may ask, did it now assume a fresh degree of violence? For two reasons, one of which was due to the religious situation itself. At the time of Calvin's death and the closing of the Council of Trent, a certain inflexibility becomes apparent on both sides. Neither the rigid system of Geneva nor that of Trent allowed room for mediation or temporization. The combatants were both encased in steel. The second reason was largely political. Powerful interests of an altogether temporal nature were everywhere at work: the German princes took their stand henceforward on the famous principle *Cujus regio, hujus religio*; the French monarchs were disquieted by the sight of their kingdom threatened with cleavage; the French nobility were determined to control the State; and the Dutch bourgeoisie were exasperated with Spanish officialdom. Religious liberty, "that strange and ridiculous thing," as one contemporary German chronicler described it, was all the more inacceptable because it led to a kind of permanent conspiracy against the security of States, a conspiracy in which revolutionaries at home were supported by foreign powers. Elevated thus to the height of a major conflict, in which factions, governments and whole peoples were opposed, the religious problem sought solution in bloodshed, the horror of which was aggravated by the almost unlimited means at its disposal.

5. Calvin treated Castellio as "a poisonous beast."

2. CATHOLICISM AND POLITICS: SPAIN UNDER PHILIP II

PHILIP II (1556–1598) occupied the throne of Spain during the second half of a century that witnessed his country's highest achievements. He is a man of mystery, haloed in glory yet bearing the unmistakable impress of defeat. The fact that he represented a complete fusion of the religious and the political order, in which the latter received from the former not only its principles, but also its means of action, makes it hard to speak dispassionately of a man who, even in his own lifetime, was the object of contradictory but always violent judgments. He was called by some "the Demon of the South," by others "the Wise King"; but neither term is exactly true, let alone both combined. That slender figure with its lanky limbs, uneasy countenance and hesitant imitation of a smile, as Titian painted him at the age of twenty-five, carried upon his shoulders the weight of a vast empire for forty years and without a moment's weakness. What was his aim? To what did he aspire? Why did he thrice commit himself to enterprises whose possible rewards were never equal to the risks involved? Was it through pride, through fanaticism, through lack of intelligence? Who can tell? No one has ever penetrated the secret of those sea-green, inexpressive eyes, of those immobile features, of that pale face which masked a Fleming become Spaniard to the very marrow of his bones. It may be that his terrible self-discipline represented a half-conscious determination to resist the forces of mental disintegration bequeathed to him by his unfortunate grandmother Juana.

His personality is reflected in the Escorial, that prodigious monument which he built in the rocky chaos of the Sierra Guadarrama,[6] three thousand feet above sea level, amid the slag of abandoned ironworks. It was a fortress, palace, convent, ministry and mausoleum all in one; planned in the form of an instrument of torture, erected to commemorate a military victory, and

6. About twenty-four miles from Madrid, an artificial capital which he created for no other reason than his dislike of the ancient cities of glory and revolution.

placed under the protection of a martyr.[7] There, in complete solitude, he strove day after day to handle the threads of that enormous skein whereby his power encircled the globe. In his austere ante-rooms, with their whitewashed walls and high, uncomfortable wooden seats, crowds awaited audience: ambassadors, prelates, conquistadors on leave and famous generals. The yellow gleam of candles lit up long, stern faces reminiscent of Greco's portraits, the white habits of Inquisitors, starched ruffs and black velvet doublets. No one spoke, unless in a whisper. On the other side of the royal door, which was padded with armorial upholstery, the puny little man sat working twelve hours a day, attending in person to the smallest details, examining every file, filling reams of paper with his fine handwriting, never stopping except at the canonical hours, when he took his breviary and prayed. The instrument that served his principles (or his dreams) was quite stupendous. On the abdication of Charles V, Philip inherited only one-half of his father's dominions; but that half sufficed to make him the most powerful sovereign of his time, ruling Spain, the Milanese, the Kingdom of Naples, Sicily, Sardinia, the Burgundian realm of Franche-Comté, Artois and the Low Countries, together with those immense and still almost unknown territories which Pizarro and other brilliant adventurers had added to his crown. A fine empire, to be sure, for a prince of twenty-five! Although he had mortgaged part of his revenues against sums advanced by the German banks, he was also by far the richest of kings—thanks to the galleons from America. His military strength was likewise unsurpassed: no fewer than one hundred fifty thousand men (a huge force at that date) were in his service, commanded by such illustrious leaders as the Duke of Alba, Don Juan of Austria and Alessandro Farnese; while "their lordships" of the *infanteria*, recruited from among the nobility, already claimed to be "invincible." Had he an idea of the lethal germs hidden in the womb of his glorious empire? Did he realize that the tide of gold and silver[8]

7. Philip II built the Escorial in memory of the victory of Saint-Quentin on the feast of St. Lawrence (August 10, 1557). Its shape is that of a grid, upon which the saint suffered martyrdom.
8. The silver mines of Potosi were discovered in 1543, and the process of treating raw silver with mercury was first used in 1554; hence the enormous influx of this metal.

flooding Spain was disorganizing the economy, accustoming men to idleness, and thus breeding a nation of hidalgos, priests and beggars; that the Spanish countryside was becoming depopulated; that his commerce was gradually passing into foreign hands; that Flanders fretted beneath the yoke of occupation; and that England, which was then discovering the Ocean, might set up as a rival to his vast Atlantic ambitions? Undoubtedly not. One needs to be more than a scrupulous administrator to fathom the drift of historical events.

The reign of Philip II was indeed the "golden age" of Spain, which not only benefited from a long and as yet intact accumulation of power, riches and strength, but revealed a wealth of creative force in every sphere. Castilian was beginning to dominate the whole kingdom and far beyond, the tongue whose "splendours, majesty and wonderful stateliness" Francisco de Medina declared "worthy to be carried to the most distant provinces in the folds of victorious banners." Miguel de Cervantes (1547–1616), who had lost an arm at Lepanto and lived in direst poverty, was preparing his masterpiece, *Don Quixote*, in which he combined the lessons of the Middle Ages with the essence of the Renaissance to exalt, even to the point of absurdity, his people's love of glory and independence. Lope de Vega and Guilhen de Castro were rebuilding the foundations of drama; while their contemporary Vittoria, a musician of consummate skill and strong emotion, came forward as the rival of Palestrina and competed with him even in Rome.[9] It was also at this time that the pictorial genius of Spain became conscious of itself and blossomed everywhere, at Valencia no less than in Catalunya and Castile. Pedro Berruguete adapted the style of Michelangelo to the old polychrome sculpture, and many foreigners sought work on the royal building sites. Meanwhile Toledo was the home of Dominikos Theotokopoulos, "El Greco" (1547–1614), heir of Byzantium and Venice, whose incomparable eye penetrated as none before or since the mystical and impassioned soul of Spain, and whose supreme technique has embodied it for ever in those intense yet secret portraits.

---

9. See above, p. 187.

Above all, the reign of Philip II was the age of St. Teresa and St. John of the Cross; and if the monarch had had to choose from all the manifold splendour of his kingdom, he would without doubt have chosen the last—the splendour of the saints. At that astonishing scene of abdication in the great hall of the palace at Brussels, Charles had passed on his burden with these final words: "My son, preserve the Catholic faith in all its purity." And Philip had replied: "Father, I will do so." Throughout his reign he endeavoured, sometimes with excessive zeal, to fulfil this undertaking. How could he have betrayed his oath? The faith was part and parcel of himself; it impregnated his whole existence. Every day he spent hours in prayer, and confessed frequently; he declared that he could not live without the Blessed Sacrament close to his room; and his reading, apart from official papers, was confined almost exclusively to the mystics, especially John of Avila and Teresa. Just before he died in atrocious agony, he spoke these words of sublime conviction: "My sins cause me more pain than do my sores." One might indeed ask what exactly was the nature of that sombre, anxious and (to use an anachronism) somewhat Jansenistic faith, which seems to have lacked mercy, the flower of spiritual refinement. But there can be no doubt whatever that his faith governed his life, bidding him serve God and defend His Church. Was it impossible for the interests of God and of the Church to be identical with those of the Spanish crown? That is the crucial question.

"I would give a hundred lives and my kingdom rather than have heretics as subjects." These words of Philip II were spoken in all sincerity; but in carrying out this resolve with implacable severity he appears at the same time to have followed the pattern of centralization and unification initiated by his ancestors Ferdinand and Isabella. In his hands the Inquisition was more than ever before an instrument of religious, political, administrative and even financial domination. A Venetian ambassador wrote: "It is fair to say that the real master of the Holy Office is the king. He personally appoints the Inquisitors. He uses this tribunal to control his subjects, and to chastise them with his characteristic secrecy and severity. The Inquisition and the Royal Council are always in step and constantly assist one another." Here indeed the confusion of religion and politics attained its zenith;

 every enemy of the king was looked upon as an enemy of the faith; and was treated as such. The outrageous methods often employed by the inquisitorial courts—calumny, uncorroborated accusations, false testimony, torture—were placed at the service of the State, so that the entire kingdom groaned beneath the weight of dictatorial terror. No one would have dared defy the all-powerful Office. It is here in Spain, during the reign of Philip II, that we must gaze upon the traditional image of the Church, which has ever since been exploited to her disadvantage: the doleful procession of condemned, clad in the *sanbenito* and accompanied by troops of priests, soldiers and monks; the *auto-da-fé*, where they receive sentence; the crowds abjectly eager to come and witness the spectacle; and lastly a column of smoke curling skyward, spreading far and wide the reek of charred human flesh.... Now which is it that bears responsibility in the royal conscience for this horror, faith or temporal policy? The two together, inseparably.

Two classes of subjects were the victims of these terrible methods of government, both considered as enemies of the faith and therefore as rebels. First we have the Moriscos, former Muslims who had been forcibly converted, "Christians in theory, Moors in fact," most of them hard-working peasants and absolutely peaceful. It was the Inquisitors Pedro Guerrero and Diego de Espinoza who "charged the royal conscience" with the duty of obliging these people to renounce their secret beliefs. Villages were raided, adults imprisoned, children kidnapped; the persecution went forward with implacable brutality. Revolt flared up, led by a descendant of the Ommayads, and the whole country from Almeria to Malaga, together with a wide area around Granada, was put to fire and sword. Merciless retaliation followed under the leadership of Don Juan and his Neapolitan troops. After four years of savage fighting thousands of Moriscos fled to Africa, abandoning their lands which Spanish agriculture never managed completely to recover until quite recent times. Such was the first stage on the road to unity of faith.

Another stage was cleared simultaneously and still more rapidly. The number of Protestants in Spain was insignificant, a few hundred perhaps; but the very existence of such heretics would not allow the king a wink of sleep. He was scarcely seated upon the throne when he organized the struggle against these vile hotbeds of iniquity, and also incidentally against the remnants of Illuminism and Erasmianism. The Grand Inquisitor, Fernando Valdès, very skillfully dispatched his agents to spy in suspect quarters, after which a number of arrests were made. Seville and Valladolid, the main heretical centres, suffered severely. Five great *autos-da-fé* during the years 1559 and 1560 practically annihilated such elements of Lutheranism, Erasmianism and Calvinism as the peninsula had harboured. On the day of his arrival in Spain, Philip II had been required by the Grand Inquisitor to uphold the faith and to entrust the Holy Office with that task. He had sworn upon the naked sword to do so, and no oath was ever more strictly observed. At one *auto-da-fé* an Italian captain on his way to the stake called out to the king: "How can you, a gentleman, allow another gentleman to perish at the hands of these monks?" Raising his voice for once, Philip replied: "If my son were as perverse as you I would myself bring wood for the stake that was to burn him."

It might be possible to destroy by fire the small Protestant groups in Spain; but the same means were not so easily employed in those possessions of the Crown where heresy was already entrenched. It was while attempting to apply them in the Low Countries that Philip II suffered one of the major setbacks of his reign: the revolt of the "Beggars," the exhausting struggle against the insurgents, and the final secession of the United Provinces. Catholic dictatorship and the methods of force could make no headway against the Dutch Calvinists and their determination to be free.

It is not only in home affairs that we can detect Philip II's constant identification of his personal interests with those of the religion he claimed to defend. His foreign policy affords no less striking examples. The evidence suggests that religious conviction was not invariably the primary source of his imperialism; all the same, it was so closely bound up with his temporal planning that it is almost impossible to discern where ambition and pride began, and where the designs of faith ceased to operate. Considered as a whole, his reign appears to have been a multiple endeavour to protect the interests of Catholicism and the authority of the Church in every field of

 European politics; nor indeed have historians hesitated to represent it as such. But this familiar portrait of Philip as champion of the faith requires a good deal of retouching.

After his victory over the French at Saint-Quentin, he found another adversary in Pope Paul IV,[10] who was thoroughly alarmed by the rapid spread of Spanish power in Italy; and the "Catholic king" promptly hurled Alba's mercenaries against the holy capital of the Church. What was the policy he recommended in England as husband of Mary Tudor? High-handed restoration of the faith, the same policy of repression as he applied in his own country? By no means. He favoured temporization, perhaps in order to keep England in a state of weakness that would be profitable to his own interests. During the negotiations at Cateau-Cambrésis, when there was question of a Franco-Spanish offensive against the Protestants of Germany or Geneva, Philip II showed much less enthusiasm than Henri II. He did not finally set himself up as the champion of intransigence until he realized that by doing so he would become leader of the Catholic world. Thus it was largely his vigorous efforts that ensured the successful issue of the Council under Pius IV; but at Trent his enormous delegation, consisting of more than two hundred prelates and ambassadors, so often gave an impression of serving the interests of Spain, rather than those of the Church, that they were several times openly rebuked.

From this Catholic imperialism Philip II did not always obtain the happiest results. On one occasion indeed the whole world beheld him lead the arms of Christendom to victory. This was at the battle of Lepanto (1571), where his fleet, blessed by Pope Pius V, escorted by the prayers of all Catholics, and commanded by his own illegitimate half-brother Don Juan of Austria, sank three hundred of Sultan Selim III's vessels, thus showing Islam that any attempt to invade the western Mediterranean was doomed to failure.

The *Te Deum*, however, which the ascetic and imperturbable monarch icily intoned when he received the glorious news, was to be the last of his

10. See above, Chapter II, section 5.

career as champion of the faith. For this magnificent picture is offset by another of a very different kind, in which we see Philip's ambition disappointed and the failure of his schemes for the restoration of Catholicism. A second enterprise upon the waters ended in disaster. It is doubtful whether his declaration of war against Elizabeth of England was dictated solely by the Catholic cause. There were many political and economic factors, both in the Low Countries and on the high seas, to account for mutual hostility; the bleeding head of Mary Stuart was a mere pretext. The huge Spanish expedition included one hundred thirty ships carrying twenty-seven hundred cannons, ten thousand sailors and nineteen thousand troops, while an army of thirty thousand men was concentrated in Flanders; and it seemed certain that this mighty host would repeat against heretical England the victorious operation conducted seventeen years earlier against the Turk. But Providence decided otherwise, and we know what became of the "Invincible Armada" (1588), buffeted by storm, pursued by the English fireships, scattered along the coasts of Scotland and driven on the rocks. Sixty-five ships lost and twenty thousand dead: such was the debit of that enormous crusade in which too many altogether temporal interests were at play.

In France the "Catholic" policy of Philip II had no more success, though it suffered no comparable disaster. We may doubt whether it was in the single and unselfish hope of rendering France true to her ancient loyalties that he set out to profit by the bloody crisis in which the kingdom of the Valois was then struggling, that he sided with the rigorists so as to exert influence by their means in the royal counsels, that he perhaps even incited the Massacre of St. Bartholomew, and that he assisted the League with money and with men. Coligny spoke the truth when he taunted his adversaries with "having in their bellies the red cross of Spain." The interlocking of political and religious interests was never so apparent as in these complex and tragic affairs, and the underlying motive of the ambitious Spaniard was certainly to have his own daughter Isabella ruling in the Louvre. The result was disappointing. It is beyond question that the appearance of Spanish troops in the streets of Paris helped not a little to provoke the national upheaval which enabled Henri IV to establish himself firmly on the throne of France. Even French Catholics could not welcome the indiscreet hand of a foreigner meddling, upon pretext of faith, in the affairs of their country.[11]

In the end how futile Philip's "Catholic policy" appears. He left his kingdom weaker than when he received it, exhausted by so many colossal undertakings, ruined by bankruptcy, unable to prevent English corsairs from insulting Cadiz, and already on the downward path that would reach its lowest point in the seventeenth century. As regards the Catholic cause, Spanish arms had led it to victory neither in the Low Countries nor in England nor in France; it won the day in Spain only by means of the *auto-da-fé* and blood-stained repression. Must it then stand condemned? In the secret places of the human heart the most upright intentions can mingle, almost unconsciously, with so many selfish motives; and it is very probable that that ascetic prince, whose strongest wish was unquestionably to be a saint, remained sincerely convinced that in following his own interests he was defending also those of his faith, those of the Church and those of humanity. Such is the conviction (or the pretext) of all despots. In this case it may in fact have been true; for as Joseph de Maistre observed long ago, "of all European countries, that which shed least blood was the kingdom of Philip II, the Spain of Catholic authoritarianism." The Inquisition in the Hispanic peninsula certainly claimed far fewer victims than the wars of religion in France and Germany or than the tribunals of Henry VIII, Edward VI, Mary Tudor and Elizabeth in England. It was perhaps part of the cruel genius of that age to make evil means serve the very best of causes.

11. No religious pretext was invoked to justify the most fruitful imperialist measure of Philip II's reign. The annexation of Portugal took place in 1580 after her heroic King Sebastian, Philip's nephew through his mother, had been killed during a glorious but foolhardy crusade in Morocco. Portugal remained Spanish until 1641.

3. THIRTY-SIX YEARS OF HORROR IN FRANCE

ON March 1, 1562, the bloody affray of Vassy[12] set in motion that drama which every intelligent Frenchman had known to be inevitable ever since matters of religion had tended to become political affairs and the two Churches had organized themselves into opposing factions. The method of temporization tried by the diplomatic Catherine dei Medici, acting as regent for young Charles IX (1560–1574), had failed completely. The Conference of Poissy had proved fruitless. Twenty-eight Protestants had been killed in a barn in Champagne, and a hundred wounded had only just escaped death. In various parts of France there were spontaneous and savage outbreaks of violence: at Tours two hundred Calvinists were drowned; at Sens their temple was destroyed, and in the ensuing riot both Huguenots and Catholics went "to revictual the fishes of the Yonne." The tragedy was beginning, and was destined to last for thirty-six years.

Two parties were at loggerheads. The nobles were adhering to the Reformation in ever-increasing numbers, some through conviction, others for the more or less conscious purpose of recovering for their caste that authority which the monarchy had been steadily undermining during the past hundred years. The Bourbons and Chatillons could not leave the profit of this undertaking to the Guises; in going over to the heretical camp they took with them, willy-nilly, whole villages of their tenants, and thus obtained troops. The Catholics, however, seeing power in the hands of an unreliable Italian woman and a frail little king, turned to the strong men who seemed capable of defending their faith with more courage. In fact Michel de Castelnau's *Mémoires* show clearly that from about 1560 bishops, priests and preachers looked upon the royal authority as no longer sufficient to guarantee the rights and fortunes of Catholicism. All the makings of a civil war were combined, including the vague feeling of anger which was noticeable throughout a kingdom which was severely shaken by economic difficulties resulting in rising prices, and in which the termination of hostilities with

---

12. See *A Religious Revolution: The Protestant Reformation*, Volume 2, Chapter VII, p. 650.

 Austria by the Treaty of Cateau-Cambrésis had thrown officers and men out of work. If one side were to begin the conflict the whole kingdom would quickly be alight. It was the Protestants, fearful for their safety, who took this responsibility.[13] Among them were honest Coligny and ambitious Condé, who were followed before long by a whole section of the aristocracy. Most of their pastors, even those who, like François Morel and Antoine de la Roche-Chandieu, belonged to the aristocracy, tried to prevent armed insurrection, but were overruled by their troops. Christ of the Gospels gave place to Ronsard's "Christ under arms."

What a strange spectacle of paradox is France in the second half of the sixteenth century, running with blood yet glittering with art, with gold and beauty. For we cannot forget, while narrating the various episodes of this tragedy, that they are exactly contemporary with the fertile period during which, as we learn from historians of art and literature, the High Renaissance reached its full development in France. Just when the hideous conflict was beginning there rose from the ground those delightful buildings whose architecture combines in single harmony the French tradition with the tradition of antiquity from beyond the Alps. Everywhere illustrious painters were at work, covering great stretches of canvas or expressing every slightest detail in the most wonderful portraits. Musicians also were busy revising the fundamentals of their art. Nor perhaps has France ever witnessed such an outpouring of prose, and especially of verse, as at this time when her language, "protected and ennobled" by the hand of inspiration, became fully conscious of its excellence. This literary activity plays a part in the politico-religious drama, sometimes merely by way of narrative, as, for example, the *Commentaires* of Montluc and Castelnau's *Mémoires.* Sometimes, however, it enters directly into the struggle, so that we have a Protestant

13. Not without anxiety and hesitation. Agrippa d'Aubigné's *Histoire universelle* describes the pathetic scene when Admiral Coligny's wife urged him to take arms in defence of his co-religionists. She persuaded him only by declaring that on Judgment Day she would bear witness against him unless he did his duty. Lucien Remier in particular has asked whether that was not a grave mistake, whether the Protestants would not have done better to temporize all they could while continuing their propaganda, so as not to give the superior Catholic forces an opportunity to crush them.

literature, which, from Agrippa d'Aubigné to the anonymous authors of popular laments, occupies a place in the struggles of the Reformation. But alongside this "literature on active service" there developed another and far richer type, whose outlook was more agreeable, hedonistic, and even pagan. The same is true of art, where the most important work seems designed both to make room for and to celebrate the joy of living, even in that unhappy age. The sculpture of Ligier Richier (1500–1567)[14] may be held to reflect the atmosphere of his time, but it may equally be considered as re-echoing the anguish of the fifteenth century.

The Wars of Religion did not prevent the erection of such masterpieces as the châteaux at Chambord, Amboise, Azay-le-Rideau, Écouen, Dampierre, Valençay and many others, all of which were visited in turn by the kings and their courts. Pierre Lescot (1510–1571) built the Louvre; Philibert Delorme rivalled him with the Château d'Anet; the brilliant and mysterious chisel of Jean Goujon (1515–1563) intuitively rediscovered the beauty of ancient works of art; and Germain Pilon (1535–1590) moved during an eventful life from firm and serene realism to the tomb of Chancellor Birague with the joyous grace of its nymphs whom he called virtues. Bernard Palissy (1510–1590), with face scorched at the mouth of his furnace, but with soul on fire despite his many sufferings, gave a new dignity to ceramics; while Léonard Limosin (1505–1577) opened up fresh fields to the art of enamelling. Primaticcio (1504–1570) completed those enormous sculptural decorations which made Fontainebleau the centre of a school, and Benvenuto Cellini laboured with incomparable skill. It is hard to say whether Jean Clouet or his son François penetrated more deeply, with unerring assurance, into the thoughts and feelings of those whose features they have immortalized. This was also the period when Palestrina's master Goudimel (1510–1572), Roland de Lassus with his delightful motets, and Antoine de Baif (1532–1589) were preparing new perspectives for music. What shall we say of literature? Ronsard (1524–1585), Remi Belleau and Noël du Fail

14. Particularly the tomb of René de Chalons at Bar-le-Duc, where a magnificent skeleton brandishes its heart.

 survived Joachim du Bellay (1522–1560) to witness the Massacre of St. Bartholomew. The *Discours des misères de ce temps* shows that not all were indifferent to the anguish of their country. It is amid the noise of gunfire that we hear a gentle voice sing, "*Mignonne, allons voir si la rose...*" to the music of Jehan Chardavoine. This was the tune whistled by Henri de Guise as he strode across the courtyard of the château at Blois to meet his assassins. The great wisdom of La Boétie (1530–1563) and of Montaigne (1533–1592) was in large measure a reaction against the blood-stained follies of their time.

In order to appreciate the vitality of sixteenth-century France we need only point to the extraordinary fact that she was quickly revived by a few years of prudence and good order once the crisis had passed. It was because she felt young and vigorous that she lashed herself with such fury and seemed to place so small a value upon life. None of the generals who led her opposing armies was more than twenty-five years old, an age at which men loved fighting for its own sake, but were no less fond of magnificent velvet doublets, impeccable ruffs, elegant embossed breast-plates and plumed caps. They danced and killed and died. Ladies of quality wore the *vertugarde*, but that was a poor defence of somewhat easy virtue. The pitiless conflict had its festive side: opera, for example, reached France, with the *Ballet Comique de la Reine*, only a few weeks before the assassination of Henri III.

It is against this variegated background of France with all her brilliance, pleasure-seeking yet productive of so much beauty, that we must visualize the monstrous stains of massacre committed in the name of Faith. Never in all her history, except perhaps during the Revolutionary terror, has that nation, which claims to be so wise and moderate, provided such an example of unrestrained violence and inhuman ferocity. We find assassination, murder of the wounded, massacre of whole populations after the capture of a city, and the same contempt of human life, aggravated of course by a common fanaticism but no more frenzied on one side than the other. "It would be impossible to recount the barbarous cruelties perpetrated by each of the opposing factions," says the jurist Pasquier,[15] an impartial witness and tolerant Catholic.

15. *Recherches de la France* (1560).

"Where the Huguenot is master he destroys all the images, demolishes the sepulchres and funeral monuments, carries off all sacred property. The Catholic, in retaliation, kills, murders, drowns all those whom he knows to belong to this sect, and gluts the rivers with their bodies." The *Commentaires* of Montluc, Marshal of France and illustrious veteran of the Italian wars, coldly recite the numerous executions of Calvinists for which he was responsible in Guienne. "It was possible thus to tell where I had passed, for the remains of those whom I had hanged were to be seen suspended from the wayside trees." And he adds this practical observation: "One man hanged was more frightening than a hundred in action." Having learned that the inhabitants of Terraube, near Lectoure in Gers, were sheltering heretics, he sent a company with orders to "dispatch everyone they found there." His orders were faithfully carried out; and when all were dead their corpses were thrown into the city well, "which was very deep, but was so full that one could touch them with the hand." Here are the gallant butcher's concluding words: "It was a very good riddance of very wicked fellows." In the south-east, however, a Calvinist leader, Baron des Adrets, committed such horrors that Coligny described him as a "mad beast." Having taken Montbrison, he forced the defenders to throw themselves from the walls on to the raised pikes of his soldiers. Castelnau informs us that at Mornas, near Orange, "when some of those who were flung from the windows tried clinging to the bars, the baron most inhumanly had their fingers cut off." But after he had quarrelled with the Calvinists and became reconciled with the court, his earlier conduct did not prevent him receiving the Collar of St. Michael and from calmly declaring that he had never acted except by way of reprisal or intimidation.

The population of France, however, did not consist entirely of unbridled brutes[16] devoid of all but pitiless ambition. The very Catholics who

16. Montaigne relates that Montluc himself, "having lost his son, a gallant nobleman and one of great promise, who died in the island of Madeira, mentioned particularly among other regrets, how bitterly grieved he felt at never having written to him, and at having, as a result of paternal coldness and reserve, lost the advantage of knowing and appreciating his son, and also of assuring him of the great good will he bore him and the high opinion he entertained of his virtue." So this ferocious man had a heart accessible to feeling.

 formed the armies of these bloodthirsty captains used to crowd the churches and remain to pray long after Mass, for fervour was never more keen. Their Protestant adversaries, too, would sing in all purity of heart their affecting psalms of love and mercy. But antagonism had become so strong as to expel every humane feeling. We learn from La Noüe that before joining battle on the plain of Dreux, in the first great fratricidal combat, "everyone present stood firm, revolving in his mind that the men whom he saw coming against him were neither Spaniards, nor Englishmen, nor Italians, but Frenchmen, nay even the bravest of Frenchmen, among whom were some of his own companions, friends and relations, and that within an hour they would have to kill one another—a thought which inspired them with some degree of horror, but without diminishing their courage." These last five words perhaps supply the key to those souls; they were not without feeling, but believed they must be ruthless in the name of Christ.

Such was the climate of what the seventeenth century called "the Wars of Religion" in order to discredit the faith which had caused such crime and misery. Contemporaries spoke simply of "the troubles." On the religious plane they were among the worst manifestations of the great upheaval into which the Protestant revolt had precipitated the Church of Christ. On the political plane they were one of the major episodes in the development of monarchical dictatorship. It is usual to reckon eight of these wars between 1562 and 1593; but in reality there was a single conflict lasting for nearly thirty years, though interrupted by periods of truce. The whole of France was involved; there was fighting almost everywhere. The principal encounters took place in Normandy, where English reinforcements might be landed; but the two sides clashed also in the region of the middle Loire, in those radiant provinces where the Valois trailed their courts from one château to another, where Condé dreamed of carving for himself a State within the State to serve as a base for his offensives, with Orleans as capital—Orleans, beneath whose walls François de Guise was shot down by Poltrot de Mere. Nor was the south-west spared. Here the Protestants were able to conduct some dangerous operations, being securely established from Saintonge to Languedoc and Béarn, and also in the remote districts of the Rhone and the

Alps, which were less accessible to central authority than were the plains.
Nevertheless, however appalling may be the spectacle of a whole kingdom drenched in blood, we must not, when speaking of the "Wars of Religion," imagine large-scale operations employing huge armies like those of today. There were few great battles. At Dreux, on November 19, 1562, neither side had more than twelve thousand men; at Jarnac, Condé charged with three hundred cavalry to rescue Coligny; at Montcour, on October 15, 1569, the Catholics numbered twenty-four thousand against some twenty thouasnd Protestants. As the years went by it became increasingly difficult to pay mercenaries, operations were reduced to a succession of local episodes, and the forces engaged dwindled accordingly. This war, with its classic eight-fold division, cannot be understood in terms of highly organized strategical maneuvers. One would need rather to follow its course province by province, city by city, and even village by village; to imagine a fanatical clique at work in such-and-such a town, or the passage of an armed band bent on murder, loot and rape; to think of a more or less general reign of terror causing intermittent but none the less atrocious suffering. Perhaps the nearest modern parallel is to be found in the Spanish Civil War of 1936–1939.

A final complication, just as in the last-named conflict, took the form of foreign intervention, the machinery of which is perfectly described by Michel de l'Hôpital in an address to the States-General: "We see that an Englishman and a Frenchman whose religion is the same have more affection and friendship for one another than two (French) citizens who belong to the same city and are subject to the same over-lord, but who adhere to different religions." Both sides then sought victory in reliance upon foreign powers. The Catholics relied upon Spain, with whom they maintained such close relations that the Spanish ambassador in his secret correspondence referred to Cardinal de Lorraine[17] simply as "*el amigo.*" The Protestants looked to Protestant England. An atmosphere seeming to our eyes very much like treason hung over all these military operations, in which Frenchmen

17. Nephew of the man who founded the seminary at Rheims, of which place, however, he was archbishop, as his uncle had been.

sacrificed the interests of France to their fanaticism. The Reformers actually delivered Le Havre to the English, while the Catholics went so far as to admit Spanish troops into Paris; and very few were shocked by such proceedings. Thus throughout those thirty blood-stained years international politics were bound up with home affairs. With a view to securing power for his daughter Isabella, Philip II endeavoured to obtain control of France, playing a subtle game by assisting the Protestants and humouring the Valois. All this foreign intervention balanced the contending forces, and thereby did much to prolong the fratricidal strife in which neither adversary was strong enough to administer a decisive blow, but in which the fury of both sides ended by turning a beautiful kingdom into what Pasquier called the "Corpse of France."

4. CATHERINE AND COLIGNY: ST. BARTHOLOMEW

THE Wars of Religion, like a tragedy on the stage, consist of three main acts, during each of which some outstanding personality played the leading part. The drama was eventually terminated by Henri IV, when France, exhausted and sick of so much bloodshed, became once more accessible to reason. The central and culminating act was dominated by Henri III, a vacillating prince, torn this way and that, inspired by sombre passion and ungoverned instinct. The principal character of the first act was Catherine dei Medici, whose portraits declare the enigma of her personality. Balzac describes the "secretive, unhealthy face nestling in its white ruff, with forehead bulging beneath the tip of a gloomy veil, and large round eyes, dark and prominent—the mask of an abbess, withdrawn and emaciated, wary and inquisitive." Although she was alert and energetic, fond of riding, feasts and buffoonery, there was another side of her nature in harmony with the widow's weeds she never laid aside: like her fellow countryman Machiavelli, she was obsessed with a sombre passion for intrigue and lacked the slightest trace of moral principles. Nor was this true only in the realm of politics. We know for what purposes she employed the charming bevy of her maids of honour; these poor little pawns on the queen's chessboard were trained to servile obedience by every possible means, including the roughest chastisement, which Her Majesty administered in person. From the religious standpoint she practised a kind of indifference, superior alike to dogma and to jurisdiction. Thus she wrote a most curious letter to Pope Pius IV, suggesting that he reduce religion to a few elementary precepts (those of the Decalogue), which would enable all men to consider themselves Christians adhering to a single faith. In dealing with opposite factions such a woman would certainly never indulge a spirit of religious fanaticism; her sole ambition would be to command and to defend by every means at her disposal the throne entrusted to her care. She would pursue that policy not only with her accustomed cynicism, but also with natural dignity, practical intelligence and undeniable ability.

The intention of Catherine dei Medici was certainly to maintain the royal prestige above internal disorders, and she managed to do so for about ten years. When death rid her, almost at a single stroke, of Antoine de Bourbon, Francois de Guise and Maréchal de Saint-André, she imposed the first "religious peace," the Edict of Amboise (March 1563), which gave France four years of peace; and she took advantage of this lull to mount an expedition which recovered Le Havre from the English. Then, during the years 1564 and 1565, by way of divertlng the French in accordance with the advice of François I, she staged a slow and magnificent journey through the provinces in order to show her people young Charles IX, who, having attained his thirteenth year, had just been declared of age.

This truce, however, was most precarious. Condé and Coligny suspected the good faith of the Queen-Mother; they feared that Pope Pius V was urging her to adopt repressive measures, and that Philip II had made her certain promises with the same end in view. Though defeated at Dreux, the Protestants by no means considered themselves crushed. As for Catherine, she seemed to dread a decisive Catholic victory, which would have delivered her into the hands of the Catholic reformers. At all events she granted the heretics freedom of worship in the suburbs of such towns as were subject to the jurisdiction of a bailiff or were the residences of those having a right to administer justice within the limits of their estates; and this privilege was later extended to all places (Paris alone excepted) where Protestants delivered sermons in public. Montluc, aware of her purpose, exclaimed in fury: "We win by force of arms, but the Protestants win with their damned writings!"

Hostilities were resumed in 1567 and 1568; Montmorency was killed in battle at Saint-Denis while trying to deliver Paris from blockade by Condé. The Calvinists were beaten at Jarnac and Montcour, but Coligny stood firm and regained the advantage. This alternation of success was so favourable to the queen's interests that she could not but encourage it. Officially she was angered beyond measure by an insolent attempt of the Huguenots to kidnap the king at Monceaux; but she was at the same time negotiating a marriage between her daughter Marguerite de Valois and young King Henri of Navarre, who had become leader of the Calvinist party at the age of fifteen.

At this period also the star of Gaspard de Coligny (1517–1572) was in the ascendant. "He was looked upon," says Brantôme, "as a distinguished nobleman, a wise, mature and upright man, a shrewd politician, a bold critic, a sound judge of opportunity, loving honour and virtue." It was with regret and, as we have seen, after much hesitation that he agreed to take part in civil war, and he often used to tell his companions "that there was nothing on earth he detested so much." He was a handsome man of serious aspect, with bright blue eyes and face that betokened energy. As good a Frenchman as he was a fervent Protestant, he desired above all things the prosperity of his country. "It is indeed true," says Brantôme again, "that he was very ambitious on behalf of his king, yearning and striving to make him great."

Summoned to court by Charles IX in 1571, Admiral Coligny at once became an influential member of the Royal Council, and promised the young monarch great things. He considered it a matter of vital importance to renew the traditional anti-Spanish policy and to form a grand alliance with England, the Lutheran princes of Germany, the Tuscan Medicis, the Swiss cantons and the Turks. The Low Countries had just rebelled; it was time "to throw war from within to without"; Huguenot volunteers under La Noüe were even then helping Louis of Nassau to occupy Mons and

Valenciennes. The Huguenot nobility, which had assembled in Paris for the wedding of Henri de Navarre (August 18, 1572), seemed suddenly to have the upper hand.

Catherine was not at all pleased. She would not agree to be supplanted in the guardianship of her son. She was also aware of the difficulties confronting the proposed foreign alliance. Elizabeth was not disposed to commit herself; the Lutheran princes felt no sympathy for the Dutch Calvinists; the Turks had recently been overwhelmed at Lepanto; and an army of reinforcements under Genlis had been annihilated before reaching Mons. The admiral's cold and haughty airs at length exasperated the queen. She accordingly laid her plans in conjunction with François de Guise's son Henri (1550–1588), a good-looking lad of twenty-one, strongly ambitious and ruthlessly enterprising, who saw in an ultra-Catholic policy the supreme opportunity of his career. Philip II likewise encouraged her schemes. And so, on August 22, four days after the royal wedding, a man named Maurevert, who belonged to the Guise faction, hid himself in a house at the corner of the Rue des Fossés-Saint-Germain and the Rue des Poulies, and fired on Coligny as he came out of the Louvre. One of the admiral's fingers was severed, another shot ripped open his left arm; but he was still alive, and he knew who had armed the assassin.

Charles IX was beside himself with rage: "Am I never to have a moment's peace? Trouble, trouble, always fresh trouble!" He called on the wounded man and assured him he would avenge the crime "in a frightful manner." That evening Catherine pestered him, as she well knew how, to tell her what the admiral had said to him in secret. Charles was then twenty-two years old, but in the presence of his mother he was still a little boy. Coligny, he said, had advised him to rule by himself. Catherine panicked. Surely all these Huguenot nobles who had come to Paris for the wedding were preparing to get rid of her; Coligny would undoubtedly sway the feeble mind of her child; the first shot had misfired, she would have to begin again and cut down all the leaders of the Reformation. Such was the advice given her by a number of persons, among them perhaps the Spanish ambassador and certainly the young firebrand Guise. This appalling crime, undoubtedly the

214 most terrible ever perpetrated in the name of Faith, would prove after all to be nothing but the desperate expedient of a great ambition brought to bay.

On the evening of the August 23, Catherine visited her son and spent two hours representing to him the peril of his crown, the danger threatening his brothers, the hand of England secretly at work in the affairs of France. Motherly, provocative and imperious by turns, she inflamed the young man's sickly sensibility to such an extent that he completely lost his head. One after another the most trusted of his counsellors threw their weight into the balance: Birague, the Italian Gonzaga, Due de Nevers, Maréchal Tavannes and the Chevalier d'Angoulême—all insisted that France was again on the threshold of civil war. Then, in a moment of blind fury bordering upon insanity, he gave the celebrated order: "Kill the lot! Not one must live to reproach me." Plans for the massacre were settled at dead of night. Guise took charge. It was decided that only Condé and Navarre would be granted their lives, because of the royal blood in their veins. Operations were to begin at dawn on August 24, conducted by the city militia and the Swiss Guard. At the last moment the royal family, seized with dread, tried to suspend the whole business; but it was too late: the tocsin was already sounding from Saint-Germain-l'Auxerrois. Dawn was breaking over Paris, the dawn of a heinous day: it was the feast of St. Bartholomew, apostle and martyr.

Henri de Guise went straight to Coligny's residence, where the door was forced and the guards jostled aside. The admiral, awakened by the noise, appeared in his dressing-gown. A Czech mercenary, one John Yanowitz called Besme, demanded: "Are you the admiral?" "I am," he replied, then added: "Would to God I had been killed by a man instead of a menial." He was struck in the stomach and then stabbed, but he continued to breathe. Down in the street Guise was shouting at the assassins to make haste, and they threw the dying man from a window. Henri recognized him, spurned him with his foot and went off without another word. The head of the Grand Admiral of France was cut off for dispatch to Rome; his body was carried to the gallows at Montfaucon like that of a condemned criminal. There followed an orgy of murder, a contagion, as it were, of blood. It had been intended that only the leaders should be killed, but there were in fact more than two thousand victims. The populace awoke and joined in the game: innumerable Protestants were dragged from their beds and butchered or drowned by frenzied termagants and half-wits. There was slaughter in the corridors of the Louvre, and even in the young Queen of Navarre's bedchamber, where her squire, the Vicomte de Léron, was discovered hiding under the bed. Condé and Navarre, summoned to the king's presence, were offered "Mass, death or the Bastille." They abjured. On the afternoon of the twenty-fourth, Charles IX gave instructions that the carnage—and the looting, which was also in full swing—must cease. But his order went unheeded, and it was not until the twenty-seventh that the besotted people quietened down. In the provinces, Meaux, Orleans, Rouen, Troyes, Toulouse and Lyons imitated Paris; but the Catholic governors of Dauphine, Burgundy and Auvergne managed to prevent a repetition of such scenes within their territories. It is not known exactly how many victims there were in the whole of France; estimates vary between eight and thirty thousand. Among these were the great humanist Ramus and the musician Goudimel. Michel de l'Hôpital, who lay sick at Vignay, was forgotten, but he died of grief a few months later. Charles IX, alternately frozen with horror and drunk with blood, never forgot those abominations for which he had been responsible; they proved too much for his mental equilibrium.

International repercussions were considerable. "What a crushing blow for us!" exclaimed William the Silent, leader of the rebels in the Netherlands. As for Philip II, the Massacre of St. Bartholomew was one of the great joys of his life. What was the Pope's attitude? It has been severely criticized, but always on a superficial basis. St. Pius V had certainly urged Catherine for a long time to "the complete extermination of heretics," as appears from a letter of 1569. What he desired, however, was open warfare, not collective butchery. His successor, Gregory XIII, shared his views, and when he heard that the French Court was planning the assassination of Coligny and Condé he expressed his disapproval in no uncertain terms. He was likewise furiously indignant when he learned that Cardinal de Lorraine had entered the Vatican in company with Maurevert, who had fired on the admiral. "The man's a murderer," he cried. The Papacy therefore bore no responsibility whatever, directly or indirectly, for the Massacre of St. Bartholomew. But Gregory XIII, deceived by tendentious reports reaching him from Paris, thought that the news referred to some great battle lately won, and this misunderstanding caused him to exclaim that the information was "more welcome than fifty victories of Lepanto"—an exaggeration in true southern style. He then proceeded to have a commemorative medal struck, and directed Vasari to immortalize this latest triumph of the Church on the walls of the Sacred Palace.[18]

At home the Massacre of St. Bartholomew resulted in a very grave turn of events, for the French reform underwent yet another transformation. It had been, as Leonard aptly remarks, "an opinion, then a Church, then a political party in arms"; now it became in Michelet's phrase, "a Protestant republic," a counter-state. When the nobility adopted it they were thinking almost exclusively of their religious liberties; many were now dead, and five hundred and twenty-seven of them had abjured, together with Condé and Henri de Navarre. The terrified middle class fled to Geneva or London. But in the market towns and countryside the cause was taken up anew by the common people, headed by the small landowners of Béarn, Languedoc and Rouergue. With Nîmes, Montauban, Sancerre and La Rochelle as its key points, the "Protestant Republic" took shape, assisted in large measure by the old communal traditions of the South. In December 1574 an Assembly at Millau drafted the constitution for this scattered and fluctuating State; its articles provided for a military structure, the creation of elective consuls and the levying of troops. The Calvinist democracy poured out a stream of tracts and lampoons denouncing the rule of the assassins. While one of these pamphlets ridiculed the *Life, Actions and Misdeeds of Catherine dei Medici*, Theodore Beza's *Rights of Magistrates over their Subjects*, Hotman's *Franco-Gallia* and the anonymous *Vindiciae contra*

18. Gregory has been bitterly censured for this mistake. See Vacandard, "Les Papes et la Saint-Barthélemy," in *Études de critique et d'histoire religieuse*, vol. 1, p. 221; K. Remier, "Les Événements de Rome et la préméditation du Massacre," in *Rome au XVI Siècle* (1913), p. 529.

Tyrranos[19] were laying the juridical bases of an insurrection, developing (a century in advance of their time) the theory of Social Contract, and demanding convocation of the Estates-General to appoint a new king. Montluc says that this propaganda spread throughout France, that the Calvinist peasantry was everywhere proclaiming themselves, the sovereign people, to be the rightful rulers of France. The situation which Catherine had foolishly hoped to improve by means of an abominable massacre had greatly deteriorated.

Charles IX was dying, ravaged with tuberculosis, worn out with the pleasures of love, awakened by hideous nightmares in which he beheld his former friends covered with blood and bitterly reproaching him. He rendered up his soul on May 30, 1574, weighing with terror the consequences of his act, the curse called down upon his kingdom by the blood which he had shed, the curse of which Agrippa d'Aubigné would one day write:

> Cités ivres de sang et de sang altérés,
> Vous sentirez, de Dieu l' épouvantable main.
> Vos terres seront fer et votre ciel d'airain...

5. HENRI III AND THE HOLY LEAGUE

WHEN he learned of his brother's death, Catherine's third and favourite son Henri, whom she had made King of Poland, left Cracow in secret and hurried to occupy the throne of France. He was twenty-three years old, "a tall, thin and slightly stooping figure, who looked down at one without affectation, with a majestic grace and at the same time much ease and much reserve. Though his intelligence was of a high order, he suffered from periodical failures of will-power, which made him seem indifferent to public affairs, whereas in fact he had them much at heart. Like Charles VII, he sometimes lacked firmness until the moment when he needed it for everyone's sake. He was as frivolous in the small things of life as he was grave in matters of state, and his

19. Attributed to Duplessis-Mornay or Languet.

 extravagance, his whims and fads, which were sometimes carried to absurd lengths, would disconcert and then exasperate men whose good opinion was often kept alive by nothing else but his talents as an orator and statesman."[20] He was thus a highly complex personality, passing from the most scandalous masquerades to the most exaggerated forms of devotion,[21] surrounding himself with undesirable favourites, yet marrying for love and adoring his wife. Indeed he was the first king of France to receive from his subjects the official style of "Majesty," and he fully deserved it. But was he equal to the terrible responsibilities which circumstances placed upon his shoulders?

The reign of Henri III (1574–1589) was the period of France's worst ordeal, fifteen dreadful years of unrelenting civil war and large-scale foreign intervention. Three factions henceforth divided the kingdom: (1) The Protestants, organized as the Calvinist Union, a "State within the State" as Richelieu later described it. (2) The violent Catholic group, exalted by what they regarded as their victory and resolved to impose their ideas by every possible means. (3) A third party, for which it was not difficult to discover antecedents, if only in the ideas of Michel de l'Hôpital,[22] but which became an actuality through force of circumstances, detestation of bloodshed and instinctive common sense. The members of this last association were known as "politicals" or "malcontents," two words that indicated clearly both their feelings and their programme. Governors who had refused to authorize the massacres, Catholics horrified by so much bloodshed, moderate Huguenots who saw that in the long run war would be fatal to their doctrines, and recent converts—all desired national reconciliation and peaceful tolerance. Their leaders were Henri Montmorency, Governor Damville of Languedoc and François, Duc d'Alençon.[23]

---

20. Due de Mirepoix, *Guerres de Religion.*
21. On one occasion, at Lyons, he took part in a procession stripped to the waist and taking the discipline.
22. For example, "Gentleness will do more good than violence."
23. D'Alençon's connection with the party was unfortunate. Youngest brother of the king, dissatisfied with his lot and ready for anything, he was a mischief-maker whose ambition was not always of service to this noble cause.

Very soon after that tragic night in August 1572, the Protestants had restored their fortunes, thanks to the new party and to the indomitable resistance of La Rochelle and Sancerre. Henri III, hoping to soothe everyone and urged thereto by Catherine dei Medici, granted the Peace of Beaulieu (May 1576). The reformed worship was permitted everywhere, except at Paris; eight strongholds were conceded as the regular arsenals of a faction that could henceforward regard itself as legally mobilized for war; free access was allowed to all the frontiers; while in the Parliaments mixed tribunals were created to try cases in which Protestants were involved. The Crown was thus recognizing "a State within the State." 219

Now those Catholics who had chosen the way of violence could not agree to a measure which appeared as an act of surrender by the king, and their retaliation took shape in an organization intended to oppose the Protestant union. Armed confederations had come into being here and there during the first years of the "troubles"; but on the morrow of the Peace of Beaulieu, when Condé was appointed governor of Picardy, and Navarre governor of Guienne, the cry went up of "Treason!" At Péronne, d'Humières called upon the Catholics to form "a holy Christian union" which should prevent Condé taking possession of his province, and "restore the holy service of God and obedience to His Majesty the King." Thus was born the League. The same course was followed in Languedoc, Champagne, Nivernais and Burgundy. Paris, ardently attached to Roman orthodoxy and responsible for the extent of the massacres, responded to the fanatical appeal of monks and parish priests who went about stirring up the mob. In this way there arose a second "State within the State," led by a man of implacable audacity, Henri de Guise, nicknamed *Le Balafré* (the Scarred) because of a wound lately received at the battle of Dormans. The party's aims, hastily set out by the Jesuits, were comprised in four words: "Full reinstatement of Catholicism." Loyalty to the king was earnestly proclaimed; but there was also talk of summoning the States-General in the event of the sovereign failing to carry out the suggested programme. To make assurance doubly sure Guise had the genealogists prepare a family tree showing his descent from Charlemagne! Meanwhile Philip II's emissaries were promising the League subsidies and reinforcements.

220 The position of Henri III was thus extremely serious. Was he fully aware of the fact? History has discarded the traditional picture of a painted puppet, interested only in lapdogs and mummery. The king was far from a non-entity; he was indeed the first of the Capetians who conceived the idea of a general code[24] to reorganize the French economy by bringing all trades within the guild system. But in those critical days the realm of the fleurs-de-lis needed at its head someone very different from this scion of an ancient and doomed race.

Confronted with the League, Henri could think of nothing better to do than to declare himself its leader and, after another passage of arms, to issue the Edict of Poitiers (October 1577) restricting the benefits conferred upon the Huguenots in the previous year. Having made these concessions he ordered the League to dissolve, imagining rather naively that the two sides would thus be rendered powerless. He was sincerely anxious to restore his country to peace and order, as well as to revive the prestige of his crown; and it was at this time that he instituted the Order of the Holy Ghost, whose members would swear obedience to himself. In the domain of foreign politics he played a subtle game, allowing his young brother Francois to intervene in the Low Countries against Spain, but not preventing many others of his nobles from associating their names with the grand project of a crusade against Elizabeth of England, which a group of enthusiastic Jesuits was attempting to organize. This seesaw policy, however, was doomed to failure. Among the Leaguers, Henri de Guise would never willingly step down among the rank and file; nor had the Protestants any intention of renouncing the advantages they already enjoyed, particularly as the Calvinist Union now possessed a first-class military leader in the person of Henri de Navarre who had returned to heresy and fled from Paris.

A new and indecisive period of hostilities seemed to promise some kind of understanding when the question of succession once again fanned the embers into flame. Henri III had no children, and appeared to be impotent. His heir, the turbulent François, died on June 19, 1584, after a tubercular

24. The three hundred sixty articles of the Grand Ordinance of Blois.

hemorrhage, and the right of succession passed by virtue of the Salic Law to Henri de Bourbon, "King of Navarre," who was accordingly recognized by Henri III. Indignation ran high among the Catholics: was it possible, they asked, that a traitorous renegade should occupy the throne of St. Louis? It was an alarming situation, which the heir apparent took care not to exploit for the time being. Remaining at Nérac, where he competed with his wife "Queen Margot" in gallant escapades, he had the good sense, says d'Aubigné, "to hide behind himself." But his mere existence was enough to exasperate the feelings of others.

The League reappeared spontaneously and in several parts of the kingdom, even before the three Guises (Henri le Balafré, the cardinal and Charles, Duc de Mayenne) had returned to the scene. A great majority of those Catholics who had defended their faith for so many years thought it inconceivable that a Huguenot should become King of France. There was, of course, the Salic Law, but above it there was this more fundamental law: "Jesus Christ, King of France, with His lieutenant there administering justice, and always a Christian." Such was the spontaneous reaction of the people, who instinctively upheld this principle before all political interests. At Paris the League's propaganda won over the middle class, the Parliament, the legal fraternity, the butchers' guild and the small tradesmen. Châlons-sur-Marne, Dijon, Mâcon and other places were secured by various members of the nobility in preparation for the coming struggle. Henri de Guise sent word to Philip II, who promised a monthly subsidy of fifty thousand crowns. An idea began to take shape that in the event of the king's death the Catholics would recognize as sovereign the aged Cardinal de Bourbon, uncle of Henri de Navarre; and Pope Sixtus V signed a Bull declaring the Béarnais incapable of succeeding to the throne of France. Civil war was impending, and would be more savagely contested than ever before. The North, the East, the West and nearly all the large cities took arms against "those who were trying to subvert the Catholic religion and the State." Cardinal de Lorraine himself called upon the king to summon the States-General.

Henri III was in a fix. The Duc d'Épernon undertook a fruitless mission to beg Henri de Navarre to return to the bosom of the Church; the heir apparent, as usual, would give no more than vague promises and assurances of loyalty. The Catholic protest now became an ultimatum. In July 1585 the king allowed his mother to sign the Treaty of Nemours: Protestant worship was forbidden, its adherents were commanded to abjure within six months under pain of exile and Navarre lost his right to the crown. The League had triumphed. This was the signal for what is usually called "the eighth War of Religion," the longest[25] and the most violent. Foreign intervention became more and more active, so that the unity of France had never been in such peril since the days of the Armagnacs and Burgundians.

The popularity of Henri de Guise steadily increased. "France," wrote a contemporary, "is crazy about that man; 'in love with him' would be an understatement." While Henri de Navarre, who controlled the south-west, was crushing the Duc de Joyeuse (one of the king's favourites) at Coutras, Guise won two small engagements in Champagne, which clever propaganda represented as major victories achieved by the "new Maccabeus." The League gradually enlarged its authority to include three-quarters of the kingdom. It drew up a programme intended to link the reformed French clergy with Rome, to restore to the nobility and towns their privileges and immunities, and to support Philip II's great expedition against England. Henri III found himself completely outstripped by events. Through Montaigne he kept in contact with Navarre. It was Guise whom he mistrusted most, and when the latter sent word that he was on his way to Paris, the king forbade him to enter the city. Guise, however, ignored the royal interdiction and was rapturously acclaimed. Was he going to depose his sovereign? Rumour said as much, and it was also whispered that Henri III, who had just brought troops into the capital, was preparing to arrest and perhaps to assassinate his rival. On May 12, 1588, the "Day of Barricades," there was a sudden outbreak of rioting, during which sixty of the king's soldiers were killed; and only the authority of Guise was capable of ending it.

Henri III was furious, and fled to Chartres. There he played a redoubtable game with masterly cunning. He pretended to grant his fortunate rival

25. It lasted for eight years.

everything required. Guise was appointed lieutenant-general of the realm. In the States-General, which met at Blois in October 1588, he showed himself conciliatory towards the demands of the League and even went beyond them. Publish the decrees of the Council of Trent? Certainly. Include the banishment of heretics among the fundamental laws? With pleasure. He was not unaware, however, that the young fools of Guise's *entourage*, particularly his sister Catherine, Duchesse de Montpensier, were in the habit of showing their visitors the scissors they would use to tonsure the king as if he were some common Merovingian idler; and he secretly prepared to take revenge.

On Saturday, December 23, two days before Christmas, the Duke was summoned to His Majesty's apartment. Eight noblemen were there, all staunch supporters of the king. Guise entered and bowed. The eight stood up as if to show their respect—then set to work. Stabbed in front and from behind, his loins pierced by their swords, Guise called in vain for help. Being a man of unusual strength, he was able, on the very threshold of death, to drag the whole gang of assassins as far as the royal bed, where he collapsed. Next day Cardinal de Lorraine was murdered and Cardinal de Bourbon thrown into prison.

"Now I'm king!" cried Henri III. "I'm determined no longer to tolerate insult or injury."

Events followed with pitiless logic. Paris revolted and set up a General Council to co-ordinate Catholic action; almost every city hurried to join the League; the Duc de Mayenne was appointed "Lieutenant-General of the State and Crown of France"; the king and Henri de Navarre were reconciled; and the Pope summoned Henri III to Rome, to answer for the murder of Cardinal de Lorraine. The aged Catherine had died, broken-hearted, in January. Henri III, though denounced as "perjurer, abettor of heresy and sacrilegious assassin," faced the storm with a courage remarkable in one so effeminate. Allied with the Protestants of Navarre, he went and besieged his capital with thirty thousand men, firmly resolved to have nothing more to do with the League.

But one dagger attracts another. Paris under blockade was in the grip of wild excitement. Furious sermons, pamphlets and pictures exhibited in the streets as well as in the churches raised public imagination to white heat. Many good people sincerely believed that both Henri III and Henri de Navarre, if victorious, would employ the same violent methods as Elizabeth of England in dealing with her Catholic subjects. The idea of necessary regicide came to dominate men's minds. A young Jacobin friar aged twenty-two, one Jacques Clément, an uncouth fellow of peasant stock and low intelligence, decided to make himself the instrument of divine justice. Having prayed, fasted and, as he said, been encouraged by mystical visions, he entered the royal camp at Saint-Cloud on August 1, 1589, obtained audience of Henri III on pretext of having secrets to deliver, and forthwith plunged a large kitchen knife into his belly. Then, with arms crossed, he waited to be cut down by the guards. Before dying the king had time to bless his successor, who had ridden at full speed from Meudon.

6. HENRI IV THE PEACEMAKER

A new reign was beginning, destined to be one of the most glorious in French history (1589–1610); but it was beginning amid the worst possible confusion. D'Aubigné, an eye-witness, has left us an account of the agitation reigning at Saint-Cloud, where the late king's body lay in state, watched by two friars of the Order of Minims. Great lords clapped on their hats, or flung them to ground exclaiming angrily: "Better a thousand deaths than a Huguenot king." The princes and high officers of State recognized Henri de Navarre as King of France, but he could not be unaware of the difficulties confronting him. On the other hand he was never one to despair.

Henri IV: no king of France has bequeathed to the national conscience a memory of greater friendliness and forbearance. Nevertheless he had many defects: he was "a creature of foreign race, very firm as a soldier, but in all else changeable as water"; an inconstant lover, an unfaithful friend; a braggart and more prodigal of compliments than of gold; quick to forget favours no less than injuries. Though not, as Shakespeare says, "lying water," he was the very opposite of a reliable man. All the same, those virtues which he did possess were solid: a profound understanding of men and events, patience and courage, the rare gift of being able to choose the right man for the right place, and inexhaustible common sense. Opposed to stern measures, and giving his orders the appearance of requests, he desired, says Pasquier, "in the handling of affairs of State to be trusted absolutely." This whole complex web of merit and demerit, together with his straightforward and familiar ways, his slightly contemptuous good nature, his easy benevolence, his bravery, his confidence in himself and in his star, made him the kind of hero in whom the French delight. None could resist his ingratiating manners, his keen glance, his caressing voice, his tears, his witticisms, or his laughter. All these qualities were so many trump cards in his hand, and he knew how to play them.

Henri took in the situation at a glance. The League held Paris, the larger towns and some of the provinces. Cardinal de Bourbon, who had lain in prison since the murder of Guise, had been proclaimed king as Charles X by the Duc de Mayenne. The Protestants were urging the new monarch not to exchange their proven loyalty for the inconstant backing of sworn enemies. The "politicals" were reminding him that, as head of a confessional minority, he could not rule over a people the majority of whom were still attached to the Roman Church. Henri IV, uplifted by the conviction of his legitimacy, "pale with anger and fear," as d'Aubigné relates, protested against "the violence with which he was assailed at the moment of his accession... with which he was bidden to strip his heart and soul upon entering the regal state." Nevertheless, albeit he had declared, with his invaluable gift for striking phrases, that he had on his side "all those among the Catholics who loved France and honour" and that "he was king of the brave and would not be abandoned except by cowards," he understood that he must return to the faith of his ancestors if he wished to reign.

On August 4, he announced that he would uphold "the Catholic, Apostolic and Roman religion in all its fullness, without any innovation or change," and that "he was ready and desired nothing more than to be instructed in the said religion by a good, lawful and free general council of the nation." He was not the sceptic that some of his more intemperate remarks might lead us to suppose; but recent history and his experience as a leader had shown him a sufficient intermingling of temporal and religious loyalties to convince him that God knows His own beneath ritual and even doctrinal differences, so that salvation is to be had in either confession. Moreover he possessed so lofty a notion of monarchy, so keen a sense of France's needs, that he would not hesitate to sacrifice his own scruples.

For the moment, however, since half the troops investing Paris had deserted, the only solution was to withdraw into Normandy and thus maintain contact with England. Mayenne followed in pursuit, but was defeated in two bitter engagements. The first of these (September 1589) took place at Arques, near Dieppe; the second (March 1590) at Ivry, near Evreux, where, with his tremendous charges—the *panache blanc* of Ivry—Henry IV won his unshakable reputation as a dauntless and irresistible commander. But, while making his provisional capital at Tours, the cunning Béarnais knew well that so long as his present circumstances continued a change of faith would be barren of results, appearing simply as a desperate maneuver. Patiently therefore he laid plans for his attack.

It was because the question of Henri's personal religion was far less important than the extreme danger of France that the lawful king, awaited by the nation and helped by a good sense that taught him the necessary steps, triumphed over the worst difficulties. Spain hoped to attract France into her orbit. Philip II therefore, abandoning the reconquest of the northern Low Countries, ordered his best general, Alessandro Farnese, to relieve Paris, which had lain under siege since the battle of Ivry, and to throw a garrison into the city; and, since the Catholic candidate "Charles X" was at the point of death, he tried to have his daughter Isabella Clara Eugenia[26] recognized as Queen of France. In promising dismemberment of the kingdom he was acting in concert with other pretenders. Among these was Charles Emmanuel, Duke of Savoy, a nephew of Henri III, who took possession of Aix and Marseilles; Charles III, Duke of Lorraine, son-in-law of Henri II, who laid claim to the eastern districts; and the Duc de Mercoeur, a cadet of the house of Lorraine, who roused Brittany and placed Spanish garrisons on

---

26. She was granddaughter of Henri II through her mother, Elizabeth de Valois.

the northern coast of the peninsula. Surely the nation would react to these treasonable proceedings.

The thirty thousand fanatics who organized armed processions in Paris, and supported the terrorist government of the representatives of the "sixteen quarters," offered no resistance; but the middle class and particularly the better members of the Parliament, being more or less Gallican, objected to the thunderbolts launched by the Holy See against a man whom the Salic Law had brought to the throne of France, and wished for an understanding with the Béarnais. As the insurrectionary committee at Paris hanged the first president and some counsellors of the Parliament, Mayenne was obliged to execute four members of the municipality which sided with the League. But all this led nowhere.

Henri IV, "a king without a crown, a general without money, a husband without a wife," then understood that it was wrong to disappoint the secret hopes of those who awaited him. The League held its States-General at the beginning of 1593, and the presence of the Duke of Feria, ambassador extraordinary of Philip II, showed that the choice of Isabella would undoubtedly be proposed. Henri forthwith suggested a conference of reconciliation, and delegates met at Suresnes on May 5. Renaud de Beaune, Archbishop of Bourges, supported the principle of monarchical legitimacy, to which Pierre d'Espinac opposed the necessity of a Catholic sovereign. Then, two weeks later, Beaune announced that the king would embrace Catholicism.

Abundant contemporary evidence reveals the psychology of Henri IV in those decisive hours. Events were crowding upon him. He would have preferred to make himself master of Paris before changing his religion, but there was no hope of that; any further delay would be disastrous. There was no mincing of words by politicians on either side. "Take your choice," said the Marquis d'O, a Catholic; "either satisfy your Gascon prophets by returning to evil ways and leaving us to do the best we can to protect ourselves, or else conquer the League, which fears from you nothing so much as your conversion...and thereby become within a month absolute King of France, gaining more in an hour at Mass than you will do by twenty victories in the field or twenty years of labour and peril."

228 His friend Rosny, afterwards Due de Sully, re-echoes much the same feeling on the Huguenot side:

> You will never obtain complete possession and peaceful enjoyment of your kingdom except in one of two ways. The first of these is force of arms, which will necessitate the use of strong decisions, severity, harshness and violence—all of which are contrary to your temperament and inclination. It will also necessitate your having to endure countless difficulties, fatigues, pains, vexations, dangers and toils; you will have to be continually in the saddle, wearing helmet and breast-plate, grasping pistol and sword. Even worse, you will have to bid farewell to repose, pleasures, pastimes, love-making, mistresses, games, dogs, birds and buildings; for you will escape from such troubles only at the price of many towns captured, many battles fought, signal victories won and much shedding of blood. The second way is to fall in with the wishes of the majority of your subjects as regards religion. If you do that, you will not meet with so much embarrassment, so many anxieties and hazards in *this* world. I don't know so much about the next.... You will not expect me as a Protestant to advise you to hear Mass; but I will go so far as to say that by doing so you will employ the quickest and easiest means of over-throwing every monopoly and of bringing all malicious designs to nothing....

The famous sally, "Paris is worth a Mass," is no doubt apocryphal; but it does express one of the causes of Henri's inevitable choice. Nevertheless he looked deeper into the political setting. Thus, when Pastor La Faye endeavoured to hold him back, he appealed to the national interest. "If I followed your advice," he answered, "there would soon be neither king nor kingdom in France." In order to sway the man as distinct from the politician, Gabrielle d'Estrées added her entreaties. Was she then, as the irreconcilable d'Aubigné maintains, "the final instrument which did more than all the rest"? The intransigent Catholics scoffed at her behaviour. She owed them a grudge. "When the hope of attaining royal status by matrimony was strengthened in the mind of this lady," says the Calvinist historian, "and when she was made to understand that all the ministers together could not dissolve the first marriage and that only the Pope was able to strike such a blow, she was strongly encouraged by those who boast of having changed their minds after a careful scrutiny of the earlier view; and thereafter she took advantage of her great beauty and every convenient hour of the day and night to discuss the benefits of a change." Besides, had not Henri been promising for the last four years to receive instruction? Surrounded by Huguenot ministers, who were unwilling to let him go and whom he overwhelmed with fine promises, as well as by prelates who vowed their skillful and meritorious services, he had come to the conclusion that "the difference between the two religions was not great, except for the animosity of their preachers, and that one day his authority would be able to resolve it."

He therefore convoked a meeting of some twenty bishops, theologians and parish priests at Mantes. Then, on July 23, at Saint-Denis, he heard "an account of all the main controversial topics of the age." This conference lasted five hours, and Henri listened attentively. When the subject of Purgatory was raised he could not help interrupting: "Now there the Church has a splendid source of income!" But when they came to discuss the reality of Christ's presence in the Eucharist he assured them: "I have no doubt of it, for I have always believed as much." The account of his conversion which he gave to the first presidents of the Parliaments of Paris and Rouen was so tactfully worded as to reconcile his own goodwill with reasons of State and the operation of Divine Grace. "He assured us," notes Claude Groulart of Rouen, "that ever since God called him to the crown his whole desire had been to seek the means of his salvation, which he valued above all worldly goods, and had prayed the Divine Majesty to open the road for him, but especially during the last few days since he came to realize that his Catholic subjects desired it; that he had put himself into the hands of some theologians, and had derived so much profit from conferring with them that he had been induced and had at length determined to profess the Catholic religion; and that although he had in his early years been brought up in the contrary profession and confirmed therein, he was nevertheless beginning, by the grace of the Holy Spirit, to appreciate the arguments which had been urged upon him."

He was not, however, aware of the consequences of his act. While foreseeing the loss of some support, he did not weigh the corresponding advantages; and it is in the light of this ignorance that we must understand the well-authenticated words scribbled in a note to Gabrielle d'Estrées: "I shall make the perilous leap on Sunday." On July 25, 1593, an enormous crowd, inquisitive but well behaved, filled Saint-Denis. Henri IV entered the famous abbey, where the Archbishop of Bourges awaited him at the bottom of the nave. "Who are you?" "I am the king." "What do you ask?" "I ask to be received into the bosom of the Catholic, Apostolic and Roman Church." "Do you wish it?" "Yes, I wish and desire it." He read his profession of faith, signed and returned it to the archbishop, and received absolution. Then he disappeared behind the altar to make his confession while the *Te Deum* pealed forth; after which he heard Mass and communicated.

Military operations were suspended for three months. The good folk of Paris would flock together on the look-out for His Majesty, whom they wildly acclaimed. He was winning men's hearts. A pamphlet had been circulating clandestinely since the beginning of spring; it was the work of a group of poets and parliamentarians, and had appeared first at Tours under the title *Menippean Satire.* By ridiculing the League States, Mayenne, the intransigent monks, the legate and the Spanish ambassador, it hastened the dissolution of the League. Since Rheims was held by a friend of the Guises, Henri IV had himself crowned at Chartres on February 27, 1594; he also touched for the king's evil, for he was now monarch by holy unction. He was able to enter Paris on March 22, and to watch, from a house near the Porte Saint-Denis, the departure of the Spanish troops. Pope Clement VIII, disillusioned by the poor results of Philip II's diplomacy, advised also by several enlightened Jesuits and by his confessor St. Philip Neri, who threatened to refuse him absolution unless he recognized Henri, showed himself more tractable. On September 17, 1595, after the Abbé d'Ossat and Bishop du Perron of Evreux had acknowledged on behalf of their sovereign the invalidity of the absolution at Saint-Denis and had promised publication of the Tridentine decrees in France, he granted the official pardon of the Church.

Henri IV had won the day, but this did not mean that he had overcome every trace of malice, which was never fully disarmed. Shortly before his conversion a soldier of the League, at the instigation of two Jesuits, had formed a plan to assassinate him, but had been caught and broken on the wheel. A few days after the ceremony at Saint-Denis, one Chatel, a pupil of the same Jesuits, also tried to kill him, but only cut his lip. Chatel was quartered, one of the Fathers was hanged and the Society was expelled from France. The king of tolerance was destined to live beneath the constant threat of murderers lurking in the shadows, even to the day of Ravaillac's knife.

Meanwhile the situation was completely reversed. Henri was now the lawful sovereign, and he profited by the invaluable support of those who longed for an end to this era of misery and slaughter, the support of the whole French people who were prepared to love him from the moment of his reconciliation with the Church. It must not be imagined, on the other hand, that all difficulties were annulled by a single act. The League had been so powerful, Spain had been so deeply involved, and the king was so short of military and financial resources, that it was impossible to hope for the immediate and undisputed submission and pacification of the country. Burgundy under Mayenne, Picardy under the Duc d'Aumale and Brittany under Mercoeur—all stood as bastions of resistance. But Henri was equal to the situation. By means of a loud and commanding voice offset by a skillful mask of affability, by distribution of offices and confirmation of privileges, by recourse to arms and still more frequent use of money as a timely bait,[27] and by constant activity in every field, he managed within four years to rally the whole of France. Under the auspices of the papal nuncio, who was anxious to effect a reconciliation between the two principal Catholic states, the Treaty of Vervins (May 2, 1598) put an end to the Spanish war; its articles were similar to the conditions of peace laid down at Cateau-Cambrésis forty years earlier.

27. In order, as he subsequently declared, "to buy his kingdom rather than conquer it."

232 The attempt to solve the religious problem by warfare had miscarried, and the status of French Protestants had still to be decided. Their numbers had been reduced and most of the leaders had disappeared; but their communities, encouraged by the pastors, co-ordinated by periodical assemblies and hardened by suffering, had become one of the irreducible elements of national life. The king's relations with his former co-religionists were strained. The Edict of Poitiers had been revived in 1591, and Henri wished to preserve and guarantee its essential provisions. When negotiations with Spain drew to a close, the Protestants understood that they could do nothing but accept another edict, which was accordingly signed at Nantes on April 13, 1598.

This celebrated document contained ninety-two main articles and fifty-six articles of application. Defining the religious rights of the reformers, it granted them unlimited freedom of conscience, but it restricted their liberty of worship to the places authorized at Poitiers in 1577 and to those localities where it was practised in 1597. It likewise forbade all Protestant ceremonies in Paris, in the episcopal cities within a radius of five leagues therefrom, in the royal residences and in the armies. The Huguenot minority was allowed full civic rights and admission to all offices, as well as to the universities and hospitals; and with a view to the impartial administration of justice, tribunals composed of members belonging to both confessions and known as *chambres mi-parties*, were set up at Paris, Grenoble, Castres and Nérac.

Such was the "general, clear and absolute law" which is still its maker's chief title to glory. The Edict of Nantes has often been described as "a milestone in the world's history." Whereas in Germany, Spain and England governments imposed a single faith upon their subjects, France was the first to adopt religious liberty. We must not, however, exaggerate the importance of a measure which was accepted by Frenchmen for very different reasons—political discretion or (as in the case of Sully) indifference to Churches and ecclesiastical loyalties far more often than respect for the spiritual freedom of souls. Henri IV had a hard struggle to secure registration of the Edict by the Parliaments. "You still have something Spanish in your bellies," he told the counsellors of Toulouse. There was the same sort of resistance on the Protestant side, and the king was obliged to add two warrants. By the first of these he undertook to defray the expenses of the reformed worship; by the second he allowed the Huguenots an eight-year tenure of one hundred "strong places," whose garrisons he himself would pay. It would be anachronistic to represent this edict of pacification as welcomed with unanimous cries of joy. We must not forget that when he read its text Pope Clement VIII exclaimed: "This crucifies me!" and that he added some words very similar to those once heard on the lips of Calvin and Theodore Beza: "Liberty of conscience for each and every one is the worst thing in the world." Such were the ideas of the age.

France emerged from the terrible ordeal ravaged and drenched in blood, her land lying fallow, her peasants starving and ready to revolt, her commerce ruined. She needed, as King Henri said, "to recover breath." The Catholic Church was in a way victorious, because the sovereign, in order to establish his authority, had been forced to submit to her; but the separation of so many of her sons remained an open wound in her side. This work of plain common sense and sound policy, so far in advance of contemporary feeling, might have proved dangerous and short-lived, but for the appearance of a king who took a completely fresh view of the religious problem. Unity of faith was declared in the preamble of the edict to be the supreme advantage; circumstances alone had inspired common-sense arrangements, which would henceforward be the rule.

SELECT BIBLIOGRAPHY

THESE are the most important works cited by the author in his extensive bibliographical notes. I have substituted English translations wherever possible. For the benefit of readers to whom the numerous French and German works may be inaccessible, I have added a short supplement of English books covering much of the same field.

GENERAL

A. Dufourcq, *Histoire moderne de l'église*, vol. 18, 7th ed. (1933).

L. von Pastor, *History of the Popes Since the End of the Middle Ages* (English translation, 1891–1938).

CHAPTER I. THE AWAKENING OF THE CATHOLIC SOUL: ST IGNATIUS OF LOYOLA

P. Pourrat, *La Spiritualité chrétienne*, 2 vols. (1921).

M. Bataillon, *Erasme et l'Espagne* (1937).

D. Barrand, *Les Ideés philosophiques de Bernardin Ochin* (1924).

236 M. De La Claviere, *Saint Gaétan* (1902).

G. Chastel, *Saint Antoine-Marie Zaccaria, Barnabite* (1930).

J. Cherprenet, Preface to translation of John of Avila's *Audi Filia.*

P. Dominique, *La Politique des Jésuites* (1955).

A. Brou, *Les Jésuites de la Légende*, 2 vols. (1906–1907).

H. Pinard de la Boullaye, *La Spiritualité Ignatienne* (1936).

J. Gautier, *La Spiritualité Catholique* (1953).

P. Suau, *Histoire de Saint François Borgia* (1910).

CHAPTER II. THE COUNCIL OF TRENT AND THE WORK OF THE SAINTS

L. Cristiani, *L'Église à l'époque du Concile de Trente* (1948).

C. J. Hefele–H. Leclercq, *Histoire des Conciles*, vols. 9 and 10 (1930–1938).

Dom Ancel, *L'Activité reformatrice de Paul II* (1909); *La Disgrace et le procès des Carafa* (1909).

P. Richard, *Le Concile de Trente* (1930–1931).

G. Grente, *Saint Pie V* (1914).

C. Hirschauer, *Politique de Sainte Pie V en France* (1922).

R. Deslandres, *Saint Pie V l'Islamisme* (1911).

R. Hoonaert, *Sainte Thérèse* (1925).

J. Galzy, *Sainte Thérèse d'Avila* (1927).

L. Bertrand, *Sainte Thérèse* (1927).

Fr. Bruno, O.D.C., *St. John of the Cross* (English translation, 1933).

L. Ponnelle and L. Bordet, *St. Philip Neri and the Roman Society of his Times* (English translation, 1937).

E. Mâle, *L'Art religieux après le Concile de Trente* (1932); republished as *L'Art religieux de la fin du XVI Siècle* (1951).

P. Fierens, *L'Art Flamand* (1945).

CHAPTER III. THE RENDING OF CHRISTIAN EUROPE, PART ONE

N. Paulus, *Protestantism und Toleranz in 16. Jahrhundert* (1911).

F. Buisson, *Sébastien Castellio* (1892).

E. Girau, *Sébastien Castellio et la Réforme Calviniste* (1916).

S. Zweig, *The Right to Heresy: Castellio Against Calvin* (English translation, 1936).

Due de Levis Mirepoix, *Les Guerres de religion* (1950).

Reinhart, *Henri IV ou la France Sauvée* (1924).

R. Ritter (ed.), *Lettres du Cardinal de Florence* (1955).

L. Bertrand, *Philippe II à l'Escorial* (1929); *Philippe II, Une Ténébreuse Affaire* (1929) [both favourable].

J. Cassou, *La Vie de Philippe II* (1929) [unfavourable].

H. Pirenne, *Histoire de Belgique* (1923–1924).

X. Carton de Wiart, *Marguerite d'Autriche, Régente des Pays-Bas* (1939); *La Jeunesse du Taciturne* (1945).

J. Neale, *Queen Elisabeth* (1934).

M. Humber-Seller, *Elisabeth I, Reine d'Angleterre* (1953).

J. Chastenet, *Elisabeth I* (1951).

E. Waugh, *Edmund Campion* (1935).

W. L. Mathieson, *Politics and Religion in Scotland* (1902).

R. Chauviré, *Le Secret de Marie Stuart* (1937).

J. B. Bossuet, *History of the Variations of the Protestant Churches* (English translation, 1829).

P. Janin, *Les Églises séparées d'Orient* (1937).

P. Hughes, *A History of the Church*, 2nd ed. (1948); *A Popular History of the Reformation* (1957).

P. A. Kunkel, *The Theatines in the History of Catholic Reform* (1941).

C. Hollis, *Saint Ignatius* (1931).

W. H. Longridge (ed. and trans.), *The Spiritual Exercises* (1919).

T. J. Campbell, *The Jesuits, 1534–1921* (1932).

M. P. Harvey, *The Jesuits in History* (1941).

A. M. Clarke, *The Life of St. Francis Borgia* (1894).

C. C. Martindale, *In God's Army*, vol. 2 (1917).

C. M. Antony, *The Life of St. Pius V* (1911).

M. Yeo, *A Prince of Pastors: St. Charles Borromeos* (1938).

E. A. Peers, *Mother of Carmel* (1945); *St. John of the Cross* (1932); *Spirit of Flame* (1943).

R. H. Allpost, *Henry of Navarre* (1920).

G. Slocombe, *Henry of Navarre* (1931).

D. Loth, *Philip II of Spain* (1932).

W. Walsh, *Philip II* (1938).

240 C. V. Wedgwood, *William the Silent* (1944).

E. Linklater, *Mary, Queen of Scots* (1933).

S. Zweig, *Mary Stuart* (English translation, 1935).

V. Cronin, *The Wise Man from the West* [Fr. M. Ricci] (1955); *A Pearl to India: The Life of Roberto de Nobili* (1959).

C. F. Lummis, *Spanish Pioneers* (1930).

H. Biggar (ed.), *The Voyages of Jacques Cartier* (1924).

J. Brodrick, *St. Peter Canisius* (1935).

A. M. Boase, *The Fortunes of Montaigne* (1935).

C. C. Martindale, *Life of St. Camillus* (1946).

H. Burton, *Life of St. Francis de Sales*, 2. vols. (1925–1929).

M. De La Bedoyere, *St. Francis de Sales* (1959).

M. S. Briggs, *Baroque Architecture* (1913).

S. Sitwell, *Southern Baroque Art* (1924).